Interactive
Mathematics Program®

INTEGRATED HIGH SCHOOL MATHEMATICS

FIRST EDITION AUTHORS:

Dan Fendel, Diane Resek, Lynne Alper, and Sherry Fraser

CONTRIBUTORS TO THE SECOND EDITION:

Sherry Fraser, IMP for the 21st Century

Jean Klanica, IMP for the 21st Century

Brian Lawler, California State University San Marcos

Eric Robinson, Ithaca College, NY

Lew Romagnano, Metropolitan State College of Denver, CO

Rick Marks, Sonoma State University, CA

Dan Brutlag, Meaningful Mathematics

Alan Olds, Colorado Writing Project

Mike Bryant, Santa Maria High School, CA

Jeri P. Philbrick, Oxnard High School, CA

Lori Green, Lincoln High School, CA

Matt Bremer, Berkeley High School, CA

Margaret DeArmond, Kern High School District, CA

Key Curriculum

Year 3
Second Edition   I M P

This material is based upon work supported by the National Science Foundation under award numbers ESI-9255262, ESI-0137805, and ESI-0627821. Any opinions, findings, and conclusions or recommendations expressed in this publication are those of the authors and do not necessarily reflect the views of the National Science Foundation.

Key Curriculum
1150 65th Street
Emeryville, California 94608
email: editorial@keypress.com
www.keycurriculum.com
10 9 8 7 6 5 4 3 2   14 13 12
ISBN 978-1-60440-046-5
Printed in the United States of America

Project Editors
Mali Apple, Josephine Noah, Sharon Taylor

Project Administrators
Emily Reed, Juliana Tringali

Professional Reviewers
Rick Marks, Sonoma State University, CA
D. Michael Bryant, Santa Maria High School, CA, retired

Accuracy Checker
Carrie Gongaware

First Edition Teacher Reviewers
Daniel R. Bennett, Moloka'i High School, HI
Maureen Burkhart, Northridge Academy High School, CA
Dwight Fuller, Ponderosa High School, CA
Daniel S. Johnson, Silver Creek High School, CA
Brian Lawler, California State University San Marcos, CA
Brent McClain, Vernonia School District, OR
Susan Miller, St. Francis of Assisi Parish School, PA
Amy C. Roszak, Cottage Grove High School, OR
Carmen C. Rubino, Silver Creek High School, CA
Barbara Schallau, East Side Union High School District, CA
Kathleen H. Spivack, Wilbur Cross High School, CT
Wendy Tokumine, Farrington High School, HI

First Edition Multicultural Reviewers
Genevieve Lau, Ph.D., Skyline College, CA
Arthur Ramirez, Ph.D., Sonoma State University, CA
Marilyn Strutchens, Ph.D., Auburn University, AL

Copyeditor
Brandy Vickers

Interior Designer
Marilyn Perry

Production Editor
Andrew Jones

Production Director
Christine Osborne

Editorial Production Supervisor
Kristin Ferraioli

Compositor
Lapiz Digital Services, Kristin Ferraioli

Art Editor/Photo Researcher
Maya Melenchuk

Technical Artists
Lapiz Digital Services, Laurel Technical Services, Maya Melenchuk

Illustrators
Taylor Bruce, Deborah Drummond, Tom Fowler, Briana Miller, Evangelia Philippidis, Sara Swan, Diane Varner, Martha Weston, April Goodman Willy

Cover Designer
Jeff Williams

Printer
RR Donnelley

Mathematics Product Manager
Elizabeth DeCarli

Executive Editor
Josephine Noah

Publisher
Steven Rasmussen

Foreword

Students must be prepared for the world that they will inherit. Whether or not they choose to enter college immediately after high school, we must equip them to handle new problems with confidence and perseverance. Our ever-changing world requires that students grow into critically thinking adults who are prepared to absorb new ideas and who will become lifelong learners. The Interactive Mathematics Program® (IMP™) aids in this development.

IMP enhances students' understanding of mathematics by obliging them to present reasoned arguments. The group activities in IMP foster teamwork and the development of oral and written communication skills. These skills are honed by requiring students to write intelligible explanations about the processes that they followed to reach their conclusions.

As a parent of an IMP student, I have found that IMP enables students to experience mathematics in action and to recognize that mathematics is not simply an esoteric subject. On the other hand, IMP also offers students the opportunity to experience how beautiful and open-ended mathematics is.

As a professional mathematician, I believe that IMP teaches mathematics in the way that it should be taught. Mathematics does not arise naturally in nicely defined semester-long modules labeled Algebra I, Geometry, Algebra II, and Trigonometry/Precalculus. IMP effectively breaks down the artificial barriers created by such divisions.

I have found the Problems of the Week exceedingly interesting and intellectually stimulating—sufficiently so that I have shared several of them with members of my faculty. It is refreshing to interact with my son around mathematics that is quite challenging to me also. He can appreciate my excitement and that mathematics can be fun.

As a parent and educator, I know the concerns that students, parents, school officials, and others have about colleges' expectations of entering students. What I value most, as do many of my colleagues at other top institutions, is that students have experienced good teaching in well-constructed courses that emphasize communication and creative thinking, and in which the learning that takes place is genuine and meaningful.

At Colorado School of Mines, a school of engineering and applied science, we require that our students develop strong communication skills and learn to work effectively as team members. To help our students enhance these skills further, we have established a writing center staffed by qualified professionals. In the beginning courses in calculus in our Department of Mathematical and Computer Sciences, we emphasize the working of real problems provided by the science and engineering disciplines. Students learn to think creatively and not be tied to one notation system. We also require our seniors to take turns at presenting reports on a research topic at weekly seminars. The other students submit reviews of their classmates' presentations and learn from the preparation of their assessments, in addition to providing valuable feedback to the presenter.

We expect that our students will not simply reflect their professors' thinking. Students have a responsibility to engage in independent thinking and to understand the power of thought as distinct from the power of authority. Students have a head start when they enter college courses with prior knowledge in solving complex problems that go beyond calculation and in coping with ambiguity.

The Interactive Mathematics Program helps prepare students for life, not just for calculus. Because IMP emphasizes creative thinking, communication skills, and teamwork, it should serve our students well.

Graeme Fairweather
Professor and Head
Department of Mathematical and Computer Sciences
Colorado School of Mines

NOTE TO STUDENTS

This textbook represents the third year of a four-year program of mathematics learning and investigation. As in the first two years, the program is organized around interesting, complex problems, and the concepts you learn grow out of what you'll need to solve those problems.

If you studied IMP Year 1 or 2

If you studied IMP Year 1 or 2, then you know the excitement of problem-based mathematical study. The Year 3 program extends and expands the challenges that you worked with previously. For instance:

- In Year 1, you learned how to use variables to describe relationships, and you solved linear equations algebraically. In Year 2, you worked with quadratic equations and functions. In Year 3, you'll learn to use exponential functions to solve problems involving rates of growth.

- In Year 1, you used the normal distribution to help predict the period of a 30-foot pendulum. In Year 2, you learned about the chi-square statistic to understand statistical comparisons of populations. In Year 3, you'll learn about the binomial distribution and apply it to a variety of situations including a baseball pennant race.

You'll also use ideas from geometry to see how to make a "hideout" from an array of trees, you'll use matrix algebra to help a city decide how to allocate land resources, and you'll study rates of change and derivatives in order to make predictions about world population growth.

If you didn't study IMP Year 1 or Year 2

If this is your first experience with the Interactive Mathematics Program (IMP), you can rely on your classmates and your teacher to fill in what you've missed. Meanwhile, here are some things you should know about the program, how it was developed, and how it is organized.

The Interactive Mathematics Program is the product of a collaboration of teachers and mathematicians who have been working together since 1989 to reform the way high school mathematics is taught. Over 500,000 students and 2,000 teachers have used these materials since the first edition was published in 1996. This second edition reflects the experiences, reactions, and ideas of students and teachers who have used the first edition for many years.

Our goal is to give you the mathematics you need in order to succeed in this changing world. We will present mathematics to you in a manner that reflects how mathematics is used and that reflects the different ways people work and learn together. Through this perspective on mathematics, you will be prepared both for continued study of mathematics in college and for the world of work.

This book contains the tasks that will be your work during Year 3 of the program. As you will see, these problems require ideas from many branches of mathematics, including algebra, geometry, probability, graphing, statistics, and trigonometry. Rather than present each of these areas separately, we have integrated them and presented them in meaningful contexts, so you will see how they relate to each other and to our world.

Although the IMP program is not organized into courses called "Algebra," "Geometry," and so on, you will be learning all the essential mathematical concepts that are part of those traditional courses. You will also be learning concepts from branches of mathematics—especially statistics and probability—that are not part of a traditional high school program.

Each unit in this four-year program has a central problem or theme and focuses on several major mathematical ideas. Supplemental problems at the end of the main material for each unit provide additional opportunities for you to strengthen your understanding of the core material or to explore new ideas related to the unit.

To accomplish your goals, you will have to be an active learner. You will experiment, investigate, ask questions, make and test conjectures, reflect on your work, and then communicate your ideas and conclusions both orally and in writing. You will do some of your work in collaboration with fellow students, just as users of mathematics in the real world often work in teams. At other times, you will work on your own. You will talk about what you are doing and why, and you will present your results to the class.

We hope you will enjoy the challenges that the Interactive Mathematics Program presents. And we hope that your experiences give you a deeper appreciation of the meaning and importance of mathematics.

Dan Fendel   *Diane Resek*

Lynne Alper   *Sherry Fraser*

CONTENTS

Orchard Hideout—Circles and Coordinate Geometry

Meadows or Malls?—Three-Variable Equations, Three-Dimensional Coordinates, and Matrix Algebra

Small World, Isn't It?—Slope, Derivatives, and Exponential Growth

Pennant Fever—Permutations, Combinations, and the Binomial Distribution

High Dive—Circular Functions and the Physics of Falling Objects

Orchard Hideout

Circles and Coordinate Geometry

Orchard Hideout—Circles and Coordinate Geometry

Orchards and Mini-Orchards

Have you ever stared into an orchard as you passed it on the road? From one perspective, you see that the trees are planted in straight rows. But as you move to a different spot, all you see is a mass of trees.

The main characters of this unit, Madie and Clyde, have planted an orchard. They want to know how long it will take the trees to grow before they can no longer see from the center of the orchard to the outside world.

You will begin the unit by looking at their overall problem, and then you'll examine some simpler cases. You will also explore some activities related to the first POW of the unit.

Annie Tam and Ryan Tran work to develop the mathematical definition for a circle.

Orchard Hideout

Madie and Clyde want some peace and quiet. Most of all, they want privacy. So they leave the city and buy a piece of land in the countryside.

Their lot is in the shape of a circle. They decide to plant an orchard on the lot in nice neat rows.

Here's how they set up their orchard.

They plant their first row of trees along an east-west line through the center of the circle. They space the trees equally, except they leave out the tree that would have been at the circle's exact center. There are 50 trees to the east of the center and 50 to the west. The trees at the ends of this east-west row are exactly on the boundary of the property.

Madie and Clyde then plant a north-south line of trees through the center, using the same spacing as before and omitting the tree at the center. Again, there are 50 trees to the north of the center and 50 to the south. And the trees at the ends of this north-south row are exactly on the boundary of the property.

They use each tree in the north-south row as the center of an east-west row, filling in the orchard with rows of trees. They use the same distance between trees in every row.

Madie and Clyde realize that as the trees grow, their trunks will become so big that it will eventually be impossible to see out from the center of the orchard. The center of the orchard would then be like a hideout.

continued

Here is the main question of this unit.

How soon after Madie and Clyde plant their orchard will the center of the lot become a true "orchard hideout"?

1. Study the problem. Make a model of the situation, perhaps using a smaller orchard as an example.

2. Make a list of questions you need to ask to understand this problem better. Try to answer some of your questions.

Adapted from "The Orchard Problem" in *Mathematical Gems I,* by Ross Honsberger (Washington, DC: Mathematical Association of America, 1973).

A Geometric Summary

As you can see, the central problem of this unit involves circles, straight lines, and all sorts of distances. To solve the problem, you will use many ideas from geometry, including trigonometry.

Here is a summary of basic definitions and essential principles from geometry that were presented in Years 1 and 2 of the Interactive Mathematics Program. Over the course of this unit, you will develop other key ideas.

I. Polygon Angle Sums

The *angle sum property* for triangles is as follows:

In any triangle, the sum of the measures of the angles is exactly 180°.

One proof of this principle is based on properties of parallel lines, discussed in Part V.

In general, the sum of the measures of the angles of a polygon depends only on how many sides the polygon has. This sum is always a multiple of 180°.

II. Similarity

Two polygons are considered similar if they have the same shape (though not necessarily the same size). Here is the formal definition.

> ***Definition*** Two polygons are *similar* if their corresponding angles are equal and their corresponding sides are proportional in length.

Recall that when we say two angles are equal, we really mean their measures, or sizes, are equal.

Here are two basic principles for proving similarity of triangles.

If the corresponding angles of two triangles are equal, then the triangles must be similar.

If the corresponding sides of two triangles are proportional in length, then the triangles must be similar.

continued ▶

The angle sum property for triangles leads to a simpler version of the *corresponding angles* principle.

If two angles of one triangle are equal to two angles of another triangle, then the triangles must be similar.

III. Congruence

Congruence is a special case of similarity. Two polygons are considered congruent if they have the same shape and the same size. This means they are similar and the ratio of corresponding sides is 1:1. Here is the formal definition.

Definition Two polygons are *congruent* if their corresponding angles are equal and their corresponding sides are equal in length.

Here are two principles for proving congruence. The first applies to all polygons, and the second is specifically for triangles.

If two polygons are similar and some pair of corresponding sides are equal in length, then the polygons must be congruent.

If two sides and the angle they form in one triangle are equal to the corresponding parts of another triangle, then the triangles must be congruent.

IV. Right Triangles

A right triangle is a triangle in which one of the angles is a right angle. The sides of a right triangle have special names.

Definition In a right triangle, the sides forming the right angle are the *legs*. The side opposite the right angle is the *hypotenuse*.

The relationship between the lengths of the sides of a right triangle is summed up in the **Pythagorean theorem.**

In any right triangle, the sum of the squares of the lengths of the legs is equal to the square of the length of the hypotenuse.

continued ▶

The trigonometric functions describe ratios within a right triangle. Here are the basic definitions.

> **Definition** If $\triangle ABC$ is a right triangle with a right angle at C, the trigonometric functions **sine, cosine,** and **tangent** for $\angle A$ are defined by these ratios.

$$\sin A = \frac{BC}{AB} \quad \cos A = \frac{AC}{AB} \quad \tan A = \frac{BC}{AC}$$

Each trigonometric function has an **inverse trigonometric function** that is used to determine an angle if the value of the trigonometric function is known. For example, if x is a number between 0 and 1, the inverse sine of x (written $\sin^{-1} x$) is the angle between 0° and 90° whose sine is x.

V. Parallel Lines

Certain parts of a diagram like the one shown below have special names.

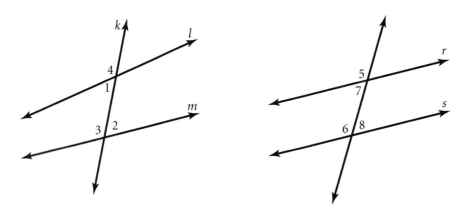

> **Definition** If two lines l and m are intersected by a third line k, the line k is a *transversal.* A pair of angles like angles 1 and 2 are *alternate interior angles.* A pair of angles like angles 3 and 4 are *corresponding angles.*

Whether two lines intersected by a transversal are parallel is related to whether certain angles formed are equal.

For instance, in the diagram above, if lines r and s are parallel, then any pair of alternate interior angles (such as 7 and 8) must be equal, and

continued ▶

any pair of corresponding angles (such as 5 and 6) must be equal. Also, if any such pair of angles are known to be equal, then lines *r* and *s* must be parallel.

This gives us these principles.

> *If two parallel lines are intersected by a transversal, then any pair of alternate interior angles must be equal.*

> *If two parallel lines are intersected by a transversal, then any pair of corresponding angles must be equal.*

> *If a pair of alternate interior angles formed by a transversal intersecting two lines are equal, then the two lines must be parallel.*

> *If a pair of corresponding angles formed by a transversal intersecting two lines are equal, then the two lines must be parallel.*

This Guatemalan weaver uses wooden sticks as transversals to cross the parallel lines of her thread.

VI. Perimeter, Area, Volume, and Surface Area

Here are several basic definitions regarding perimeter, area, volume, and surface area.

> **Definition** The *perimeter* of a polygon is the sum of the lengths of its sides.

> **Definition** The *area* of a plane figure is the number of square units it contains.

> **Definition** The *volume* of a solid figure is the number of cubic units it contains.

> **Definition** A *right prism* is a three-dimensional figure formed by moving a polygon through space in a direction perpendicular to the plane it lies in. The initial and final positions of the polygon are its *bases.* The other faces form the *lateral surface* of the prism.

continued ▶

The figures shown here are prisms. Two of them are right prisms. The first figure is called an *oblique prism* because it is created by a nonperpendicular movement of the base.

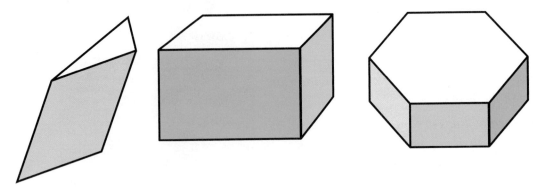

These principles describe basic formulas for finding area, volume, and surface area.

The area of a rectangle is equal to the product of its length and width.

The area of a triangle is equal to half the product of its base and the corresponding altitude.

The volume of a rectangular solid is equal to the product of its length, width, and height.

The volume of a right prism is equal to the product of its height and the area of its base.

The lateral surface area of a right prism is equal to the product of its height and the perimeter of its base.

Geometry and a Mini-Orchard

Part I: Summarizing Geometry

Read *A Geometric Summary,* which reviews ideas about geometry and trigonometry that you will need during this unit. As you read, think about what each principle or definition means, and create diagrams to help you clarify the ideas.

Part II: A Mini-Orchard

Imagine that Madie and Clyde's orchard is planted on a lot with a radius of 1 unit. At an early stage, this orchard might be represented by a diagram like this one.

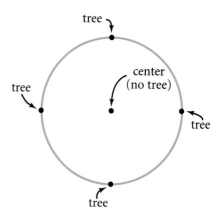

Suppose you stand in the center of this orchard. If you look due east or north or west or south, a tree will block your line of sight. If you look in any other direction, you will be able to see out of the orchard through a gap between trees. As the trees grow, the gaps between them will narrow.

Now imagine that you remain at the center of the orchard, waiting patiently as the trees grow.

1. In what direction should you look to be able to see out of the orchard for as long as possible? That is, what line of sight will be the last to get blocked by the growing trees? If there is more than one answer, be as general as possible.

2. What is the minimum radius required for each tree trunk in order to make the center of the orchard into a true "orchard hideout"? In other words, how big must the trees become so that it is impossible for you to see out of the orchard from the center?

Equally Wet

1. Two delicate flowers are planted in a garden. The gardener, Leslie, has a sprinkler that sprays water in a circle. The closer a flower is to the sprinkler, the more water it receives.

   To be sure her flowers each get the same amount of water, Leslie needs to place the sprinkler where it will be the same distance from each flower.

   What are her choices about where to put the sprinkler? Describe all the possibilities.

2. Leslie has another small garden where she wants to plant three flowers. She wants to know if it will be possible to place the sprinkler the same distance from all three.

   a. Determine which arrangements of the flowers (if any) will make this possible and which (if any) will make it impossible. As in Question 1, Leslie will be looking for a place to put the sprinkler after the flowers have been planted.

   b. For those arrangements for which it will be possible, describe how Leslie can find the correct location (or locations) for the sprinkler.

3. What about four flowers? Five flowers? Generalize as much as you can.

Your task is to explain as fully as possible, for various cases, where Leslie can place the sprinkler to give all the flowers the same amount of water. The activity *Only Two Flowers* will help get you started with Question 1 of this POW.

continued

○ *Write-up*

1. *Problem Statement:* State the problem in mathematical language without reference to the context. That is, describe the problem in geometric terms without talking about flowers or sprinklers.

2. *Process*

3. *Solution*

4. *Self-assessment*

Adapted from "Simple Math," a series of mathematics video-dramas produced by the Israeli Instructional Television Center, with academic adviser Nitsa Movshovitz-Hadar and producer Tamar Reiner.

The Standard POW Write-up

Each Problem of the Week is unique, so the form of the write-up may vary from one POW to the next. Nevertheless, most of the categories you will use for your POW write-ups will be the same throughout the year. The list below summarizes the standard categories.

Some POW write-ups will use other categories or require more specific information within a particular category. If the write-up instructions for a given POW simply list a category by name, however, use these descriptions.

1. *Problem Statement:* State the problem clearly in your own words. Your problem statement should be clear enough that someone unfamiliar with the problem could understand what you are being asked to do.

2. *Process:* Describe what you did in attempting to solve the problem. Use your notes as a reminder. Include things that didn't work out or that seemed like a waste of time. Do this part of the write-up even if you didn't solve the problem.

   If you get assistance of any kind on the problem, tell what the assistance was and how it helped you.

3. *Solution:* State your solution as clearly as you can. Explain how you know your solution is correct and complete. If you obtained only a partial solution, give that. If you were able to generalize the problem, include your general results.

   Write your explanation in a way that will be convincing to someone else—even someone who initially disagrees with your answer.

4. *Self-assessment:* Tell what you learned from this problem. Be as specific as you can. Also assign yourself a grade for your work on this POW, and explain why you think you deserve that grade.

Only Two Flowers

Your task is to answer the first question from the POW *Equally Wet*. That is, if two flowers are planted, what are the possible positions to place a sprinkler so that it is exactly the same distance from each flower?

Be sure your answer includes all possible solutions. Give your answer in two ways.

* With a diagram showing all the solutions
* With a description in words of the set of solutions

A Perpendicularity Proof

Consider this principle.

Every point on the perpendicular bisector of a line segment is equidistant from the two endpoints of the segment.

Your task is to write a proof of this principle, based on the diagram shown here. In this diagram, A and B are any two points. Point C is the midpoint of the line segment connecting A and B. Line l is the line through C that is perpendicular to $\overline{AB}$ (so l is the **perpendicular bisector** of $\overline{AB}$). Point D is some point on l.

Based on this information, prove that D is **equidistant** from A and B. In other words, prove that lengths AD and BD are equal.

From Two Flowers to Three

In *Only Two Flowers,* you determined where Leslie should place the sprinkler if she has two flowers to water. From that activity and its discussion, you should now have a simple description of Leslie's full set of options for locating the sprinkler for the case of two flowers.

Now consider a specific case using three flowers. The flowers are placed in a coordinate system at the points (4, 2), (14, 2), and (4, 8). Where can Leslie place the sprinkler so that it is equidistant from all three points? Explain in detail why the point you choose works.

More Mini-Orchards

Madie and Clyde want to know how big the radius of each tree trunk needs to be for the orchard to become a hideout. They call this the "hideout tree radius."

Of course, this value depends on the radius of the orchard itself. In *Geometry and a Mini-Orchard* you examined the case of an orchard with a radius of 1 unit. But the orchard on a lot whose radius is 1 unit is pretty dull. Madie and Clyde are glad their lot is larger than that.

Suppose, though, that their orchard is just a *little* larger.

1. Sketch a mini-orchard for a lot with radius 2. Then answer these questions.

   a. How many trees are in this mini-orchard?

   b. Approximately how big must the radius of each tree trunk become to make this orchard a true hideout? In other words, approximately what is the hideout tree radius for an orchard of radius 2?

2. Sketch a mini-orchard for a lot with radius 3. Then answer these questions.

   a. How many trees are in this mini-orchard?

   b. Approximately what is the hideout tree radius for an orchard of radius 3?

3. Find the *exact* value of the hideout tree radius for orchards of radius 2 and radius 3.

In, On, or Out?

It's convenient to use coordinates to describe situations like our orchard problem. Madie and Clyde plant a tree at every lattice point within the orchard, except at (0, 0). A **lattice point** is a point whose coordinates are both integers.

In using this system to describe the orchard, it's helpful to have a way to decide whether a given point is within the orchard. This is fairly easy for points on the axes. For other points, it can be more difficult.

For this activity, suppose the orchard has a radius of 10 (instead of 50). The center of the orchard is still at (0, 0).

Decide whether each point listed below is inside the boundary of the orchard, outside the boundary, or exactly on the boundary. In each case, explain how you decided. You may want to use diagrams to help you.

1. (11, 0)
2. (10, 0)
3. (10, 1)
4. (9, 3)
5. (9, 4)
6. (9, 5)
7. (9, 6)
8. (8, 5)
9. (8, 6)
10. (8, 7)
11. (7, 6)
12. (7, 7)
13. (7, 8)

Coordinates and Distance

Madie and Clyde have many questions about the distance
between trees and the distances from trees to various lines
of sight.

By introducing coordinates into the orchard, you've made it
possible to use the Pythagorean theorem to your advantage.
In the upcoming activities, you will encounter some important
formulas involving coordinates and distance.

*Carlos Catly uses the coordinate system to model
a mini-orchard.*

Other Trees

1. Madie and Clyde buy another circular plot of land, smaller than the first, on which to plant an orchard. They have set up coordinates as before, with the center of the orchard at (0, 0). They will plant trees at all points with integer coordinates that lie within the orchard, except at (0, 0).

   In this orchard, the tree at (5, 12) is on the boundary. What are the coordinates of the other trees that must also be on the boundary? Explain your answer.

2. Generalize Question 1 for a lot of any size. Suppose a circular orchard of any size is set up as usual with trees on the lattice points. If the point (a, b) is on the lot's boundary, what other trees must also be on the boundary? Give as complete an answer as possible. You may want to examine other examples like that in Question 1.

Sprinkler in the Orchard

Madie and Clyde are working in the scorching sun when they realize that their seedlings need water. So they haul out their trusty sprinkler and place it in the center of the orchard.

1. Suppose the sprinkler waters a circular area with a radius of 14 units. (Assume the trees do not block the water from one another.) State whether the tree at each of these locations will be watered, and explain your answers.

   a. $(-6, -13)$

   b. $(-9, 10)$

   c. $(-12, -8)$

2. Obviously, Madie and Clyde cannot reach all their trees when they place the sprinkler in the center of the orchard. After watering the trees near the center, they move the sprinkler to $(28, -19)$ to do some more watering. (Assume they temporarily uproot the tree at that location.) They also adjust the sprinkler so the water covers a circle of radius 18 units. Which of these trees will the water reach?

   a. $(16, -7)$

   b. $(38, -34)$

   c. $(20, -35)$

3. Assume the sprinkler continues to operate so that it reaches all trees within 18 units. In which locations can Madie and Clyde place the sprinkler to be able to water the entire orchard in as few waterings as possible?

   Work on this question from scratch, ignoring the waterings from $(0, 0)$ and $(28, -19)$ that are discussed in Questions 1 and 2.

The Distance Formula

There is a well-known formula in mathematics, the **distance formula,** that is closely related to the Pythagorean theorem. This activity will help you develop that formula.

The distance formula is used to find the distance between two points in the coordinate plane, say, (x_1, y_1) and (x_2, y_2). The formula gives the distance between the two points in terms of the coordinates x_1, x_2, y_1, and y_2.

1. a. Find the distance between the points (5, 3) and (7, 6).

    b. Describe in detail what you did to find your answer.

2. a. Find the distance between the points (2, 5) and (6, 3).

    b. Describe in detail what you did to find your answer.

3. Suppose (x_1, y_1) and (x_2, y_2) are the coordinates of two points. Generalize what you did in Questions 1 and 2 to create a formula or set of instructions that gives the distance between the two points.

4. Does your generalization work if any of the coordinates x_1, x_2, y_1, and y_2 are negative numbers? Explain with examples.

How Does Your Orchard Grow?

Madie and Clyde are trying to figure out how big the radius of the tree trunks must be for their orchard to become a hideout. They realize that once they figure this out, though, they still won't know how long it will take for the trees to grow to that size.

They return to the nursery where they bought the trees. The people at the nursery can't say when the orchard will become a hideout, but they are able to tell Madie and Clyde how fast the cross-sectional area of each tree trunk will increase.

When they get home, Madie and Clyde realize they don't know the current cross-sectional area of their trees. They go out to measure. Of course, they can't simply cut a cross section in a trunk and measure the area, because that would kill the tree. Instead, they measure the circumference of the trunk.

Your Task

Imagine that Madie and Clyde know two things.

- The amount of increase each year of the cross-sectional area of the trees (This amount is the same every year.)
- The current circumference of the trees

Assume they also know the hideout tree radius. That is, they know how big the radius of each tree trunk needs to be for the orchard to become a hideout.

Develop a plan for how to use this information to figure out how long it will take the orchard to become a hideout. Identify any geometric questions you will need to answer to use your plan.

A Snack in the Middle

Some of Madie and Clyde's trees already need pruning. Every afternoon they choose the two trees that need it the most, and each of them works on one of those two trees.

Pruning makes Madie and Clyde hungry. They decide to set up a snack table at the midpoint of the segment connecting the two trees they are working on. If there happens to be a tree at that exact point, they will set up the table right next to the tree.

1. Suppose Madie is working on the tree at (24, 6) and Clyde is working on the tree at (30, 14). What are the coordinates of the point where they should set up the snack table? Prove your choice is really equidistant from (24, 6) and (30, 14).

2. If they are working on the trees at $(-3, 4)$ and (5, 12), where should they set up the table? Prove your choice is equidistant from $(-3, 4)$ and (5, 12).

3. If they are working on the trees at (6, 2) and $(11, -4)$, where should they set up the table? Prove your choice is equidistant from (6, 2) and $(11, -4)$.

4. To save them time, make up a general formula for Madie and Clyde. Suppose the trees they are pruning are at (x_1, y_1) and (x_2, y_2). Find a formula for the midpoint between these two trees in terms of x_1, y_1, x_2, and y_2. This formula is called the **midpoint formula.**

Equidistant Points and Lines

The POW *Equally Wet* involves the set of points equidistant from two or more given points. You're about to encounter some other problems that involve equal distances.

As you explore these activities, including your next POW, think about how these ideas might help Madie and Clyde with their orchard problem.

Ryan Tran works on a proof that a given quadrilateral is a square.

Proving with Distance—Part I

1. This diagram shows a quadrilateral with vertices (5, 20), (9, 23), (12, 19), and (8, 16).

   Prove this figure is a square. (Don't simply show that the figure is a rhombus. Remember, a *rhombus* is a quadrilateral with four equal sides. A *square* is a rhombus with four right angles.)

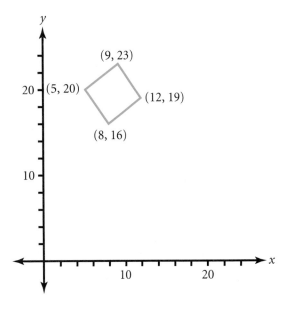

2. Choose a set of four points in the coordinate plane that form a quadrilateral. This can be any quadrilateral—it does not have to be a square. For simplicity, you may want to choose points in the first quadrant.

   a. Carefully plot the points and connect them to form a quadrilateral.

   b. Connect the midpoints of the sides of your quadrilateral to form a smaller quadrilateral.

3. Repeat Question 2 starting with a different set of four points.

4. Examine each of the smaller quadrilaterals you created.

   a. What general conjecture might you make about the lengths of the sides when you create a smaller quadrilateral this way?

   b. Find the coordinates of the midpoints in each of Questions 2 and 3. Verify your conjecture from Question 4a for each case using the distance formula.

Down the Garden Path

Leslie, the gardener in the POW *Equally Wet,* has decided to plant only two flowers. She places them in her two favorite spots in the garden.

Now she has another idea. She wants to make a straight-line path through her garden, with one flower on each side of the path.

Leslie wants the two flowers to be the same distance from the path. That way, people walking along the path will see them both equally well (though not necessarily at the same time).

1. How can Leslie design a path that is equidistant from each flower? Write simple, step-by-step instructions for her.

2. Is your path the only one possible? Describe all possible straight-line paths that are equidistant from each flower.

3. Describe what the word *equidistant* means in this situation.

Perpendicular and Vertical

1. A **tangent** to a circle is a line that intersects the circle at exactly one point.

   The first diagram shows a circle with center R and a line l that is tangent to the circle at point A. In other words, A is on both the circle and the line, and it is the only point on both.

   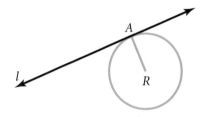

   a. Explain how you can be sure A is the point on line l that is closest to point R. In other words, show that the segment from R to A is the shortest path from point R to line l.

   b. Based on part a, what can you conclude about the relationship between $\overline{RA}$ and line l?

2. When two lines intersect, they form four angles. The angles formed by intersecting lines l and m in the diagram at the right are labeled 1, 2, 3, and 4.

   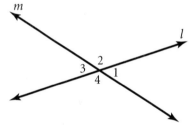

   a. Suppose $\angle 1 = 20°$. Find the measures of the other three angles.

   Pairs of opposite angles, such as the pair $\angle 1$ and $\angle 3$ or the pair $\angle 2$ and $\angle 4$, are called **vertical angles.**

   b. Prove in general that vertical angles are equal. That is, show that $\angle 1 = \angle 3$ and $\angle 2 = \angle 4$. Don't use the value $20°$ for $\angle 1$, but you can use the reasoning by which you found the other angle measures in part a.

On Patrol

You have learned that the distance from a point to a line is defined as the shortest possible distance from the point to the line. You have proved that this shortest path is perpendicular to the line. In this POW, the line is a highway and the point is a patrol station.

1. Two main highways intersect each other as they go through a certain county. The highway patrol wants to set up a station that will be the same distance from each highway. What are the possible choices for where to put the station? Assume the two highways are straight.

2. A neighboring county has three main highways. Assume all three highways are straight.

   a. Do all the highways have to intersect one another? What are the possibilities for how they might intersect? Draw some diagrams to illustrate the possibilities.

   b. Is it possible to place a patrol station the same distance from each of the three highways? How does the answer to this question depend on how the three highways intersect? Consider all possible arrangements of the highways and the possible locations of the station for each arrangement.

3. What about four highways? What about five? How can you generalize the result?

continued

○ *Write-up*

1. *Problem Statement:* State the problem in mathematical language without reference to the context. That is, describe the problem in geometric terms without talking about patrol stations or highways.

2. *Process*

3. *Solution*

4. *Self-assessment*

Adapted from "Simple Math," a series of mathematics video-dramas produced by the Israeli Instructional Television Center, with academic adviser Nitsa Movshovitz-Hadar and producer Tamar Reiner.

Proving with Distance—Part II

You showed in *Proving with Distance—Part I* that the points (5, 20), (9, 23), (12, 19), and (8, 16) are the vertices of a square.

The first diagram shows this square, as well as a circle that passes through, or intersects, the vertices of the square. We say that such a circle is **circumscribed** about the square or that the square is **inscribed** in the circle.

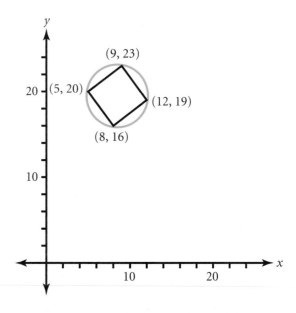

1. Find the center and radius of this circumscribed circle. Prove your answers are correct.

There is also a circle that passes through the midpoints of this square, as shown in the second diagram. The sides of the square are tangent to that circle. We say that such a circle is *inscribed* in the square or that the square is *circumscribed* about the circle.

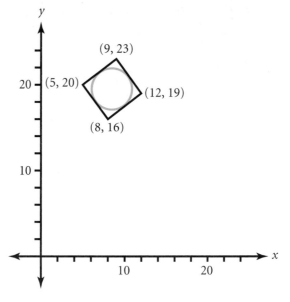

2. Find the center and radius of this inscribed circle. Prove your answers are correct.

3. Is there a circumscribed circle for every quadrilateral? Justify your answer.

All About Circles

You saw in *How Does Your Orchard Grow?* that Madie and Clyde need to understand how the circumference, area, and radius of a circle are related.

Your next task is to use polygons to help them understand the various relationships. What do circles have to do with polygons? You'll realize that the answer is as easy as pie—sort of.

A student uses a compass and straightedge to investigate the properties of a circle.

Squaring the Circle

Madie and Clyde need to know how the area and circumference of a circle are related to the radius. You will help them by completing a series of activities comparing a circle to various circumscribed regular polygons. In this first activity, you will compare the circle to the circumscribed square.

To draw such a figure, it's easiest to start by drawing a square on a sheet of grid paper. Then draw a circle inside the square so that it just touches the sides of the square. In other words, the circle is inscribed in the square.

These questions involve area, circumference, and perimeter. Find the requested numbers by making measurement estimates, rather than by using formulas.

1. a. Estimate the area of the circle. That is, estimate the number of grid squares it contains.

   b. Estimate the area of the square.

   c. Find the ratio of your answers. That is, find the value of the fraction

$$\frac{\text{area of the circle}}{\text{area of the circumscribed square}}$$

continued ▶

2. a. Estimate the circumference of the circle. You may want to use string to estimate this length.

   b. Estimate the perimeter of the square.

   c. Find the ratio of your answers. That is, find the value of the fraction

$$\frac{\text{circumference of the circle}}{\text{perimeter of the circumscribed square}}$$

3. Repeat Questions 1 and 2 for a larger circle and square. How do the ratios for the new circle-and-square pair compare to the ratios for the first pair?

4. Do you think the ratio you found in Question 1c will be the same for *any* circle? Write a careful explanation of your answer.

5. Do you think the ratio you found in Question 2c will be the same for *any* circle? Write a careful explanation of your answer.

Using the Squared Circle

In *Squaring the Circle,* you compared circles to their circumscribed squares and found ratios involving area, circumference, and perimeter.

1. Give the estimates agreed on in class for each of these ratios.

   a. $\dfrac{\text{circumference of the circle}}{\text{perimeter of the circumscribed square}}$

   b. $\dfrac{\text{area of the circle}}{\text{area of the circumscribed square}}$

2. Consider the circle and circumscribed square shown here. The circle has a radius of 10 units.

   a. Find the length of a side of the square.

   b. Find the exact perimeter of the square.

   c. Combine your ratio from Question 1a with your answer to Question 2b to get an estimate of the circle's circumference.

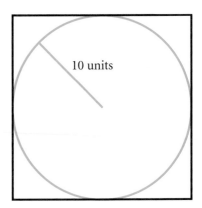

10 units

3. a. Examine the process you went through to answer Question 2c. Write a clear explanation of how to use the ratio from Question 1a to estimate the circumference of a circle from its radius.

   b. Use your explanation in Question 3a to write a formula, based on your ratio, that gives an estimate of a circle's circumference in terms of its radius.

4. a. Find the exact area of the square in Question 2.

   b. Use your answer from Question 4a and your ratio from Question 1b to estimate the circle's area.

5. a. Examine the process you went through to answer Question 4b. Write a clear explanation of how to use the ratio from Question 1b to estimate the area of a circle from its radius.

   b. Use your explanation in Question 5a to write a formula, based on your ratio, that gives an estimate of a circle's area in terms of its radius.

Hexagoning the Circle

You found approximate formulas for the circumference and area of a circle of radius r by comparing the circle to its circumscribed square.

Now you will find formulas for the perimeter and area of the regular hexagon circumscribed about that circle. These values will provide fairly good estimates of the circumference and area of the circle.

1. Begin with a circle of radius 10. Find the perimeter and area of the regular hexagon circumscribed about this circle.

2. Generalize your work to a circle of radius r. Retrace your steps from Question 1 to create formulas for the perimeter and area of the circumscribed regular hexagon in terms of r.

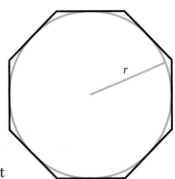

Octagoning the Circle

In *Hexagoning the Circle,* you found formulas
for the perimeter and area of a regular hexagon
circumscribed about a circle of radius r.

Your task now is to develop similar formulas for
a circumscribed regular octagon, or eight-sided
polygon.

1. Begin with a circle of radius 10. Find the perimeter
   and area of the regular octagon circumscribed about
   this circle.

2. Generalize your work to a circle of radius r. Retrace your steps from
   Question 1 to create formulas for the perimeter and area of the
   circumscribed regular octagon in terms of r.

Polygoning the Circle

The circumference C and the area A of a circle of radius r can be found from formulas of the form

$$C = k_c r \quad \text{and} \quad A = k_a r^2$$

where k_c and k_a are specific numbers called **proportionality constants** or *constants of proportionality*.

Similar formulas exist for regular polygons circumscribed about a circle. You have already developed such formulas for a square, a regular hexagon, and a regular octagon. Comparing the circle to these circumscribed polygons can give estimates of the values of k_c and k_a. The more sides a polygon has, the better the estimate.

Choose a number of sides (other than 4, 6, or 8), and develop formulas for the perimeter and area of the regular polygon with that many sides circumscribed about a circle of radius r.

Another Kind of Bisector

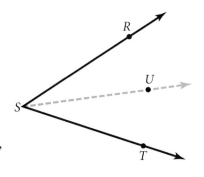

In your work on the POW *Equally Wet,* you came across the idea of a perpendicular bisector. A *perpendicular bisector* is a line that splits a line segment into two equal parts. Line segments aren't the only geometric figures that have bisectors. An **angle bisector** is a ray that splits an angle into two equal parts. For example, in the diagram at the right, if ∠*RST* is 50° and ∠*RSU* and ∠*UST* each equal 25°, then ray $\overrightarrow{SU}$ is the bisector of ∠*RST*.

Suppose two lines *l* and *m* intersect at point *A*, as shown below. In this diagram, *B* and *D* are two points on *l*, and *C* and *E* are two points on *m*. The intersecting lines *l* and *m* form four angles at *A*: ∠*BAC*, ∠*CAD*, ∠*DAE*, and ∠*EAB*.

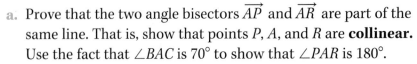

1. The diagram shows that ∠*BAC* is 70°. Find the measure of each of the other three angles.

2. In the third diagram, the dashed rays are the angle bisectors of the four angles. That is, $\overrightarrow{AP}$ bisects ∠*BAC*, $\overrightarrow{AQ}$ bisects ∠*CAD*, $\overrightarrow{AR}$ bisects ∠*DAE*, and $\overrightarrow{AS}$ bisects ∠*EAB*.

   a. Prove that the two angle bisectors $\overrightarrow{AP}$ and $\overrightarrow{AR}$ are part of the same line. That is, show that points *P*, *A*, and *R* are **collinear.** Use the fact that ∠*BAC* is 70° to show that ∠*PAR* is 180°.

   b. Prove that the angle bisectors $\overrightarrow{AQ}$ and $\overrightarrow{AS}$ are part of the same line.

   c. Prove that the line containing $\overrightarrow{AP}$ and $\overrightarrow{AR}$ is perpendicular to the line containing $\overrightarrow{AQ}$ and $\overrightarrow{AS}$.

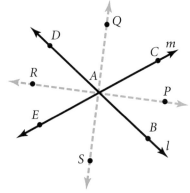

3. Your work in Question 2 was based on the fact that ∠*BAC* is 70°. Now represent ∠*BAC* as *x* and prove Questions 2a, 2b, and 2c in general. You will have to express the other angles in terms of *x*.

Proving Triples

The set of numbers 3, 4, and 5 is called a **Pythagorean triple** because $3^2 + 4^2 = 5^2$. This numeric relationship means that a triangle with side lengths 3, 4, and 5 is a right triangle.

More generally, a Pythagorean triple is defined as any trio of positive whole numbers a, b, and c that satisfy the equation $a^2 + b^2 = c^2$.

The numbers 4, 5, and 7 do not form a Pythagorean triple because $4^2 + 5^2$ does not equal 7^2. This means that a triangle with sides of these lengths is not a right triangle.

1. Show that 5, 12, and 13 form a Pythagorean triple.

2. Suppose you multiply each member of a Pythagorean triple by the same positive number. For instance, suppose you multiply 3, 4, and 5 each by 6 to get 18, 24, and 30.

   a. Determine whether 18, 24, and 30 form a Pythagorean triple.

   b. Will the process of multiplying each member of a Pythagorean triple by the same number always produce another Pythagorean triple? Give at least two more examples that support your conclusion.

3. Prove the conclusion you reached in Question 2b. There are at least two possible approaches to this question. One involves similar triangles, and the other uses the distributive property.

A Marching Strip

You might remember the economical king from *Eight Bags of Gold* and *Twelve Bags of Gold* in the Year 1 unit *The Pit and the Pendulum*. Well, he's back—with another weighty problem.

The king is planning a new rectangular courtyard in his palace. It will be laid out using square tiles. He has chosen some very pretty, but very inexpensive, tiles. However, his adviser has informed him that some of the tiles will have to be a more expensive type.

This is because visiting dignitaries will always walk along a certain diagonal, from one corner of the courtyard to the opposite corner, so the tiles along this diagonal will get lots of wear and tear. Every tile that contains a segment of the diagonal must thus be an extra-strength, more expensive tile. If a tile touches the diagonal only at a corner, it can be a regular tile.

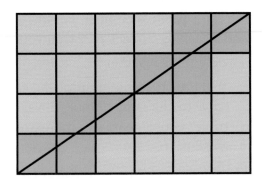

The diagram shows what the situation would look like if the king made a 4-by-6 courtyard. In this case, 8 tiles (shaded darker than the rest) include some portion of the diagonal, so these would need to be the more expensive kind.

1. The king wants to know how many of these special tiles to order. At the moment, he is planning a 63-by-90 tile courtyard. That is, it will have 63 rows of tiles with 90 tiles in each row.

   If he stays with this plan, how many special tiles will he need?

2. The king keeps changing his mind about the dimensions of the courtyard. It would be especially helpful if you could find a general formula for him.

   Suppose the courtyard has r rows with c tiles in each row. How many special tiles will the king need? (The example illustrated in the diagram, which requires 8 special tiles, is the case $r = 4$ and $c = 6$.)

continued

○ *Write-up*

1. *Problem Statement*

2. *Process*

3. *Solution*

4. *Self-assessment*

Adapted with permission from *Mathematics Teacher,* by the National Council of Teachers of Mathematics (May 1991).

Orchard Growth Revisited

In *How Does Your Orchard Grow?* you were asked to describe a plan for solving the central unit problem based on certain information. That activity led to a search for formulas for the area and circumference of a circle in terms of its radius.

Now you have those formulas, and you can carry out the plan if you are given the necessary information about the trees. Here are two key facts about the trees in Madie and Clyde's orchard.

- The cross-sectional area of a tree trunk increases by 1.5 square inches per year.
- Right now, each tree trunk has a circumference of 2.5 inches.

Although you don't yet know the hideout tree radius, you can make progress toward solving the unit problem. Your task now is to answer this question.

How long will it take for the trees to grow to a radius of 1 foot?

Cable Complications

While you've been busy learning about circles and coordinate formulas, Madie and Clyde have been dealing with another problem. There is an electrical cable that might get in the way of their planting.

While you solve this new problem, think about how it might be related to a key part of the unit problem—finding the hideout tree radius for an orchard of radius 50.

Param Gii, Kimberly Lao, and Jessica Guzman work together to solve a problem involving an electrical cable.

Cable Ready

When Madie and Clyde bought their orchard, a straight electrical cable ran along the ground from the center of the orchard, at (0, 0) in their coordinate system, to the point (30, 20).

They wanted to start their planting while they waited for the electrical company to move the cable safely underground, but they had to be sure not to plant trees right on the cable.

1. a. Could they plant a complete mini-orchard of radius 1 at the center of their lot without planting right on the cable?

   b. Answer the same question for a mini-orchard of radius 2.

   c. What is the radius of the biggest complete mini-orchard Madie and Clyde could plant without planting on the cable? Assume the tree trunks are very thin.

2. Suppose Madie and Clyde plant that biggest possible mini-orchard from Question 1c. How big will the tree trunks have to become before one of them bumps into the cable?

With your group, prepare a poster that summarizes your work on Question 2 for presentation to the class.

Going Around in Circles

1. At one time, Madie and Clyde had planned to plant a lawn instead of an orchard.

   Suppose the unit distance in their coordinate system is 10 feet. For instance, this would be the distance from (0, 0) to (1, 0).

   If a box of grass seed covers 300 square feet of ground, how many boxes would Madie and Clyde have needed for their entire lawn? Remember, the radius of their lot is 50 units, which you are assuming in this problem represents 500 feet.

2. A circular track has a diameter of 200 meters. How far is it around the track?

3. The distance around a circular pond is 100 feet. Will a 30-foot board be long enough to use as a bridge across the center of the pond?

4. A contractor has just finished installing some beautiful tiles on the floor of a circular room. Then he remembers that he is supposed to hang a banner in the room announcing the grand opening. The banner will reach across the room at its widest point, and the contractor needs to know this distance right away so he can order the banner. Unfortunately, he can't walk across the newly laid tile. He does know that he used 2830 square feet of tile for the floor.

   How long should the banner be?

Daphne's Dance Floor

Daphne has a dream of building a huge dance floor in one of the meadows on her farm. Many families live in the area, but they have no place to go dancing. Daphne thinks that with a big-name band (like the Rocking Pebbles), she'll attract a full house.

She wants a circular dance floor, 100 feet across, which means a radius of 50 feet. She needs to order wood for the floor and for the railing to surround it, so she needs to find the area and circumference of a circle with a radius of 50 feet.

She doesn't know any formulas, but she has plenty of common sense. With her trusty compass, she makes a circle that has a radius of exactly 1 foot. Then she carefully wraps a string around the circle to measure the circumference.

1. What is the circumference of a circle with a radius of 1 foot?

Because the radius of her dance floor will be exactly 50 times the radius of the circle she drew, Daphne figures the circumference of the dance floor will be 50 times the circumference of her circle. She plans to use this value to calculate how much wood to order for the railing.

continued ▶

2. a. Multiply your answer to Question 1 by 50 to get Daphne's estimate of the circumference of the dance floor.

   b. Use the formula for circumference to find the actual circumference of a circle with a radius of 50 feet.

   c. Compare your answers to parts a and b. Explain whether Daphne's method works.

Next Daphne carefully cuts out some 1-inch squares and figures out how many of them it takes, including fractions, to fill in her small circle.

3. What is the area, in square inches, of a circle with a radius of 1 foot?

As her last step, Daphne multiplies this number by 50 and figures that this tells her how many square inches of wood flooring she will need to build her dance floor.

4. a. Multiply your answer to Question 3 by 50 to get Daphne's estimate.

   b. Use the formula for area to get the actual area, in square inches, of a circle with a radius of 50 feet.

   c. Explain where Daphne's plan went wrong, and describe what she should have done instead.

Defining Circles

Earlier in this unit, you found that the equation $x^2 + y^2 = r^2$ describes the circle of radius r with center at the origin (0, 0). That is, points whose coordinates fit this equation are on the circle, and points that do not fit this equation are not on the circle.

Now you will generalize this formula to circles whose centers do not have to be at the origin.

1. Suppose the tree in the orchard at the point (6, 2) is replaced by a sprinkler and the water reaches all points within 5 units of the sprinkler. Which trees will get wet?

2. Suppose a blade of grass is growing in the open space in the orchard at the point (7.9, 6.1). Will this blade of grass get wet from the sprinkler in Question 1? How do you know?

3. Now suppose a blade of grass is growing in the open space in the orchard at the point (x, y).

   a. How can you tell if this blade of grass will get wet from the sprinkler in Question 1?

   b. Write an equation for the points on the boundary of the region watered by the sprinkler.

4. Suppose the sprinkler is at (a, b) and that the water from it reaches all points within r units. Write an equation for the circle that forms the boundary of the region the sprinkler waters.

The Standard Equation of a Circle

The Equation of a Circle

According to the distance formula, the distance from (x, y) to (a, b) is given by the expression

$$\sqrt{(x - a)^2 + (y - b)^2}$$

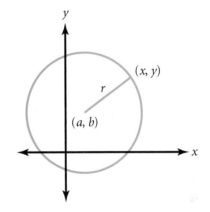

This formula can be used to write the equation of a circle, because a circle is the set of points that are some fixed distance from a given point.

The equation $\sqrt{(x - a)^2 + (y - b)^2} = r$ says, in algebraic form, that the point (x, y) is r units from (a, b). Thus the graph of this equation is the circle with center (a, b) and radius r.

For convenience, we usually square both sides of this equation to avoid the square-root symbol. The standard form for the equation of this circle is

$$(x - a)^2 + (y - b)^2 = r^2$$

For example, the equation

$$(x - 8)^2 + (y + 5)^2 = 9$$

represents the circle with center $(8, -5)$ and radius 3, as shown here.

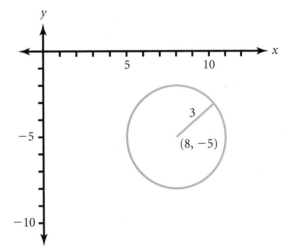

continued ▶

Transforming the Equation

Multiplying out the terms of

$$(x - 8)^2 + (y + 5)^2 = 9$$

and simplifying the result gives the equivalent equation

$$x^2 - 16x + y^2 + 10y + 80 = 0$$

More generally, the equation of a circle is always equivalent to an equation of the form

$$x^2 + cx + y^2 + dy + e = 0$$

where the coefficients c, d, and e depend on the center and radius of the circle.

Reversing the Process

This process often can be done in reverse, going from an equation of the form

$$x^2 + cx + y^2 + dy + e = 0$$

to an equation with the standard form

$$(x - a)^2 + (y - b)^2 = r^2$$

Transforming the equation in this way, when it is possible, allows you to identify the center and radius of the graph simply by looking at the equation.

This process involves the technique called **completing the square.** For example, the expression $x^2 - 16x$ suggests the perfect square $(x - 8)^2$, because expanding $(x - 8)^2$ gives $x^2 - 16x + 64$.

Completing the Square and Getting a Circle

Examine each equation. If possible, find an equivalent equation of the form

$$(x - a)^2 + (y - b)^2 = r^2$$

and identify the center and radius of the circle that the equation represents. If this is not possible, explain why not.

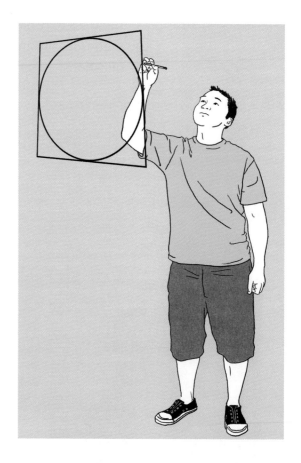

1. $x^2 - 8x + y^2 - 6y - 11 = 0$

2. $x^2 - 10x + y^2 + 12y + 28 = 0$

3. $x^2 + 3x + y^2 - 4y - 7 = 0$

4. $x^2 + 6x + y^2 + 2y + 13 = 0$

Lines of Sight

In what direction should Madie and Clyde look to see out of their orchard for as long as possible? And how long will it take until their orchard becomes a hideout?

You're closing in on the solution to the unit problem (and the trees may be closing in on you!). You will need to combine many ideas from the unit to answer Madie and Clyde's questions.

Alice Lenz uses models to help find the volume and lateral surface area of a cylinder.

The Other Gap

Using symmetry can make it much easier to locate the "last" line of sight from the center of the orchard, because some gaps between trees are like other gaps.

For instance, for an orchard of radius 3, all the gaps represented by the four shaded areas in the diagram are equivalent to the one in the first quadrant.

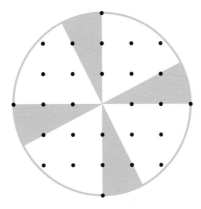

In fact, by symmetry, every gap is equivalent to one of the two gaps shown in the next diagram. The darkly shaded area represents the gap between the trees at points A and B. The lightly shaded area represents the gap between the trees at points B and C. Note that point A is at $(1, 1)$, point B is at $(2, 1)$, and point C is at $(1, 0)$.

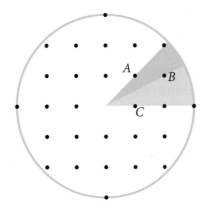

continued ▶

Within each of these two gaps, there is one optimal line of sight—
that is, a line of sight that stays unblocked as long as possible. Each is
the optimal line in its gap because it goes through the midpoint of the
segment connecting the two trees on either side of that gap. These
optimal lines of sight are shown in the next diagram.

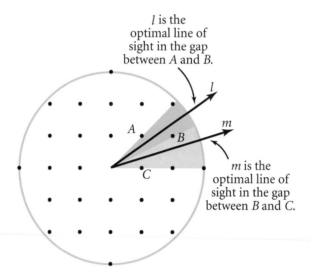

l is the
optimal line of
sight in the gap
between *A* and *B*.

m is the
optimal line of
sight in the gap
between *B* and *C*.

Note that in the context of this problem, lines of sight like *l* and *m* are
really rays from the center of the orchard. For simplicity, we can think
of them as lines.

Line *l* is in the gap between *A* and *B*. It goes through the midpoint of
$\overline{AB}$, which is $(1\frac{1}{2}, 1)$. This line of sight follows the same path as the cable
in the activity *Cable Ready*. You know from *Cable Ready* that this line
of sight becomes blocked when the tree trunks reach a radius of about
0.28 unit.

The focus of this activity is on line *m*, which is the optimal line of sight
in the gap between *B* and *C*. Line *m* goes through the midpoint of $\overline{BC}$,
which is $(1\frac{1}{2}, \frac{1}{2})$. Your task is to answer this question.

How big must the tree trunks become to block this line of sight?

Cylindrical Soda

A soft drink company sells its soda in cylindrical cans that are
12 centimeters tall and have a radius of 3 centimeters. A can of
soda this size sells for 80¢.

1. Find the volume of this can (in cubic
   centimeters). Think about how the volume of a
   box is related to the area of its base, and apply
   similar reasoning to the **cylinder.**

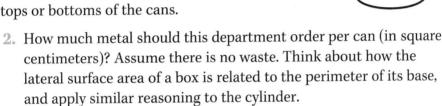

The company's Lateral Surface Department is
responsible for purchasing metal for the curved
surface of the cans. It does not buy the metal for the
tops or bottoms of the cans.

2. How much metal should this department order per can (in square
   centimeters)? Assume there is no waste. Think about how the
   lateral surface area of a box is related to the perimeter of its base,
   and apply similar reasoning to the cylinder.

3. The company decides to make a new, taller container. This tall
   can will be twice the height of the standard-size can. The top and
   bottom will still be circles with radius 3 centimeters.

   a. If the company keeps the cost per ounce of soda the same, what
      should the selling price of the tall can be?

   b. How will the metal needed for the lateral surface area of the tall
      can compare to the metal needed for the standard can?

4. The company decides to make another new
   container. This can will be three times the width
   of the standard-size can. That is, the radius
   of the base will be 9 centimeters instead of
   3 centimeters. The height of this wider can will
   be the standard 12 centimeters.

   a. If the company keeps the cost per ounce of
      soda the same, what should the selling price of the wider can be?

   b. How will the metal needed for the lateral surface area of the
      wider can compare to the metal needed for the standard can?

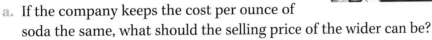

Lines of Sight for Radius Six

The last diagram in the activity *The Other Gap* suggests that *m* is one of the last lines of sight to be blocked in an orchard of radius 3. The calculations in that activity confirm this suggestion. The relevant parts of that diagram are shown here.

Line of sight *m* goes through the gap between the tree at $B = (2, 1)$ and the tree at $C = (1, 0)$. It passes through the midpoint between these two trees, which is at $(1\frac{1}{2}, \frac{1}{2})$. By symmetry, there are other lines of sight that are just as good as *m*, but no line of sight is better than *m*.

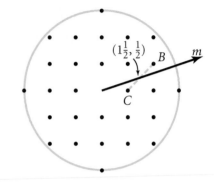

What are the last lines of sight for orchards of other sizes?

The next diagram shows the first quadrant of an orchard of radius 6. The center of the orchard is marked by a small dot, and shaded circles represent the trees.

Examine different lines of sight from the center of this orchard. Try to determine which of them will remain unblocked the longest.

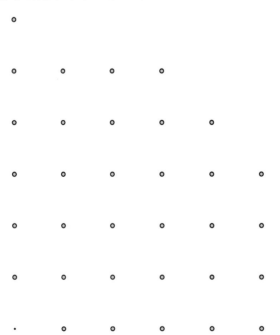

Orchard Time for Radius Three

You know that for an orchard of radius 3, the line of sight shown in the diagram is one of the last to be blocked. The perpendicular distance from the tree at $(1, 0)$ to this line is $\frac{1}{\sqrt{10}}$ unit, or approximately 0.32 unit.

Recall these facts about Madie and Clyde's orchard from the activity *Orchard Growth Revisited*.

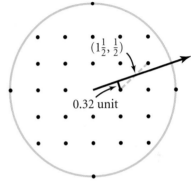

- The cross-sectional area of a tree trunk increases by 1.5 square inches per year.

- Right now, each tree trunk has a circumference of 2.5 inches.

Here is one additional piece of information about the orchard.

- The unit distance—for instance, the distance from $(0, 0)$ to $(1, 0)$—is 10 feet.

Your task is to answer this question.

How long will it take for this line of sight to be blocked?

Hiding in the Orchard

As you probably recall, Madie and Clyde planted their orchard on a circular lot of radius 50 units. They wonder how long it will take until they will no longer be able to see out of the orchard from the center.

You now have the information you need to solve their problem.

- The cross-sectional area of a tree trunk increases by 1.5 square inches per year.

- Right now, each tree trunk has a circumference of 2.5 inches.

- The unit distance—for instance, the distance from $(0, 0)$ to $(1, 0)$—is 10 feet.

- The last line of sight is the line that goes from the origin through the point $(25, \frac{1}{2})$.

Your task is to put all of this information together to answer this question.

How soon after they planted the orchard will the center of the lot become a true orchard hideout?

Big Earth, Little Earth

Suppose you were able to wrap a very long piece of string tightly around the equator of the earth. And suppose that at the same time, your friend were to wrap a piece of string tightly around the equator of a classroom globe. Of course, your friend's string would be much shorter.

For simplicity, assume the earth is a perfect sphere with a radius of 4000 miles (this isn't far off) and that the globe is a perfect sphere with a radius of 6 inches. Remember that 1 mile is equal to 5280 feet.

1. Find the length of each piece of string.

Now suppose you each replace your string with a piece 1 foot longer. Of course, your strings will no longer fit tightly around their equators. But if the earth's radius got a little bit bigger, your string would be tight again. And if the globe's radius grew a little bit, your friend's string would be tight again.

2. By how much would each radius have to increase? Which radius would have to grow more—the earth's or the globe's—for the string to fit tightly? Justify your answer.

Beginning Portfolios

A Coordinate Summary

Many of the ideas in this unit involve the coordinate system. For example, you developed a formula for finding the distance between two points in the coordinate plane in terms of their coordinates.

Write a summary of the main ideas about coordinates that you learned or used in this unit. Include important formulas and equations and their explanations as well as examples of how coordinates played a role in solving the unit problem. Also indicate which activities played an important role in your understanding of these ideas.

Me, Myself, and Pi

Maybe you knew something about the number π before starting this unit. Whether you did or not, your work in this unit with circles and circumscribed polygons will have given you insight into this important number.

Write an essay on what you thought about π before this unit and what you think now. Include any misconceptions you had that you have now corrected. In your essay, indicate which activities played an important role in your understanding of π.

Orchard Hideout Portfolio

You will now put together your portfolio for *Orchard Hideout*.
This process has three steps.

- Write a cover letter that summarizes the unit.
- Choose papers to include from your work in the unit.
- Discuss your personal growth during the unit, especially with regard to the relationship between geometry and algebra.

Cover Letter

Look back over *Orchard Hideout* and describe the central problem of the unit and the key mathematical ideas. Your description should give an overview of how the key ideas were developed and how they were used to solve the central problem.

In compiling your portfolio, you will select some activities you think were important in developing the unit's key ideas. Your cover letter should include an explanation of why you selected each item.

Selecting Papers

Your portfolio for *Orchard Hideout* should contain these items.

- *Hiding in the Orchard*
- A Problem of the Week

  Select any one of the three POWs you completed in this unit: *Equally Wet, On Patrol,* or *A Marching Strip.*

- *Beginning Portfolios*

  Include the write-up you did for this activity as well as the activities you discussed in it.

Arta Gharib Parsa selects work for his portfolio.

continued ▶

- Other key activities

  Identify two concepts you think were important in this unit (other than those discussed in *Beginning Portfolios*). For each concept, choose one or two activities that improved your understanding, and explain how the activities helped.

Personal Growth

Your cover letter for *Orchard Hideout* describes how the mathematical ideas developed in the unit. In addition, write about your own personal development during this unit. You may want to address this question.

How did the unit improve your understanding of the relationship between algebra and geometry?

Include any thoughts about your experiences that you wish to share with a reader of your portfolio.

SUPPLEMENTAL ACTIVITIES

The supplemental activities in *Orchard Hideout* expand the geometry themes from the unit. Here are some examples.

- *The Perpendicular Bisector Converse* and *Why Do They Always Meet?* follow up on ideas from the POW *Equally Wet*.

- *Inscribed Angles* and *Angles In and Out* are among several activities involving angles and angle measurement.

- *Right in the Center* and *Hypotenuse Median* are related activities involving coordinates.

Right and Isosceles

Right triangles are special, and so are isosceles triangles. Some triangles have the special property of fitting into both categories.

Triangle ABC has a right angle at C, and $\overline{AC}$ and $\overline{BC}$ have the same length.

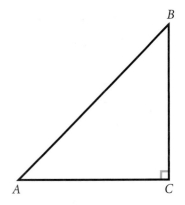

1. What is the size, or measure, of $\angle A$? Justify your answer.

2. Find the exact values of $\sin A$, $\cos A$, and $\tan A$, based on geometric principles. In other words, do not use a calculator to get your answers.

The Perpendicular Bisector Converse

In the POW *Equally Wet,* you investigated where a sprinkler could be placed to water two flowers equally. In mathematical terms, this means finding the set of points in a plane that are equidistant from two given points. You saw that this set forms the perpendicular bisector of the segment connecting the two points.

One part of this result involved proving this "if-then" statement, which you did in the activity *A Perpendicularity Proof.*

> *If D is on the perpendicular bisector of the segment connecting points A and B, then the distances AD and BD are equal.*

In this statement, the hypothesis is "*D* is on the perpendicular bisector of the segment connecting points *A* and *B.*" The conclusion is "the distances *AD* and *BD* are equal."

When the hypothesis and conclusion of an "if-then" statement are interchanged, the result is called the **converse** of the original statement. For some true "if-then" statements, the converse is true. For others, the converse is false.

continued ▶

Your Task

Your task is to prove that the converse of the statement you proved earlier is also true. That is, prove this statement.

If the distances AD and BD are equal, then D is on the perpendicular bisector of the segment connecting points A and B.

Start with a diagram like the one here, and assume the hypothesis is true. That is, assume $AD = BD$.

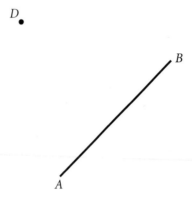

Then draw a perpendicular segment from D to $\overline{AB}$, as in the next diagram.

At this point you know that $\overline{DC}$ is perpendicular to $\overline{AB}$, but you don't know whether it bisects $\overline{AB}$. You need to show that C is the midpoint of $\overline{AB}$. In other words, show that $AC = BC$. The key is finding a way to use the hypothesis that AD and BD are equal.

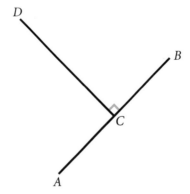

Counting Trees

If Madie and Clyde plant their orchard on a lot of radius 1, it will include only the four trees on the axes. All four of those trees lie on the boundary of the orchard.

If they expand to a lot of radius 2, their orchard will include 12 trees. Again, there will be exactly four trees on the boundary.

1. Sketch an orchard of radius 3. Find out how many trees it has on its boundary.

2. Sketch an orchard of radius 5. Find out how many trees it has on its boundary.

3. Is it possible for an orchard to have on its boundary a tree whose coordinates are equal? Assume the radius of the lot is a positive integer.

4. Use your examples and your answer to Question 3 to develop a general statement about the number of trees on the boundary of an orchard. You may find your work on the activity *Other Trees* useful.

Perpendicular Bisectors by Algebra

The perpendicular bisector of a line segment is the set of points that are equidistant from the endpoints of the segment. The coordinate system provides a way to think about perpendicular bisectors algebraically.

1. Start with the two points $(4, 3)$ and $(8, 5)$ and a general point (x, y).

   a. Write an expression for the distance from (x, y) to $(4, 3)$.

   b. Write an expression for the distance from (x, y) to $(8, 5)$.

   c. Form an equation by setting the two expressions equal.

Your equation from Question 1c says, in effect, "(x, y) is equidistant from $(4, 3)$ and $(8, 5)$." This means it should be the equation of the perpendicular bisector of the segment connecting those two points.

2. Simplify your equation as much as possible. You should be able to simplify it so that it becomes a linear equation.

3. a. Find the coordinates of the midpoint of the segment connecting $(4, 3)$ and $(8, 5)$.

   b. Verify that the coordinates you found fit the equation from Question 2.

   c. Explain why the coordinates of the midpoint *should* fit the equation.

4. Plot the points $(4, 3)$ and $(8, 5)$ and draw the segment connecting them. Then graph your equation from Question 2. Does the result fit your expectations? Explain.

5. Suppose (a, b) and (c, d) are any two points. Use the steps in Questions 1 and 2 to write the equation of the set of points equidistant from these two points. That is, find a linear equation for the perpendicular bisector of the segment connecting (a, b) and (c, d).

Midpoint Proof

In the activity *A Snack in the Middle,* you were asked to find the midpoint of the segment connecting (24, 6) and (30, 14). The answer is (27, 10). Part of your task was to prove that (27, 10) is equidistant from the two endpoints of the segment.

Unfortunately, this doesn't prove that (27, 10) is the midpoint, because *any* point on the perpendicular bisector of the segment will be equidistant from the two endpoints.

1. Find at least two other points that are equidistant from (24, 6) and (30, 14).

2. Explain how you know that (27, 10) is actually on the line segment connecting (24, 6) and (30, 14). To do this, you will need to find a linear equation whose graph includes those two points, and show that (27, 10) also fits the equation.

3. How would you prove in general that the midpoint formula actually gives the midpoint?

Why Do They Always Meet?

Start with any triangle. Draw the perpendicular bisector of one of the triangle's sides. Then draw the perpendicular bisector of a different side.

Because these two perpendicular bisectors aren't parallel, they must meet at some point.

1. Prove that the third perpendicular bisector must go through this same point. In other words, show that all three perpendicular bisectors meet in a single point. Use the principle that the perpendicular bisector of a line segment consists of all points equidistant from the endpoints of the segment.

2. Explain how your result from Question 1 shows that every triangle has a circumscribed circle.

3. Explain how this idea applies to the three-flower case in the POW *Equally Wet.*

4. If you didn't answer the sprinkler problem for four flowers or more in your POW, work on it some more, using the ideas from Questions 1 to 3.

Inscribed Angles

In examining the three-flower case in the POW *Equally Wet*, you may have realized that any triangle can be inscribed in a circle. You can find the center of this circle by looking for the place where the perpendicular bisectors of the three sides of the triangle meet. That point is equidistant from all three vertices. (The supplemental activity *Why Do They Always Meet?* asks you to prove that the three perpendicular bisectors all meet in one point.)

Now you will look at the special case in which the center of the circle is actually on one of the sides of the triangle.

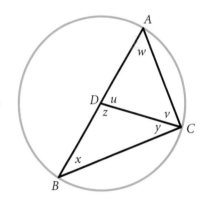

In this diagram, $\triangle ABC$ is inscribed in a circle whose center, point D, is on side $\overline{AB}$. Because $\overline{AB}$ is a diameter of the circle, we say that $\triangle ACB$ is *inscribed in a semicircle*. The diagram also shows the radius from D to C and uses the letters u, v, w, x, y, and z to represent the measures of the indicated angles. For example, u is the measure of $\angle ADC$.

Your task is to prove this statement.

> *An angle inscribed in a semicircle must be a right angle.*

You can use these steps to construct a proof.

1. Explain why $x = y$ and $v = w$.

2. Explain why $u + z = 180°$.

3. Write equations showing the sums of the angles of various triangles.

4. Combine your findings from Questions 1 to 3 to prove that $v + y = 90°$. In other words, prove that $\angle ACB$ is a right angle.

More Inscribed Angles

The supplemental activity *Inscribed Angles* asked you to prove that an angle inscribed in a semicircle must be a right angle. This is actually a special case of a more general principle. To state this general principle, we need to introduce some terminology.

If an angle *ABC* is situated with points *A*, *B*, and *C* on a circle, as shown at the right, we say the angle is *inscribed in the circle*.

The angle formed by the radii from the center *D* to points *A* and *C*, which is ∠*ADC*, is called the **central angle** that corresponds to inscribed ∠*ABC*.

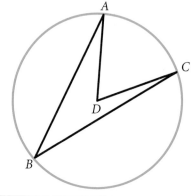

Here is the general principle.

An angle inscribed in a circle is half the size of the corresponding central angle.

Before proving the general principle, you need to consider first the case in which $\overline{AB}$ is actually a diameter of the circle, as shown in the second diagram. (This diagram is part of the diagram from the activity *Inscribed Angles*.)

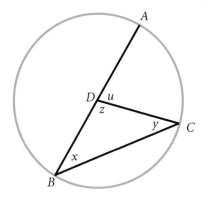

1. Prove in this case that ∠*ABC* is half the size of ∠*ADC*. (Look at the relevant parts of Questions 1 to 3 of *Inscribed Angles*.)

2. Apply the special case from Question 1 to prove the general case. You will need to show that ∠*ABE* in the third diagram is half the size of ∠*ADE* and that ∠*CBE* is half the size of ∠*CDE*.

3. Explain why the result from *Inscribed Angles* is a special case of this principle.

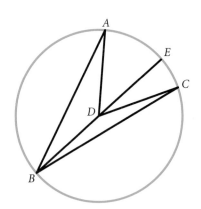

Angles In and Out

If you worked on either of the supplemental activities *Inscribed Angles* or *More Inscribed Angles,* you saw a diagram like this one.

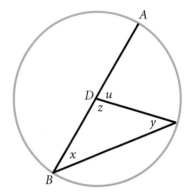

In the course of your work, you may have realized that $u = x + y$. In fact, this is a special case of a more general principle that has nothing to do with circles or inscribed angles.

Consider the second diagram, in which $\triangle PQR$ is an arbitrary triangle and S is a point on the extension of $\overline{PQ}$. The letters a, b, c, and d represent the measures of the indicated angles.

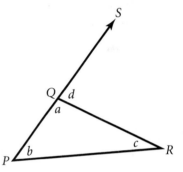

You may recall that an angle such as $\angle SQR$ is called an **exterior angle** for $\triangle PQR$. In addition, $\angle PQR$ is called the **adjacent interior angle** for this exterior angle, and $\angle QPR$ and $\angle QRP$ are called the **nonadjacent interior angles.**

Your task in this activity is to prove this statement.

> *In any triangle, each exterior angle is equal to the sum of the two nonadjacent interior angles.*

In other words, prove that $d = b + c$.

Midpoint Quadrilaterals

In Question 2 of the activity *Proving with Distance—Part I,* you picked four points in the coordinate plane and connected them to form a quadrilateral.

You then found the midpoints of the sides of that quadrilateral and connected them to form a new quadrilateral, which we will call the *midpoint quadrilateral.*

Your final diagram probably looked something like the pair of quadrilaterals shown here.

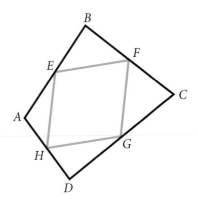

It turns out, as you may have conjectured, that the midpoint quadrilateral is always a parallelogram, no matter what quadrilateral you start with. Your task now is to prove this. (In *Proving with Distance—Part I,* you were asked to prove that the opposite sides of that specific quadrilateral had equal lengths.)

Before beginning, recall that a *parallelogram* is defined as a quadrilateral with opposite sides that are parallel.

An Outline Using Triangles

This activity provides a three-part outline to help you construct a proof. (Parts I and II involve only triangles.)

The diagram at the right is formed from part of the original diagram and shows the diagonal $\overline{AC}$ of the original quadrilateral. So $\triangle ABC$ could be any triangle, and E and F are the midpoints of $\overline{AB}$ and $\overline{BC}$.

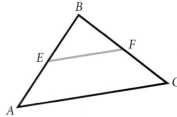

In $\triangle ABC$, we will refer to $\overline{AC}$ as the *base* and to $\overline{EF}$ as the **midline** (because it connects two midpoints).

continued ▶

In Parts I and II, you will prove two statements about this diagram.

- *EF* is half *AC*. (In other words, the length of $\overline{EF}$ is half the length of $\overline{AC}$.)
- $\overline{EF}$ is parallel to $\overline{AC}$.

You may want to think ahead about how you would use the second statement to prove *EFGH* is a parallelogram. (That's Part III.) Keep in mind that these statements apply to any triangle.

Part I: The Length of the Midline Is Half the Length of the Base

The proof of this statement suggested in Questions 1 and 2 uses coordinates. (The study of geometry using coordinates is called **analytic geometry.**)

To make things completely general, suppose that point *A* is (r, s), *B* is (t, u), and *C* is (v, w).

1. Find expressions for *EF* and *AC* in terms of these coordinates.

2. Use your expressions from Question 1 to prove that *EF* is half *AC*.

Part II: The Midline Is Parallel to the Base

The proof of this statement suggested in Questions 3 and 4 uses similarity but does not involve coordinates. (The more general study of geometry, without coordinates, is sometimes called **synthetic geometry.**)

3. Prove that $\triangle EBF$ is similar to $\triangle ABC$. Use the result from Question 2 to show that corresponding sides of these two triangles are proportional.

4. Prove that $\overline{EF}$ is parallel to $\overline{AC}$. Use the result from Question 3 to show that $\angle BEF = \angle BAC$. Then use ideas about transversals and their corresponding angles.

Part III: EFGH Is a Parallelogram

5. Prove that quadrilateral *EFGH* is a parallelogram. Use the fact that for any triangle, the midline is parallel to the base. Also use the definition of a parallelogram.

Equidistant Lines

As part of your discussion of the activity *Down the Garden Path,* you proved this statement.

If a line goes through the midpoint of $\overline{AB}$, then it is equidistant from points A and B.

Your task now is to prove the converse of this statement, which is the conjecture the class came up with by drawing various lines in *Down the Garden Path.* In other words, prove this statement.

If a line is equidistant from points A and B, then it goes through the midpoint of $\overline{AB}$.

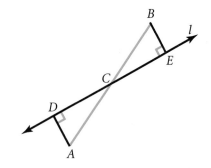

You can use the diagram here to set up the problem. The diagram shows two points A and B and a line l. Point C is where l meets $\overline{AB}$.

The hypothesis says to assume that l is equidistant from A and B. This means the perpendicular distances AD and BE are equal.

You need to prove that C is the midpoint of $\overline{AB}$.

Right in the Center

1. Consider the triangle whose vertices are (4, 1), (12, 7), and (24, −9).

   a. Prove this is a right triangle.

   b. Find the midpoint of the hypotenuse of this triangle.

   c. Show that the midpoint of the hypotenuse is equidistant from all three vertices.

2. Use the results from Question 1 to find the center and radius of a circle that goes through all three vertices of the triangle.

3. Find the equation for the circle in Question 2. Verify that the coordinates of the points (4, 1), (12, 7), and (24, −9) all fit the equation. (This requires ideas from the activity *Defining Circles*.)

Thirty-Sixty-Ninety

Triangle *ABC* in this diagram is equilateral, and $\overline{AD}$ is the altitude from *A* to $\overline{BC}$.

The supplemental activity *Right and Isosceles* focused on one special type of triangle. The focus now is on the equilateral triangle.

1. Find the angle measures in right triangle *ABD*.

2. Use the diagram to find the exact values of sin 30°, cos 30°, tan 30°, sin 60°, cos 60°, and tan 60°. Do not rely on a calculator for your answers.

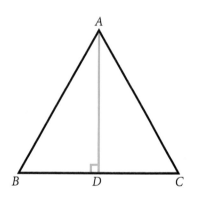

Darts

To pass the time while their trees are growing, Madie and Clyde hang a dartboard on one of the trees. The dartboard looks like the one shown here, in which the radii of the circles are in the ratio 1:2:3.

A dart that lands in the white ring around the outside earns 10 points. A dart in the shaded ring earns 30 points. A dart that hits the innermost darkly shaded circle earns 50 points.

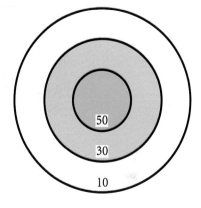

Assume that Madie and Clyde always hit the board and that darts have an equal chance of landing at any location on the board. What is the expected value for their score per dart? (*Reminder:* You can find the expected value by taking an average over a large number of trials.)

Adapted with permission from the *Mathematics Teacher*, by the National Council of Teachers of Mathematics (December 1990).

More About Triples

As you have seen, a Pythagorean triple is any trio of positive whole numbers a, b, and c that satisfy the equation $a^2 + b^2 = c^2$. The triple 3, 4, and 5 and the triple 5, 12, and 13 are two of the most familiar examples.

Your task in this activity is to learn more about Pythagorean triples. Here are two questions to get you started, but don't be limited by them. In fact, the study of problems like these is part of a branch of mathematics called *number theory*. You may want to consult a book on number theory for ideas.

1. Is it possible to have a Pythagorean triple a, b, and c in which a and b are equal? Justify your answer.

A *primitive* Pythagorean triple is one in which a, b, and c have no common whole-number factor (other than 1).

2. Assume a, b, and c form a primitive Pythagorean triple, with $a^2 + b^2 = c^2$.

   a. Prove that a and b cannot both be even numbers.

   b. Prove that a and b cannot both be odd numbers. (This is harder than part a.)

   c. Prove that c must be an odd number.

The Inscribed Circle

You saw in the POW *On Patrol* that a point on an angle bisector is equidistant from the two lines that form that angle.

This fact and its converse can be used to prove that every triangle has an inscribed circle. (This is similar to the result from Question 2 of the supplemental activity *Why Do They Always Meet?*) An *inscribed circle* is a circle to which the sides of the triangle are all tangent.

Consider $\triangle ABC$, shown here. Suppose rays l and m are the bisectors of $\angle BAC$ and $\angle BCA$. Point D is where these two rays meet.

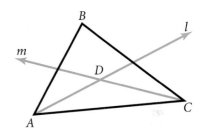

1. Prove that the ray from B through D bisects $\angle ABC$. Use the general principle about angle bisectors from *On Patrol*.

2. Explain how your result proves that every triangle has an inscribed circle.

Medians and Altitudes

If you worked on the supplemental activity *Why Do They Always Meet?*, you saw why the perpendicular bisectors of the sides of a triangle all meet in a single point. That point is called the *circumcenter* of the triangle, because it is the center of the circumscribed circle. The diagram at the right shows a triangle, its perpendicular bisectors, and the circumscribed circle.

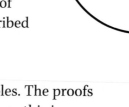

A similar principle holds for angle bisectors. That is, the three angle bisectors of a triangle all meet in a single point. That point is called the *incenter* of the triangle, because it is the center of the inscribed circle. (This principle was established in the supplemental activity *The Inscribed Circle*.)

This activity involves two other, similar principles. The proofs of these two principles are much more difficult, so this is a very challenging activity.

Part I: Medians

In any triangle, the line segment connecting a vertex to the midpoint of the opposite side is called a **median.** For example, in $\triangle RST$, point W is the midpoint of $\overline{RS}$, so $\overline{TW}$ is a median.

Prove that in any triangle, the three medians meet in a single point.

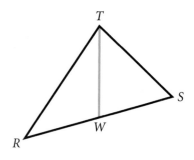

continued ▶

Part II: Altitudes

In any triangle, the line segment from a vertex perpendicular to the line containing the opposite side is called an *altitude*. For example, in $\triangle FGH$, $\overline{GK}$ is perpendicular to $\overline{FH}$, so $\overline{GK}$ is an altitude.

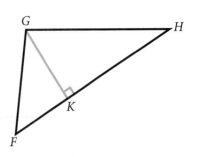

Prove that in any triangle, the three altitudes meet in a single point.

Hypotenuse Median

In the supplemental activity *Right in the Center,* you were asked to show that the midpoint of the hypotenuse of a certain right triangle is equidistant from all three vertices. As you may have guessed, this is not a coincidence. Your task now is to prove the general principle.

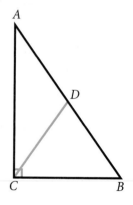

In any triangle, the line segment connecting a vertex to the midpoint of the opposite side is called a *median.* So, $\overline{CD}$ in the diagram is the median to the hypotenuse. In this diagram, $\triangle ABC$ is a right triangle and D is the midpoint of $\overline{AB}$.

The goal of this activity is to prove this principle.

> *The length of the median to the hypotenuse is half the length of the hypotenuse.*

We will call this principle the *median-to-the-hypotenuse property.*

Here are outlines for two ways to prove this principle. Try to prove it both ways.

1. First prove that the two diagonals of any rectangle are the same length and bisect each other. Draw $\triangle ABC$, draw in the full rectangle around $\triangle ABC$, and use this fact about the diagonals of a rectangle to prove the median-to-the-hypotenuse property.

2. Place the triangle in the coordinate system with point C at the origin and points A and B on the axes. Assign coordinates to A and B in a way that makes $\triangle ABC$ a general right triangle. Then find the coordinates of D and use the result to prove the median-to-the-hypotenuse property.

Not Quite a Circle

You've seen that $x^2 + y^2 = r^2$ is the equation of a circle with center $(0, 0)$ and radius r. A point with coordinates (x, y) is on this circle if and only if the coordinates fit the equation.

Your task in this activity is to experiment with variations of this equation to determine what shapes they define.

Specifically, think of the equation in the form $1 \cdot x^2 + 1 \cdot y^2 = r^2$, and examine what happens to the graph of the equation if numbers other than 1 are used as coefficients for x^2 and y^2. That is, consider equations such as these.

$$9x^2 + 16y^2 = 144$$
$$25x^2 + 16y^2 = 400$$
$$4x^2 + 4y^2 = 25$$

Restrict yourself to coefficients and **constant terms** that are perfect squares, as in these examples. This will allow you to write these numbers as squares of other numbers. For example, the equation $9x^2 + 16y^2 = 144$ can be written $3^2 \cdot x^2 + 4^2 \cdot y^2 = 12^2$.

Investigate specific examples and report on what you learn about the graphs of equations of the form $a^2x^2 + b^2y^2 = c^2$.

Knitting

As the years go by, Madie and Clyde decide to start a family. They spend their afternoons sitting out among the trees, knitting booties and doing geometry problems.

They figure that a ball of yarn with about a 3-inch diameter will be needed for each bootie.

1. Madie has a ball of yarn with a 1-foot diameter. How many booties will it yield?

2. How many booties will they get from a ball of yarn with a 2-foot diameter? How does this compare with your answer to Question 1?

Adapted with permission from *Mathematics Teacher,* by the National Council of Teachers of Mathematics (December 1990).

What's a Parabola?

In the Year 2 unit *Fireworks,* you described graphs for $y = x^2$ and similar quadratic functions as parabolas. But what exactly is a parabola? Is it any curve that goes down and then up (or up and then down)?

In fact, this term has a precise geometric meaning that can be described in two distinct ways.

The Parabola as a Conic Section

The **parabola** is one of several shapes, called *conic sections,* that you can get by taking the intersection of a plane with a cone. In mathematics, a cone consists of two parts, sort of like one ice cream cone inverted on top of another and extending infinitely in both directions.

By changing the angle of the plane, you get different conic sections. These include the familiar shape known as an **ellipse** (which includes the circle as a special case) and another shape called a **hyperbola.** When the plane is parallel to the edge of the cone, the result is a parabola.

The Parabola in the Coordinate Plane

A second geometric definition of *parabola,* which you will explore in this activity, involves the coordinate plane. This approach can be

continued ▶

applied to the other conic sections as well. The definition begins by choosing a point P, called the **focus,** and a line l (not containing P), called the **directrix.** The parabola defined by that point and line consists of every point Q whose distance from P is the same as its distance from l.

To illustrate this, the diagram uses the point $(0, 1)$ for P and the line $y = -1$ for l.

The origin $(0, 0)$ is exactly one unit from P and one unit from l, so it is on the parabola defined by this point and line.

The diagram also shows a general point Q, with coordinates (x, y), and the segments connecting Q to P and to l. This particular point Q appears to be farther from P than it is from l, so this point Q is not on the parabola.

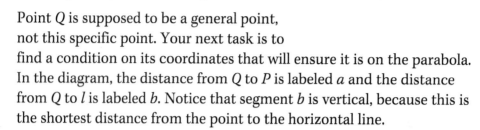

1. Estimate the distance from Q to P and the distance from Q to l to confirm that this point Q is not on the parabola.

Point Q is supposed to be a general point, not this specific point. Your next task is to find a condition on its coordinates that will ensure it is on the parabola. In the diagram, the distance from Q to P is labeled a and the distance from Q to l is labeled b. Notice that segment b is vertical, because this is the shortest distance from the point to the horizontal line.

2. a. Write an expression for distance a using the coordinates of P and Q.

   b. Write an expression for distance b using the coordinates of Q and the equation of line l.

3. Use your work from Question 2 to create an equation that states that the distances a and b are equal.

4. Simplify your equation until it looks like a familiar quadratic function.

continued ▶

In the example in Questions 1 to 4, point P is on the y-axis. Also, the distance from P to the x-axis is the same as the distance from l to the x-axis. This makes the algebra as simple as possible.

5. Suppose the focus P is the point $(2, 1)$ and the directrix l is the line $y = -3$.

   a. Find a simple equation for the parabola defined by this choice of P and l.

   b. Where is the vertex of this parabola in relation to P and l? Why?

6. Imagine choosing some other point for P and some other horizontal line for l. If you create and simplify the equation for the parabola defined by that choice of focus and directrix, do you think you will get a quadratic function? Justify your answer.

Creating Parabolas

In the supplemental activity *What's a Parabola?* you were given specific combinations of a point P and a line l not containing that point. In each case, you had to find an equation for the parabola defined by that combination of focus and directrix.

Now you will work the other way, starting with the equation of a parabola and trying to find the parabola's focus and directrix. You may find it helpful to refer to your work on *What's a Parabola?*

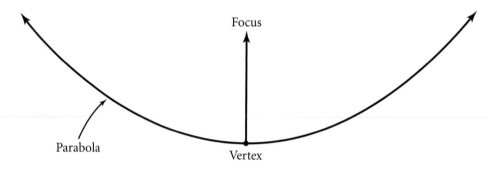

1. Find the choice of P and l that leads to the equation $y = x^2$.

2. Find the choice of P and l that leads to the equation
   $y = (x + 1)^2 - 2$.

3. Find the choice of P and l that leads to the equation
   $y = 4(x - 3)^2 + 1$.

Coordinate Ellipses and Hyperbolas

In the supplemental activity *What's a Parabola?* you looked at a coordinate definition of the term *parabola*. Given a particular point *P* and a line *l* that doesn't pass through *P*, the parabola they define consists of every point *Q* whose distance from the focus *P* is the same as its distance from the directrix *l*.

Replacing "the same as" by something else leads to a way of defining the other two classes of conic sections: ellipses and hyperbolas.

Suppose *k* is some fixed positive number. Let the set *S* consist of every point *Q* whose distance from *P* is exactly *k* times its distance from *l*. If $k = 1$, you already know the set *S* is a parabola.

1. Using the point (0, 1) for *P* and the line $y = -1$ for *l*, as in the diagram, and using the value $\frac{1}{2}$ for *k*, sketch the set *S*. Begin by looking for points on the *y*-axis whose distance from *P* are exactly half their distance from *l*. For more general points, you might consider whether the specific location of *Q* in the diagram would belong to set *S*, and why.

2. Use the coordinates in the diagram to write an equation stating that the general point *Q* is exactly half as far from *P* as it is from *l*.

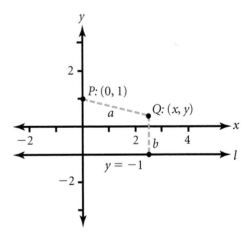

3. Simplify your equation as much as you can.

4. Describe the shape of the graph in general terms.

5. Using the same point and line, go through the steps in Questions 1 to 4 using the value 2 for *k*. You should get points below *l* as well as points above *l*.

continued ▶

Conic Sections Defined

The three types of conic sections—parabola, ellipse, and hyperbola—can all be defined in terms of a point P, a line l not containing P, and a positive constant k (called the *eccentricity*).

- If $k < 1$, the set of points whose distance from P are exactly k times their distance from l is an ellipse.

- If $k > 1$, the set of points whose distance from P are exactly k times their distance from l is a hyperbola.

- If $k = 1$, the set of points whose distance from P are exactly k times their distance from l is a parabola.

In this scheme, a circle is considered a special case of an ellipse, but often the circle is described as a fourth kind of conic section.

Another View of Ellipses and Hyperbolas

In the supplemental activity *Coordinate Ellipses and Hyperbolas,* the ellipse and hyperbola were defined starting with a point P and a line l. There is an alternate definition based on two points.

Suppose P_1 and P_2 are two points and d is a fixed positive number.

- The ellipse defined by P_1, P_2, and d is the set of points Q for which the sum of the distance from Q to P_1 and the distance from Q to P_2 is equal to d.

- The hyperbola defined by P_1, P_2, and d is the set of points Q for which the difference between the distance from Q to P_1 and the distance from Q to P_2 is equal to d.

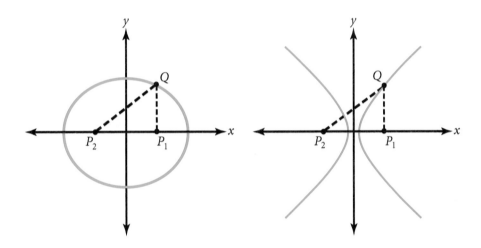

Sketching an Ellipse

Suppose P_1 is the point $(2, 0)$, P_2 is the point $(-2, 0)$, and $d = 8$. Consider the ellipse determined by these values according to the definition just stated.

1. Verify that the point $Q = (2, 3)$ is on this ellipse. In other words, show that $P_1Q + P_2Q = 8$.

continued ▶

2. Find all the points on either axis that are on the ellipse.

3. Find at least three more points on the ellipse.

4. Sketch the ellipse, using your points from Questions 1 to 3 as a guideline.

Sketching a Hyperbola

Suppose P_1 is the point $(2, 0)$ and P_2 is the point $(-2, 0)$, but this time let $d = 2$. Now consider the hyperbola determined by these values according to the definition stated earlier.

5. Verify that the point $Q = (2, 3)$ is on this hyperbola. Because Q is closer to P_1 than to P_2, this means showing that $P_2Q - P_1Q = 2$.

6. Find a point on the hyperbola that is closer to P_2 than to P_1. In other words, find a point Q for which $P_1Q - P_2Q = 2$.

7. Use symmetry to find two more points on the hyperbola.

8. Find all the points on either axis that are on the hyperbola.

9. Sketch the hyperbola, using your points from Questions 5 to 8 as a guideline.

It turns out that for an ellipse, d must be greater than the distance from P_1 to P_2, but for a hyperbola, d must be less than the distance from P_1 to P_2.

10. Explain the two parts of the last statement, as follows.

   a. For the case of the ellipse: What happens if d is equal to the distance from P_1 to P_2? What happens if d is less than the distance from P_1 to P_2?

   b. For the case of the hyperbola: What happens if d is equal to the distance from P_1 to P_2? What happens if d is more than the distance from P_1 to P_2?

Ellipses and Hyperbolas by Points and Algebra

In the supplemental activity *Another View of Ellipses and Hyperbolas,* you saw these two definitions, based on a choice of two points P_1 and P_2 and a fixed positive number d.

- The ellipse defined by P_1, P_2, and d is the set of points Q for which the sum of the distance from Q to P_1 and the distance from Q to P_2 is equal to d.

- The hyperbola defined by P_1, P_2, and d is the set of points Q for which the difference between the distance from Q to P_1 and the distance from Q to P_2 is equal to d.

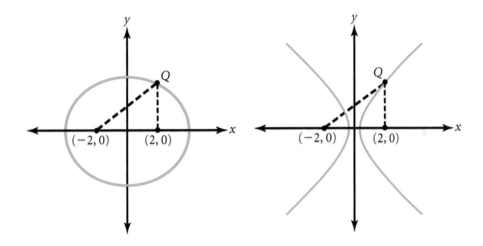

Now you will develop equations for the specific examples from *Another View of Ellipses and Hyperbolas.*

In both cases, P_1 is the point $(2, 0)$ and P_2 is the point $(-2, 0)$. Although these points make the algebra about as simple as possible, it's still very messy.

continued ▶

In each situation, you will likely start with an equation that involves two square-root expressions. Start by writing an equivalent equation in which these square-root expressions are on opposite sides of the equation. Then square both sides of the equation and simplify to isolate the square-root expression you still have. Then square again and simplify one more time.

1. Suppose $d = 8$. Create and simplify an equation for the ellipse defined by the points P_1 and P_2 and the constant d. That is, consider a general point Q with coordinates (x, y) and write an equation using x and y that says $P_1Q + P_2Q = 8$.

2. Suppose $d = 2$. Create and simplify an equation for the hyperbola defined by the points P_1 and P_2 and the constant d. That is, consider a general point Q with coordinates (x, y) and write an equation using x and y that says either $P_1Q - P_2Q = 2$ or $P_2Q - P_1Q = 2$.

Generalizing the Ellipse

In the supplemental activity *Ellipses and Hyperbolas by Points and Algebra,* you saw that an ellipse can be defined as the set of all points the sum of whose distances from two fixed points is a given positive constant. Those two points are called the **foci** of the ellipse.

Suppose the ellipse is in "standard position," with its center at the origin and its foci on the x-axis at $(c, 0)$ and $(-c, 0)$. (The earlier activity examined the case of $c = 2$.)

The ellipse meets the x-axis in two points, labeled $(a, 0)$ and $(-a, 0)$ in the diagram. It meets the y-axis in two points, labeled $(0, b)$ and $(0, -b)$.

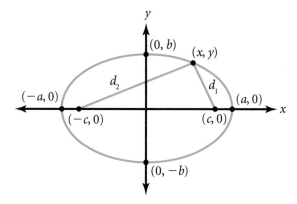

If (x, y) represents a general point on the ellipse, then the distances from (x, y) to the foci are given by the equations

$$d_1 = \sqrt{(x - c)^2 + y^2} \quad \text{and} \quad d_2 = \sqrt{(x + c)^2 + y^2}$$

For the special case in which $(x, y) = (a, 0)$, the sum of the distances to the foci is $2a$. Therefore the equation of the ellipse is $d_1 + d_2 = 2a$. (This shows that the case examined in *Ellipses and Hyperbolas by Points and Algebra* used $a = 4$.)

1. Show that $a^2 = b^2 + c^2$.

2. Show that the equation of the ellipse can be simplified to

$$\frac{x^2}{a^2} + \frac{y^2}{b^2} = 1$$

Moving the Ellipse

In the supplemental activity *Generalizing the Ellipse,* you considered an ellipse whose center is at the origin and whose critical points are $(a, 0)$, $(-a, 0)$, $(0, b)$, and $(0, -b)$.

The equation for this ellipse is

$$\frac{x^2}{a^2} + \frac{y^2}{b^2} = 1$$

This ellipse is shown in the diagram.

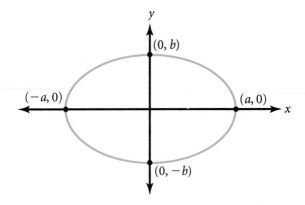

If the center of the ellipse is not at the origin, then the equation is a bit more complicated.

Suppose the ellipse with equation $\frac{x^2}{a^2} + \frac{y^2}{b^2} = 1$ has been moved h units to the right and k units up. Its center is now at the point (h, k). If h or k is negative, then the ellipse has been translated left or down.

1. Find the equation of this translated ellipse. Also find the coordinates of its foci.

2. How is this equation similar to the equation of a circle with center at (h, k)?

Meadows or Malls?

Three-Variable Equations, Three-Dimensional Coordinates, and Matrix Algebra

Meadows or Malls?—Three-Variable Equations, Three-Dimensional Coordinates, and Matrix Algebra

Recreation Versus Development: A Complex Problem

The people of River City have a decision to make. They must decide how much of the city's land to use for recreation and how much to use for development, and exactly which land to use for each purpose.

To help them with their decision, you will apply many ideas about algebra, geometry, and the relationship between the two. The first stage is simply to make some sense of this complicated situation.

Daniel Kurek thinks about how to represent the constraints algebraically.

Meadows or Malls?

Who would have thought that so much good fortune could cause so much trouble? Well, it surely has in River City. Actually, there are three separate pieces of good fortune.

First, when Mr. Goodfellow died, he left his 300-acre farm to the city. His will had no stipulations, so the city can do whatever it wishes with the property.

Then the U.S. Army closed its 100-acre base on the edge of town. The federal government gave the land to the people of River City to use in any way they choose.

Finally, 150 acres of city land was leased to a mining company 99 years ago. Now the lease is up. Because the company did not find enough minerals there to make a profit for many years, it does not wish to renew the lease. So that land is also available to River City with no restrictions on its use.

Altogether, that is 550 acres of land the city can use in any way it decides. The problem is that a city isn't exactly an "it." A city is home to many people, who don't always agree. And the people of River City definitely do not agree on how to use the 550 acres.

The controversy centers on two opposing camps. One group wants to use as much of the land as possible for *development*—that is, for stores, businesses, and housing. The other group wants to use as much of the land as possible for *recreation*—that is, for parkland, hiking trails, picnic areas, and a wildlife preserve.

The business community won an initial victory by getting the city council to agree that at least 300 acres will be used for development. The business community proposes that the more attractive sites—the army base and the mining land—should go for development, while any recreation land could come from Mr. Goodfellow's property. But the people with environmental and sporting interests believe that some of the more attractive land should be used for recreation.

continued ▶

The two groups finally arrived at a two-part compromise.

- At most, 200 acres of the army base and mining land will be used for recreation.
- The amount of army base land used for recreation and the amount of farmland used for development together must total exactly 100 acres.

Everyone realizes the city will have to improve any land used for development by putting in sewers, streets, power lines, and so on. The city will also have to spend some money on any land used for recreation.

The city manager made a table listing, for each parcel, how much each type of land use would cost the city. Everyone wants to keep the costs to River City to a minimum.

Parcel	Improvement costs per acre for recreation	Improvement costs per acre for development
Mr. Goodfellow's land	$50 GR	$500 GD
Army base	$200 AR	$2,000 AD
Mining land	$100 MR	$1,000 MD

The city manager has to decide how to split the land use between development and recreation so that the cost of necessary improvements is minimized. She also must ensure that at least 300 acres go for development and that the two-part compromise is followed.

Because of her full schedule, she decides to turn the matter over to a consulting firm of city planners.

$$\text{cost} = G_R(50) + A_R(200) +$$

continued ▶

Your Task

Your group, functioning as the consulting firm, will work on this problem over the course of the unit. Your task for now is to find out as much as you can about the problem. By the end of the unit, you will identify the best solution.

1. Find one way to allocate the land and satisfy the constraints. Find the cost to the city for this solution (even though you may recognize that it is not the least costly allocation).

2. What approaches to solving this problem might you try if you had more time? What approaches did you try that didn't seem to work?

Meadows, Malls, and Variables

1. Use the variables defined below to write a set of constraints that express the *Meadows or Malls?* problem.

   - G_R is the number of acres of Mr. Goodfellow's land to be used for recreation.
   - A_R is the number of acres of army land to be used for recreation.
   - M_R is the number of acres of mining land to be used for recreation.
   - G_D is the number of acres of Mr. Goodfellow's land to be used for development.
   - A_D is the number of acres of army land to be used for development.
   - M_D is the number of acres of mining land to be used for development.

2. Use the variables from Question 1 to write an algebraic expression for the city's cost based on how the land is allocated.

3. Check whether each of these allocations satisfies the constraints you defined in Question 1. If it does, find the cost to the city. If it does not, show which **constraint** or constraints it violates.

   a. $G_R = 250$
   $A_R = 50$
   $M_R = 150$
   $G_D = 50$
   $A_D = 50$
   $M_D = 0$

   b. $G_R = 200$
   $A_R = 0$
   $M_R = 0$
   $G_D = 100$
   $A_D = 100$
   $M_D = 150$

That's Entertainment!

An entertainer has an ordinary deck of playing cards. He gives them to his subject, turns his back, and has her shuffle the deck thoroughly.

Keeping his back to her so he can't see what she's doing, he then tells her to make some piles according to these instructions.

1. First she turns over the top card of the deck.

   If this is a face card (jack, queen, or king), she puts it back somewhere in the deck and picks the new top card. She keeps going until she gets a card that is not a face card. That is, she continues until she gets an ace, 2, 3, 4, 5, 6, 7, 8, 9, or 10. Then she places that card face up on the table, as the start of a new pile.

2. Beginning with the number on that card, she starts counting to herself until she gets to 12. (Aces are treated as 1.) With each count, she takes one card from the top of the deck and places it face up on top of the new pile. When she reaches 12, she turns the pile over so that the card she started with is face down on top.

   For example, if she initially turns up an 8, she places a card on top of the 8 and silently counts "9." Then she places another card on top of the pile and silently counts "10," then another card on top and counts "11," and finally, another card on top and counts "12." At that point, she turns over the pile, with the 8 face down on top. In this example, the pile would have five cards altogether.

continued

3. As soon as this first pile is complete, she repeats instructions 1 and 2, working with the remaining cards in the original deck. She keeps creating new piles until she runs out of cards.

   If she runs out of cards while trying to complete a pile, she picks up all the cards in that incomplete pile.

The subject follows the instructions. When she is done, the entertainer turns around and asks her to give him the cards from her final, incomplete pile.

He sees she has given him five cards, but he does not look to see which cards they are. He also sees she has made six complete piles.

He then tells her to take the top card from each pile and add the values of these cards together, without showing him the cards or telling him the sum.

She does this, and he then tells her the sum she found.

○ Your Task

Your task is to figure out what the sum was and how the entertainer figured it out.

○ Write-up

1. *Problem Statement*

2. *Process*

3. *Solution*

4. *Self-assessment*

Adapted from *Mathematics: Problem Solving Through Recreational Mathematics,* by Averbach and Chein, Copyright © 1980 by W.H. Freeman and Company. Used with permission.

Heavy Flying

Lindsay is a stunt pilot, but she can't make a living just by doing stunts. So she has bought a transport plane from Philip. He agrees to help her set up her business.

Philip has two customers he no longer has time to serve: Charley's Chicken Feed and Careful Calculators. He suggests that Lindsay deliver their merchandise for them.

Charley's Chicken Feed packages its product in containers that weigh 40 pounds and are 2 cubic feet in volume. Philip has been charging a delivery fee of $2.20 per container.

Careful Calculators packages its materials in boxes that weigh 50 pounds and are 3 cubic feet in volume. Philip has been charging $3.00 per box.

The plane can hold a maximum of 2000 cubic feet of materials and carry a maximum weight of 37,000 pounds.

Charley's Chicken Feed and Careful Calculators can each give Lindsay as much business as she can handle. Of course, she wants to maximize the money she earns per flight so she can spend more time stunt flying.

Your Task

Here is your task for now.

1. Come up with several loads for Lindsay that fit the constraints. Figure out how much she will earn for each load. Assume she charges the same rates Philip did.

2. Use variables and algebra to describe the constraints on what Lindsay can carry.

A Strategy for Linear Programming

River City's problem is somewhat like the Woos' problem in the Year 2 unit *Cookies*. Both are examples of **linear programming** problems, but *Meadows or Malls?* is more complicated. It involves six variables instead of two.

Before tackling this six-variable problem, you will review what you know about two-variable linear programming problems. The goal is to develop a strategy that you might be able to adapt to the more general situation.

Caroline Williams reviews the work she did with two-variable linear programming problems in the Year 2 unit **Cookies.**

Programming and Algebra Reflections

Part I: Programming Reflections

In the Year 2 unit *Cookies,* you learned how to solve two-variable linear programming problems. You've now used ideas and methods from that unit to solve *Heavy Flying.*

To solve *Meadows or Malls?,* which has six variables, you need to generalize those methods. In preparation for creating a generalization that works for more variables, answer these questions to summarize what you know about two-variable problems.

1. What type of information are you given in a two-variable linear programming problem? What are you trying to do?

2. What do you do to solve a linear programming problem in two variables? Describe the process in as general terms as possible.

Part II: Algebra Reflections

Solve each pair of linear equations in two variables algebraically. Explain each step of the process.

3. $4x + y = 13$
   $2x + y = 7$

4. $3x - 2y = 5$
   $x + 3y = 9$

Ideas for Solving Systems

Many types of problems involve finding the common solution to a pair of linear equations. This is the same as finding the coordinates of the point where the graphs of the two equations intersect. You can often estimate the coordinates of this point by sketching the two graphs, but it's helpful to know some algebraic methods that will give you the exact solution.

No single method works best for every **system of equations,** but here are two common approaches. For simplicity, the examples have integer solutions, but the methods work on any system with a unique solution.

The "Setting *y*'s Equal" Method

In this method, you solve both equations to get expressions for one variable in terms of the other. Then you set those expressions equal to each other. Consider this pair of equations.

$$4x - y = 8$$
$$3x + y = 13$$

Adding *y* and subtracting 8 from both sides of the first equation gives $4x - 8 = y$.

Subtracting $3x$ from both sides of the second equation gives $y = 13 - 3x$.

At the point where the two lines meet, both equations hold true. That is, *y* is equal to both $4x - 8$ and $13 - 3x$, so $4x - 8 = 13 - 3x$.

Solving this equation gives $x = 3$.

Substituting 3 for *x* in either $4x - 8$ or $13 - 3x$ gives $y = 4$.

You can check that $x = 3$, $y = 4$ is a solution of both original equations.

continued

The Substitution Method

In this method, you use one of the equations to express one of the variables in terms of the other and then substitute that expression into the other equation.

Consider this pair of equations.

$$3x + 4y = 18$$
$$2x + y = 7$$

It's easiest to begin with the second equation because the **coefficient** of y is 1. Subtracting $2x$ from both sides gives the equivalent equation $y = 7 - 2x$.

At the point where the graphs of the two original equations intersect, the coordinates must satisfy this new equation. So you can substitute $7 - 2x$ for y into the first equation. In other words, x must satisfy the equation

$$3x + 4(7 - 2x) = 18$$

Solving this equation gives $x = 2$.

Once you know $x = 2$ at the point of intersection, you can substitute 2 for x in the equation $y = 7 - 2x$ to get $y = 3$.

As before, you can check your solution by substituting the values for x and y in the original equations.

Programming Puzzles

1. A Nonroutine Routine

Skateboarder Lance Stunning, who is about to enter a freestyle competition, is busy preparing his routine. His two key moves are the pool drop-in and the rail slide. Lance has to decide how many of each move to include in the routine to maximize his score.

Lance figures he has the stamina to make at most 25 of these moves in his performance. He also knows that his performance can be at most 3 minutes long.

Each pool drop-in takes 4 seconds to perform, and each rail slide takes 9 seconds. If Lance includes more than 20 of either move, the judges will get bored, and he will get a lower score.

Version a: Suppose the judges give each pool drop-in 5 points and each rail slide 10 points. What combination of moves will give Lance the best possible score?

Version b: Suppose the judges give each pool drop-in 7 points and each rail slide 5 points. What combination of moves will give Lance the best possible score?

Version c: Suppose the judges give each pool drop-in 3 points and each rail slide 8 points. What combination of moves will give Lance the best possible score?

continued ▶

2. Planning the Prom

Paige and Remy are organizing the junior prom. They plan to sell two types of tickets: individual tickets and couples tickets. The ballroom where the prom will be held holds a maximum of 400 people.

Paige believes the prom will be more successful if more people go as couples. So that at least half the people at the prom will be in couples, she and Remy decide that the number of individual tickets sold should be at most twice the number of couples tickets.

Remy orders door prizes to be handed out at the prom—one prize for each ticket, even if it's a couples ticket. Unfortunately, the supplier delivers only 225 prizes, and it's too late to get more, so they can sell a total of at most 225 tickets.

> **Version a:** Suppose individual tickets sell for $22 and couples tickets sell for $30. How many of each type of ticket should Paige and Remy sell to maximize the money they take in?
>
> **Version b:** Suppose individual tickets sell for $15 and couples tickets sell for $35. How many of each type of ticket should Paige and Remy sell to maximize the money they take in?
>
> **Version c:** Suppose individual tickets sell for $30 and couples tickets sell for $20. How many of each type of ticket should Paige and Remy sell to maximize the money they take in?

continued ▶

3. Working Two Jobs

Raj works as a health aide at both a hospital and a neighborhood clinic. Because he is also going to school part-time, Raj can work no more than 20 hours per week.

Raj likes working at the clinic better than the hospital, so he always wants to work at least as many hours there as at the hospital. However, he wants to keep his job at the hospital in hopes of getting a better position there eventually. To keep the hospital job, he must work there at least 4 hours per week.

Version a: Suppose Raj earns $20 per hour at the hospital and $15 at the clinic. How many hours should he work at each job to maximize his earnings?

Version b: Suppose Raj earns $17 per hour at the hospital and $19 at the clinic. How many hours should he work at each job to maximize his earnings?

Version c: Suppose Raj earns $18 per hour at the hospital and $16 at the clinic. How many hours should he work at each job to maximize his earnings?

Donovan Meets the Beatles

Aji and Sunshine want to make a CD of songs from the 1960s to donate to their school library to be broadcast during school picnics. Sunshine's parents were big fans of the 60s singer Donovan, and they named her after his song "Sunshine Superman." Aji's folks were devotees of the Beatles. Aji and Sunshine want their CD to consist entirely of songs by Donovan and the Beatles.

Because Sunshine is named after a Donovan song, she wants to include at least as many Donovan songs as Beatles songs. Aji agrees. In return, Sunshine agrees to include at least five Beatles songs.

To provide enough variety to make the mix interesting, they decide to include at least 20 songs altogether.

Suppose Aji and Sunshine have to pay $11 in royalties for each Beatles song and $7 for each Donovan song. How many of each type should they put on their CD to minimize their royalty costs?

Finding Corners Without the Graph

When a profit function is linear and the **feasible region** is a polygon, the **profit function** will always achieve its maximum at a corner point of the feasible region. But for problems involving three variables, drawing the feasible region can be difficult. (And it's impossible for more than three variables!)

It's helpful to be able to locate the corner points without actually drawing the region. As preparation for more complex cases, consider the two-variable feasible region defined by these linear inequalities.

$$x + 2y \le 8$$
$$2x + y \le 13$$
$$y \le 3$$
$$x \ge 0$$
$$y \ge 0$$

1. Each of these inequalities has a corresponding linear equation, whose graph is a straight line. Each corner point of the feasible region is the intersection of two of these lines. How many combinations of these equations are there, taking them two at a time?

2. For each of your combinations from Question 1, find the intersection point for the pair of lines. If there is no intersection point, explain why not.

3. Which intersection points from Question 2 are actually corner points of the feasible region defined by the inequalities? Explain how you know.

What Wood Would Woody Want?

Woody, a character in the Year 1 unit *Shadows,* is very interested in trees, especially measuring them. Well, he has developed his hobby into a trade and is opening a carpentry shop that makes tables and chairs.

The wood Woody buys is sold in terms of a unit called a *board foot,* which is based on boards with a thickness of 1 inch and a width of 1 foot. For example, a board 9 feet long, 1 inch thick, and 1 foot wide consists of 9 board feet of lumber.

Woody has found that each chair requires 3 board feet of lumber and 2 hours of labor. Each table requires 7 board feet of lumber and 8 hours of labor. His profit on each chair is $15, and his profit on each table is $45.

This week, Woody has 420 board feet of lumber and 400 hours of labor available. (He doesn't do all the work himself.) He wants to know how many chairs and how many tables he should make to maximize his profit.

Solve this problem using the general strategy for working on linear programming problems without drawing a feasible region. Use C for the number of chairs Woody makes and T for the number of tables. Explain your work carefully. If you discover places where the strategy is unclear or doesn't seem to work correctly, make a note of them.

Adapted with permission from the *Mathematics Teacher,* © May 1991, by the National Council of Teachers of Mathematics.

Widening Woody's Woodwork

Consider a variation on the situation from *What Wood Would Woody Want?* Assume as before that each chair requires 3 board feet of lumber and 2 hours of labor and that each table requires 7 board feet of lumber and 8 hours of labor.

Suppose Woody has expanded his operations so that he has 630 board feet of lumber and 560 hours of labor available each week. Also suppose he has changed his prices so that his profit on each chair is now $18 and his profit on each table is now $42.

How many chairs and how many tables should Woody make to maximize his profit?

More Equations

Part I: Pairs of Equations

In working on linear programming problems, you often need to solve pairs of linear equations. Use the **substitution method** or another algebraic method to try to solve each pair of equations. Show your work.

1. $5x + 3y = 7$ and $y = x - 3$

2. $3x + 2y = 11$ and $x + y = 4$

3. $5x - 3y = 5$ and $10x + 6y = 20$

4. $2x - 3y = 2$ and $4x - 6y = 9$

5. $2x + 4y = 12$ and $6x + 12y = 36$

Part II: Look It Up

The set of points in the xy-coordinate system is often referred to as the **coordinate plane.** You will see that planes play an important role in this unit.

The word *plane* has a specific meaning in geometry, but it has other meanings in different contexts. Look up this word in the dictionary. Write down as many meanings for it as possible, including the geometric definition.

plane *n* **1** : level surface **2** : level of existence, consciousness, or development **3** : air-plane ~ *adj* **1** : flat **2** : dealing with flat surfaces or figures

Equations, Points, Lines, and Planes

You have solved two-variable linear programming problems by looking at the intersections of lines using the *xy*-coordinate system. You will eventually return to River City and its land-use problem. But first you need to move to another level of complexity for graphs.

In the next portion of this unit, you will develop a coordinate system for three variables and see what the graph of a linear equation is in this new setting.

You will also look at how lines and planes intersect in order to generalize what you know about how lines intersect in the plane.

Gavilan Galloway and Catherine Borror create a three-dimensional coordinate system.

Being Determined

1. Do two lines uniquely determine a point? In other words, if l_1 and l_2 are lines in a plane, is there always one, and only one, point that lies on both of them?

   Explain your answer. In particular, if there are exceptions, state what they are and what happens in the exceptional cases. (Remember, in mathematics the word *line* always refers to a straight line, which does not have to be vertical or horizontal.)

2. Do two points uniquely determine a line? In other words, if P and Q are points in a plane, is there always one, and only one, line that goes through both P and Q?

   Explain your answer. In particular, if there are exceptions, state what they are and what happens in the exceptional cases.

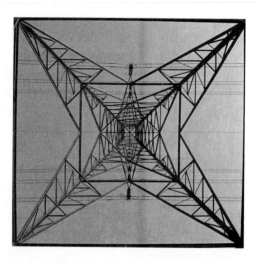

How Much After How Long?

1. The performing arts department put on its spring show on Friday and Saturday nights. The price of a ticket was the same both nights, and the cost of putting on the show was also the same both nights.

   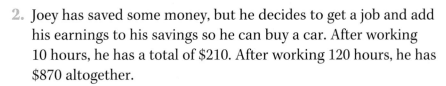

   The department made a profit of $400 on Friday when 100 people bought tickets and a profit of $500 on Saturday when 120 people bought tickets.

   a. How much did one ticket cost? What was the cost of putting on the show each time?

   b. Let t represent the number of people who buy tickets, and let p represent the amount of profit the department would make from selling that many tickets. Think of p as a function of t. Find a rule for this function, expressing p in terms of t.

2. Joey has saved some money, but he decides to get a job and add his earnings to his savings so he can buy a car. After working 10 hours, he has a total of $210. After working 120 hours, he has $870 altogether.

   a. How much money did Joey make per hour? How much money did he already have before he started working?

   b. Let h represent the number of hours Joey has worked, and let m represent the amount of money he has accumulated altogether after h hours. Think of m as a function of h. Find a rule for this function, expressing m in terms of h.

   continued ▶

3. In Question 1, you had two combinations of ticket sales and profit.
   - Selling 100 tickets produced a $400 profit.
   - Selling 120 tickets produced a $500 profit.
   a. What were the two similar combinations in Question 2?
   b. In each question, two combinations is enough information to allow you to find a rule that describes the situation. What does this have to do with the activity *Being Determined?*

4. A line passes through the points (2, 15) and (7, 45). Find an equation for the line, and explain how you got your answer.

The Points and the Equations

As you know, if P and Q are two distinct points in the plane, then there is a unique line that goes through them both. If the points are given as coordinate pairs in the xy-plane, you may want to look for an equation whose graph is that line through the points.

1. For each pair of points, find a linear equation whose graph will go through the two points. Use x to represent the first coordinate and y to represent the second coordinate.

   a. $(4, 9)$ and $(6, 13)$

   b. $(5, 13)$ and $(3, 7)$

   c. $(8, 8)$ and $(20, 14)$

   d. $(-2, 5)$ and $(1, -4)$

2. For each pair of points in Questions 1a and 1b, create a word problem that would require the solver to find the equation. Use Questions 1 and 2 of *How Much After How Long?* as sources of ideas for situations, or create your own situations.

The Three-Variable Coordinate System

The familiar *xy*-coordinate system is used to represent pairs of numbers by points in the plane. For example, the diagram to the right represents the combination of values $x = 2$ and $y = -3$.

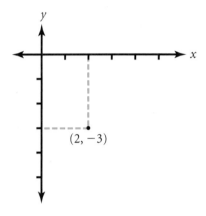

A similar system can be used to represent triples of numbers. One common way to do this is to picture the *x*-axis and *y*-axis as "lying flat" and the *z*-axis as "coming out" perpendicular to that plane. It's difficult to represent this system in two dimensions, but the diagram below suggests one way to do this.

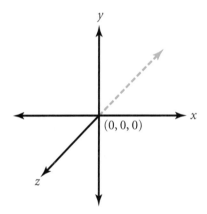

We consider the positive direction of the *z*-axis to be coming out of the page. The dashed line represents the negative portion of the *z*-axis.

As in the two-variable system, the point where the three axes meet is called the *origin*. It represents the values $x = 0$, $y = 0$, and $z = 0$. We write this point as $(0, 0, 0)$.

A triple of values represents moving the appropriate distances in the appropriate directions from the origin.

continued ▶

For instance, the point $(2, -3, 4)$ is found, as shown in the diagram at the right, by going 2 units to the right of the origin, 3 units down, and 4 units "toward you." This point represents the values $x = 2$, $y = -3$, and $z = 4$.

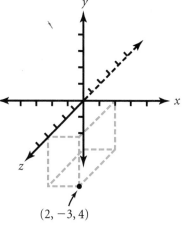

$(2, -3, 4)$

The collection of all points in this system is called the **three-dimensional coordinate system.** It is often referred to simply as **3-space.** Because our world is three dimensional, this system is very useful for describing real-world phenomena, such as the position of an object in space.

Each pair of axes defines a plane, and these planes are known as the *coordinate planes.*

In the diagram at the right, the light green plane is called the *xy-plane,* the white plane is called the *xz-plane,* and the dark green plane is called the *yz-plane.*

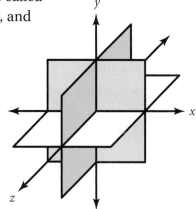

These planes divide 3-space into eight separate regions, known as **octants.** The octants are analogous to the quadrants of the two-variable coordinate system.

Although there is no standard numbering system for all the octants, the set of points whose coordinates are all positive is called the **first octant.**

What Do They Have in Common?

In the two-variable coordinate system, the points in the first quadrant all have positive *x*-coordinates and positive *y*-coordinates.

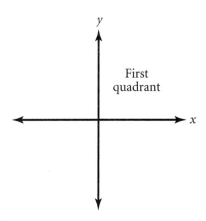

Similarly, there are sets in the three-dimensional coordinate system whose points all have one or more characteristics in common.

Questions 1 to 8 describe various sets in geometric terms. The descriptions refer to the diagram shown below. For each set, do two things.

- Give the coordinates of five specific points in the set.
- State what characteristic or characteristics the points in the set have in common, in terms of their coordinates.

1. The set of points in the *yz*-plane

2. The set of points in the *xz*-plane

3. The set of points on the *x*-axis

4. The set of points on the *z*-axis

5. The set of points above the *xz*-plane

6. The set of points behind the *xy*-plane

7. The set of points 1 unit to the left of the *yz*-plane

8. The set of points in the first octant

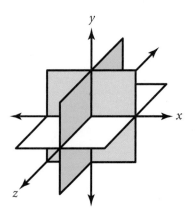

Trying Out Triples

You have been looking at the graphs of some special linear equations in three variables—namely, examples in which not all three variables appear.

Soon you will be graphing the equation $x + y + \frac{1}{2}z = 4$. This linear equation involves all three variables. As preparation, answer these questions, which concern the equation $x + y + \frac{1}{2}z = 4$.

1. Find a dozen or so triples that are solutions to this equation.

2. Organize your solutions in some way that you think might be helpful in finding the graph of this equation.

3. Describe what you think this graph will look like, or make a sketch or model.

More Cookies

Abby and Bing Woo were the bakery owners in the main problem from the Year 2 unit *Cookies*.

The Woos still make plain and iced cookies. But now, by popular demand, they're also selling chocolate chip cookies.

Here's a reminder of the ingredients needed for the original cookies.

- One dozen plain cookies requires 1 pound of cookie dough (and no icing).
- One dozen iced cookies requires 0.7 pound of cookie dough and 0.4 pound of icing.

Now you need the same information for the chocolate chip cookies.

- One dozen chocolate chip cookies requires 0.9 pound of cookie dough and 0.15 pound of chocolate chips (and no icing).

The Woos are limited by the ingredients they have on hand.

- 120 pounds of cookie dough
- 32 pounds of icing
- 18 pounds of chocolate chips

In the past, the Woos were also limited by the amount of work time available. They now have other family members to help, so work time is no longer a limitation on how many cookies they can make. They have also bought more ovens, so oven space is no longer a limitation either.

Plain cookies sell for $6.00 a dozen and cost $4.50 a dozen to make. Iced cookies sell for $7.00 a dozen and cost $5.00 a dozen to make. Chocolate chip cookies sell for $10.00 a dozen and cost $7.75 a dozen to make.

The Woos want to know how many dozens of each kind of cookie to make to maximize their profit.

continued ▶

Eventually you will need to answer the Woos' question. For now, do this.

1. Write a set of constraints that express the situation just described using these variables.

   - *P* represents the number of dozens of plain cookies.
   - *I* represents the number of dozens of iced cookies.
   - *C* represents the number of dozens of chocolate chip cookies.

2. Find four different combinations of cookies the Woos can make. Compute the total profit for each combination.

Just the Plane Facts

You have seen that two lines in a plane usually uniquely determine a point. That is, except for the special cases of parallel lines or two lines that are identical, two given lines will intersect in one and only one point.

Your task in this activity is to examine other cases of "determining," this time in 3-space. In each case, do two things.

- Describe the different ways in which the given objects can intersect.
- Explain your answers with diagrams, three-dimensional models, or other appropriate devices.

1. A line and a plane

2. Two planes

3. Three planes

4. Two lines (*Note:* Your work in Question 1 of *Being Determined* concerned lines in the same plane. Now think about the more general situation, in which the lines may or may not be in the same plane.)

5. Four planes

6. Any other combinations you'd like to investigate

Solving with Systems

You may be able to find the answers to this activity without using algebra. However, to help develop your algebraic skills for work with more difficult problems, you should define variables, write a system of equations, and use substitution to solve the systems for each question.

1. Ming is a competitive surfer. The two moves she used in her most recent competition are the off-the-lip and the cutback. The wave she caught allowed her to do a total of six moves.

   The judges awarded 6 points for each off-the-lip move and 8 points for each cutback. Ming scored a total of 40 points.

   How many moves did she make of each type?

2. In the activity *Programming Puzzles*, Paige and Remy sold two types of prom tickets: individual tickets and couples tickets.

   Suppose they sold individual tickets for $10 and couples tickets for $18 and collected $1,500 altogether. If 160 people attended the event, how many tickets of each type did they sell? (*Caution:* Remember that a couples ticket represents two people.)

Fitting a Line

Although a given line contains many points, a given *pair* of distinct lines in a plane determines a *unique* point, except when the lines are parallel. Similarly, although many lines go through a given point, a pair of distinct points always determines a unique line.

In the activity *Being Determined,* you looked at these ideas from a geometric point of view. Now you will use algebra to find the equation for a line that goes through two specific points in a plane.

Some Lines Through (1, 2)

First consider the point $(1, 2)$. You can see that this point lies on the graph of the linear equation $y = 5x - 3$ by substituting 1 for x and 2 for y. Informally, we say that the line $y = 5x - 3$ "goes through" the point $(1, 2)$.

1. Show that the line $y = -5x + 7$ also goes through $(1, 2)$.

2. Find equations for two other lines that go through $(1, 2)$.

The Family of Lines Through (1, 2)

As the diagram suggests, infinitely many functions of the form $y = ax + b$ have graphs that go through $(1, 2)$. But exactly which linear functions are they? What values of a and b give lines through this point?

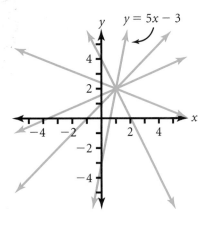

For instance, for the function $y = 5x - 3$, we have $a = 5$ and $b = -3$, so these values for a and b give a line through $(1, 2)$.

3. a. Find the values of a and b for the equation $y = -5x + 7$.

   b. Find the values of a and b for each equation you found in Question 2.

continued ▶

c. Look for a relationship between a and b that holds for all the lines that go through the point $(1, 2)$. Express this relationship as a linear equation involving a and b.

Suggestion: If you are having trouble finding a relationship, find the equations for some more lines that go through $(1, 2)$ and compile a table of values for a and b. Then look for a pattern in your table.

The Family of Lines Through $(-1, -6)$

Now consider a second point, $(-1, -6)$. Again, as the diagram suggests, infinitely many linear functions have graphs that go through this point.

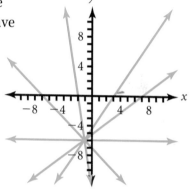

4. a. Find three examples of equations of the form $y = ax + b$ that go through this point.

   b. Find a linear equation involving a and b that must hold for any line $y = ax + b$ that goes through $(-1, -6)$. You might use a method like that suggested in Question 3c.

A Line Through Both Points

Now suppose you want a line $y = ax + b$ that goes through both points.

5. Find values for a and b so that the line $y = ax + b$ goes through both $(1, 2)$ and $(-1, -6)$.

Cookies, Cookies, Cookies

More Cookies introduced you to a linear programming problem in three variables involving the Woos' bakery. In that activity, you simply wrote the constraints and found some possible cookie combinations the Woos could make.

Now you're ready to solve that problem. To do so, you will use what you've learned about planes, linear equations in three variables, and the general strategy for solving linear programming problems.

Phi Nguyen and Kelsey Coria solve a linear programming problem.

SubDivvy

SubDivvy is a number game for two players. Here are the rules.

1. Two players cooperatively choose a starting number greater than 1. We'll call that number N.

2. Player 1 chooses a positive divisor of N that is different from N—that is, a number that divides "evenly" into N, so that the remainder is zero. Player 1 subtracts that divisor from N and gives the result of that subtraction to Player 2.

3. Player 2 works with the result of the subtraction just as Player 1 worked with N. That is, Player 2 chooses a positive divisor of that number, different from the number itself, and subtracts the chosen divisor from it. Player 2 gives the result of this subtraction to Player 1.

4. Players take turns choosing divisors and subtracting until the result reaches the number 1. The player who produces the result of 1 is the winner.

Here is a sample game, with explanations.

68	The number 68 is selected as the starting number N.
−4	Player 1 chooses 4, which is a divisor of 68, and subtracts.
64	The result of the subtraction is 64, which is given to Player 2.
−16	Player 2 chooses 16, which is a divisor of 64, and subtracts.
48	The result of the subtraction is 48, which is given to Player 1.
−24	Player 1 chooses 24, which is a divisor of 48, and subtracts.
24	The result of the subtraction is 24.
−8	Player 2 chooses 8, which is a divisor of 24, and subtracts.
16	The result of the subtraction is 16.
−8	Player 1 chooses 8, which is a divisor of 16, and subtracts.
8	The result of the subtraction is 8.
−4	Player 2 chooses 4, which is a divisor of 8, and subtracts.
4	The result of the subtraction is 4.

continued ▶

−2	Player 1 chooses 2, which is a divisor of 4, and subtracts.
2	The result of the subtraction is 2.
−1	Player 2 chooses 1, which is a divisor of 2, and subtracts.
1	The result of the subtraction is 1, so the game ends. Player 2 is the winner.

Your POW is to explore this game.

One important task is to investigate the issue of who wins. Examine whether there are certain starting numbers for which Player 1 has a winning strategy—that is, a complete strategy by which Player 1 can win no matter what Player 2 does on any turn. Are there starting numbers for which Player 2 has a winning strategy? Are there starting numbers for which no player has a winning strategy?

Consider other questions besides the issue of who wins. For instance, for different starting numbers, what can you say about the shortest game possible? The longest game possible? What generalizations can you make?

What are some other questions you might investigate about this game?

o *Write-up*

1. *Process*

2. *Solution*

3. *Evaluation*

4. *Self-assessment*

Adapted from Fendel/Resek, *Foundations of Higher Mathematics: Exploration and Proof,* content from pp. 6–7, © 1990 Addison-Wesley Publishing Company Inc. Reproduced by permission of Pearson Education, Inc.

The *More Cookies* Region and Strategy

The activity *More Cookies* introduced you to
a more complex version of the original
problem from the *Cookies* unit. We will refer
to the situation in that activity as "the *More
Cookies* problem."

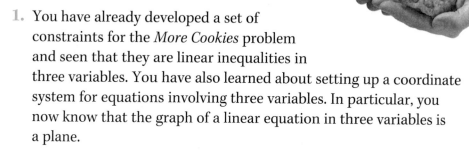

1. You have already developed a set of
   constraints for the *More Cookies* problem
   and seen that they are linear inequalities in
   three variables. You have also learned about setting up a coordinate
   system for equations involving three variables. In particular, you
   now know that the graph of a linear equation in three variables is
   a plane.

   Using that knowledge, give a general description of what the
   feasible region for the *More Cookies* problem should look like.
   For a challenge, you might sketch or build a model of this region.

2. Earlier in this unit, you developed a general strategy for solving
   two-variable linear programming problems. One element of that
   strategy was to identify corner points of the feasible region by
   finding the intersections of pairs of linear equations corresponding
   to the constraints.

   Explain how you could adapt that part of the strategy to work for
   linear programming problems involving three variables.

Finishing Off the Cookies

Your group will now develop a general plan for solving the *More Cookies* problem—that is, for finding the number of dozens of each type of cookie that will maximize the Woos' profit.

In your group, decide on an assignment for each group member so that the group can quickly solve the *More Cookies* problem together. You may decide that each person should do a different piece of the problem, or you may have several people doing the same thing as a check. It's up to you.

Your written work for this activity has three parts.

1. State your group's general plan.

2. State your individual assignment as part of that plan.

3. Describe what you did and what conclusions you reached for your part of the plan.

Equations, Equations, Equations

You've seen that solving a linear programming problem involves solving systems of linear equations.

The *More Cookies* problem has only three variables, and only one of the equations uses more than one variable. To solve the River City land-use problem, you will need to learn much more about solving such systems of equations. That's your task in the next portion of the unit.

Completing a three-variable linear programming problem will aid Randy Stevens, Emily Gubser, Kyle Abraham, and April Long in solving the more complex River City land-use problem.

Easy Does It!

To solve the *More Cookies* problem, you needed to find the common solution to some systems of three linear equations in three variables.

Those systems of equations were mostly simple ones, but real-life problems aren't always so straightforward. So here's a chance to learn more about solving such systems. (For these questions, assume there is no sales tax involved.)

1. Consider this question.

   Will bought 4 packages of batteries and 1 package of CDs for $20.00. Tania bought 5 packages of batteries and 1 package of CDs for $23.00. How much does a package of batteries cost?

   You can probably answer this question without using equations, given that Will and Tania made almost the same purchases. But write down a pair of equations anyway, and explain how your intuitive reasoning about the question could be expressed in terms of the equations.

2. Here is a similar question.

   Jennie bought 4 pens and 3 pencils for $3.75. Tanisha bought 4 pens and 6 pencils for $4.50. How much does a pencil cost? How much does a pen cost?

   Again, you can probably answer this question without using equations, but write down a pair of equations anyway. Explain how your intuitive reasoning about the question could be expressed in terms of the equations.

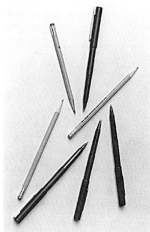

continued ▶

3. This question is not quite as easy as Question 2, but the same sort of approach works fairly well.

   Sanji bought 5 pears and 3 apples for $5.80. Ursula bought 10 pears and 7 apples for $12.20. How much does an apple cost?

   Write down a pair of equations that express the situation. Explain how your intuitive reasoning about the question could be expressed in terms of the equations.

Get Rid of Those Variables!

Read the situation described here and then move on to the questions. The situation probably sounds similar to the questions in the activity *Easy Does It!*, but be sure to follow the instructions carefully.

Erin bought 3 bottles of juice and 7 pounds of carrots and spent $12.90. Jinho bought 5 bottles of juice and 6 pounds of carrots and spent $14.70.

1. Represent the information in the situation as a pair of linear equations.

2. a. Generate a list of at least ten more combinations of purchases whose cost is easy to figure out from the combinations given in this situation. (Don't figure out the price of a bottle of juice or a pound of carrots yet.)

   b. Represent each combination from your list, with its cost, using an equation.

3. Find a pair of equations in your list that makes it easy to see what the price of a bottle of juice or a pound of carrots is. Explain how to find these prices from your pair of equations.

   If you don't find such a pair, create more combinations, until getting the individual prices is as simple as it was in *Easy Does It!*

Eliminating More Variables

Whenever you have a system of linear equations, you can create new equations by adding or subtracting two of those equations or by multiplying an equation by a **constant.**

If the coefficients match up appropriately, then adding or subtracting equations makes one of the variables "disappear," giving an equation with one less variable.

This technique for solving systems of linear equations is called the **elimination method** (or *Gaussian elimination*).

Solve each pair of equations using the elimination method. Be sure to show your work clearly.

1. $2a + 3b = 8$
   $4a + 9b = 22$

2. $4r + 3s = 18$
   $r + 2s = 7$

3. $2w + 3z = 10$
   $5w + 7z = 17$

4. $3p + 4q = 10$
   $5p - 4q = 6$

5. $-2c + 5d = 9$
   $3c + 2d = 15$

6. $2f - 6g = -16$
   $3f + 5g = 25$

Gardener's Dilemma

Part I: Leslie Returns

Leslie the landscape architect, whom you encountered in *Orchard Hideout*, is back to ask for your help with another problem.

There has been a drought this summer. Leslie would like to tell her clients how much water they will need for their gardens.

She has divided the plants she uses into three general categories: lawns, flowers, and shrubs. Her goal is to determine how much water per square foot each category of plant requires.

She looked up the water-usage records for three families she worked for during the last drought. She knows that the amounts of water these families used at that time for each type of plant were adequate without being wasteful.

The table below shows the weekly water usage of the three families. Assume the amount of water used per square foot of lawn, flowers, and shrubs is the same for each family.

	Number of square feet of lawn	Number of square feet of flowers	Number of square feet of shrubs	Number of gallons of water used
Family 1	900	120	40	1865
Family 2	0	160	800	180
Family 3	120	80	240	310

Define variables and write a system of equations that could be used to find the amount of water needed for a square foot of each category of plant. You do not need to solve this system of equations.

continued ▶

Part II: Elimination

Solve each system of equations using the elimination method.

1. $6c + 5d = 2$

   $2c + 7d = 22$

2. $5u + 9v = 13$

   $4u - 5v = 47$

3. $4x - 9y = -95$

   $18x + 20y = 480$

4. $-5r + 2s = -7$

   $3r - 4s = 3$

Elimination in Three Variables

Leslie's task in *Gardener's Dilemma* can be expressed using a system of three linear equations in three variables.

The elimination method you have used for two-variable systems can be applied to three-variable systems. The extra variable, though, makes things a bit more complicated.

Because the coefficients in Leslie's equations are fairly large, that system isn't the best one for learning the method. Here are some simpler systems involving three linear equations and three variables. Solve each of them using the elimination method.

1. $4x + 2y + z = 9$
    $2x - y - z = 2$
    $x + 2y + 3z = 9$

2. $3u + v + w = 9$
    $u + v - w = 5$
    $u + 2v + w = 4$

3. $5r - s + 3t = -10$
    $-2r + 2s + t = 11$
    $r + s + t = 2$

More Equation Elimination

In this activity, you will continue your work with the elimination method. Try to use that approach to solve each of these systems of linear equations in three variables.

1. $3a + 2b + 3c = 2$
   $2a + 5b - c = -3$
   $3b = -6$

2. $3u - v + 3w = 3$
   $2u - 4v + 5w = -10$
   $u + v + w = 1$

3. $x + y + z = 3$
   $x - y = 5$
   $y - z = -7$

4. $2d - e + f = 5$
   $d + 2e + f = 3$
   $3d + e + 2f = 8$

Equations and More Variables in Linear Programming

What do you do if one of your linear programming constraints is an equation instead of an inequality? What do you do if you have too many variables to make a graph?

In the next several activities, you will focus on two new linear programming problems: *Ming's New Maneuver* and *Eastside Westside Story*. The first problem addresses the issue of constraint equations. The second extends all of the ideas you have learned about linear programming to four variables.

Kevin Brandt refines his strategy for solving linear programming problems.

Ming's New Maneuver

Ming, from the activity *Solving with Systems,* has finally perfected the tube ride! She wants to use it along with her off-the-lip moves and cutbacks in her next competition.

The waves at this new beach are well suited for the tube ride, but Ming cannot do the same move over and over. She still needs to plan her ride to maximize the points she earns.

In this competition, Ming must make exactly 20 moves. Also, because a lip-gloss company is sponsoring the event, she is required to do at least 3 off-the-lip moves.

Ming decides she should use at most 24 seconds for her tube rides and cutbacks. She estimates the cutbacks will take 1 second each and the tube rides will take 2 seconds each.

Here is the scoring system the judges have announced.

- Off-the-lip moves: 1 point each
- Cutbacks: 4 points each
- Tube rides: 5 points each

1. Set up a system of constraints for this situation. Use L for the number of off-the-lip moves, C for the number of cutbacks, and T for the number of tube rides.

2. Determine how many of each type of move Ming should perform to maximize her point total.

Let Me Count the Ways

In solving the *More Cookies* problem, you needed to consider all combinations of constraints taken three at a time. (You may have realized that some of the resulting systems had no solution, so you could eliminate them immediately.)

This activity illustrates other situations in which you might want to make complete lists.

1. Paula's favorite pizza place is offering a special price for ordering exactly two toppings on a pizza. The two toppings have to be different.

   The store has eight toppings to choose from.

   - Anchovies
   - Onions
   - Mushrooms
   - Sausage
   - Olives
   - Zucchini
   - Peppers
   - Pineapple

   Make a complete list of all the combinations Paula can choose from for her two-topping pizza. (You may recall a similar problem from the Year 1 unit *The Game of Pig*.) It doesn't matter in what order you list the two choices. For instance, "anchovies and mushrooms" is the same choice as "mushrooms and anchovies."

continued ▶

2. Fraser School goes from seventh through twelfth grade. A Student Advisory Group has been elected that consists of six students, one from each grade level.

   a. The Student Advisory Group needs to pick a three-person committee from among their members to help plan the homecoming dance. Make a complete list of all the possible combinations of members for this committee.

   b. Suppose the group decides that the student representing the twelfth grade should definitely be on the committee, because this will be that class's last homecoming dance. List all the possible committees now.

3. Jared works afternoons at the local grocery store. He's been an employee long enough that he gets to choose which four afternoons he will work each week. The store is open seven days a week.

   Make a complete list of all his possible choices.

Three Variables, Continued

You know that the graph of a linear equation in three variables is a plane in 3-space. You also know that the intersection of three planes can be

- nothing
- a single point
- infinitely many points (either a line or a plane)

Each of these questions gives a system of three linear equations, so the graphs of the three equations are three planes. For each system, state which of the three types of intersection the graphs have, and justify your answer. If the intersection is a single point, find that point.

1. $a - b + 2c = 2$
   $2a + 2b - c = -3$
   $3a + b + c = 4$

2. $r + s + t = 2$
   $2r + 2s + 2t = 4$
   $3r + 3s + 3t = 6$

3. $u - v + w = 2$
   $u + v + w = 6$
   $u + v + 2w = 9$

4. $2x = 6$
   $3y + z = -7$
   $6x + 6y + 2z = 4$

Grind It Out

Solving systems of linear equations is an important part of various kinds of problems, including linear programming problems.

As the number of variables grows, the systems often become more difficult to solve. The central unit problem, *Meadows or Malls?*, involves six variables. This activity gets you a bit closer to that level of complexity.

1. Solve this system of four linear equations in four variables.

$$2x + y - 3z + w = 6$$
$$x + y + 2z + w = -1$$
$$y - z + w = 0$$
$$x + z - w = 5$$

2. You know that two distinct lines usually intersect in a single point, so a system of two linear equations in two variables usually has a unique solution. Similarly, as you saw in *Just the Plane Facts*, three planes in 3-space will usually have a unique point of intersection, so a system of three linear equations in three variables usually has a unique solution.

   For more than three variables, it isn't possible to draw diagrams or build models to see what's happening geometrically. Nevertheless, a system of *n* linear equations in *n* variables usually has a unique solution.

   Give the best explanation you can for why a system of four linear equations in four variables should usually have a unique solution.

People have devised many kinds of secret codes to be able to communicate privately without others understanding their messages.

○ Letter-Substitution Codes

Many messages involve words. One of the most popular ways to encode a word message is to substitute a different letter for each letter of the alphabet.

If the person who receives your message knows your system for replacing letters, it is easy to figure out your code. Even if that person does not know your system, it may not be too difficult to figure out your message, because of certain special letter combinations and the frequency with which certain letters occur.

○ A Letter-Number Code

This POW concerns codes for arithmetic problems rather than word messages. To use such a code, you start with an arithmetic problem such as

$$
\begin{array}{r}
35 \\
+\ 35 \\
\hline
70
\end{array}
$$

To create a coded version of the problem, you replace each number with a letter, always using the same letter for a particular number. For example, you might replace 3 with A, 5 with D, 7 with O, and 0 with H. The addition problem then becomes

$$
\begin{array}{r}
A\,D \\
+\ A\,D \\
\hline
O\,H
\end{array}
$$

In using such codes, be careful to distinguish between the number 0 and the letter O.

continued

○ Figuring Out the Code

It's easy to make up such a code, and it's also easy to figure out what the coded problem represents if you know the replacement system.

What's more interesting is trying to figure out a code merely by looking at the coded problem. That is, you are shown only the problem written with letters, and you have to figure out the original arithmetic problem.

○ The Rules

Problems like these usually follow certain rules.

• If a letter is used more than once in the same problem, it stands for the same number each time.

• Different letters in the same problem always stand for different single-digit numbers.

• A letter standing for 0 never starts a number with more than one digit. For example, the final arithmetic problem can't have a number like 05, but it can use 507 or 80 or even simply 0.

For some letter problems, it is easy to reconstruct the original arithmetic problem. For others, it can be quite difficult. Sometimes there is no possible answer, and sometimes there are many possible answers.

○ The Problems

See whether you can crack the codes for these problems based on the rules just listed. If you think there is only one right answer, prove it. If you think there are several possibilities, give them all and prove there are no others. You will need to keep careful track of how you arrive at your answers.

1.
$$\begin{array}{r} A\,B\,B \\ -\quad A \\ \hline D\,D \end{array}$$

2.
$$\begin{array}{r} S\,S \\ +\,E\,E \\ \hline S\,S\,T \end{array}$$

3.
$$\begin{array}{r} A\,B \\ +\,B\,C \\ \hline A\,D\,E \end{array}$$

continued ▸

4. This one is definitely harder than the others.

$$
\begin{array}{r}
\mathrm{S\,E\,N\,D} \\
+\ \mathrm{M\,O\,R\,E} \\
\hline
\mathrm{M\,O\,N\,E\,Y}
\end{array}
$$

5. Make up a problem of your own that has a unique solution, and prove the solution is unique.

○ *Write-up*

1. *Process* and *Solution:* Do a separate write-up for each of Questions 1 to 5, combining the process and solution components for each problem. You must *prove* your solutions are the only ones possible. You may find that explaining the process you went through to decipher the code will be part (or perhaps all) of your proof.

2. *Self-assessment*

Constraints Without a Context

This system of linear constraints in three variables defines a feasible region.

    a. $x + 2y + z \leq 120$

    b. $3x + 2z \leq 12$

    c. $y + z = 8$

    d. $x \leq 10$

    e. $y \leq 7$

    f. $x \geq 0$

    g. $y \geq 0$

    h. $z \geq 0$

1. Create a list of systems of equations you could solve so that the solutions to those systems would include all the corner points of this feasible region. If you can see that a particular system does not have a solution, you may omit it from your list, but you must explain how you know it has no solution.

2. Explain how you would use your list from Question 1 to determine the actual corner points of the feasible region.

Eastside Westside Story

For many years, River City had only one high school. Known simply as River High, it is located on the west side of the river. But as the city grew, the school became quite crowded.

Finally the community built a new school, on the east side of the river. They call it New High.

To promote the idea that both schools serve the entire city, the school board has mandated that at least half of the students attending New High should come from the west side of the river.

The school district has always used buses to bring students to River High. Now the district needs to provide two sets of buses. It is anxious to minimize busing costs.

Here are some facts about the situation.

- There are 300 high school students living on the east side of the river and 250 living on the west side.

- New High can handle up to 350 students, and River High can handle up to 225.

- The average cost per day of busing students is
    - $1.20 for each east-side student going to New High.
    - $2.00 for each east-side student going to River High.
    - $3.00 for each west-side student going to New High.
    - $1.50 for each west-side student going to River High.

continued

The problem facing the River City school board (and you) is to determine how many students to send to each school to minimize busing costs.

1. Write the constraints—that is, the equations and inequalities—that describe the situation. Use these variables.

    - N_e is the number of New High students who live on the east side of the river.

    - R_e is the number of River High students who live on the east side of the river.

    - N_w is the number of New High students who live on the west side of the river.

    - R_w is the number of River High students who live on the west side of the river.

2. Write the "cost of busing" expression (using the variables from Question 1).

3. List the combinations of constraints you will need to examine.

4. Solve the various combinations of equations you think you must look at.

5. Based on your solutions, write up your recommendation for the school board.

Fitting More Lines

In *Fitting a Line* your task was to find a function of the form $y = ax + b$ whose graph would go through the points $(1, 2)$ and $(-1, -6)$.

You began by finding several pairs of values for a and b for which the graph went through $(1, 2)$. You then looked for a relationship between a and b for those pairs.

You probably reached this conclusion.

> The line $y = ax + b$ goes through $(1, 2)$ if and only if the coefficients a and b fit the equation $a + b = 2$.

For example, the values $a = 7, b = -5$ fit this equation, and the line $y = 7x - 5$ goes through $(1, 2)$.

In the case of the point $(1, 2)$, the relationship between a and b is relatively simple. In this activity, you have a similar task, but you will use points for which the relationship may be somewhat harder to find.

A Line Through (3, 4) and (5, 1)

1. As with the other points you've considered, the diagram illustrates that there are infinitely many functions of the form $y = ax + b$ whose graphs go through the point $(3, 4)$.

   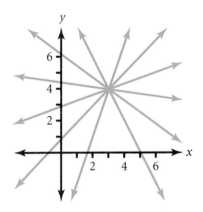

   a. Find an equation involving a and b that guarantees that the line $y = ax + b$ goes through $(3, 4)$.

   b. Find a pair of numbers for a and b that fit your equation. Check whether the resulting line $y = ax + b$ actually does go through $(3, 4)$.

continued ▶

2. The diagram shows some of the lines through the point (5, 1).

   a. Find an equation involving a and b that guarantees that the line $y = ax + b$ goes through (5, 1).

   b. Find a pair of numbers for a and b that fit your equation. Check whether the resulting line $y = ax + b$ actually does go through (5, 1).

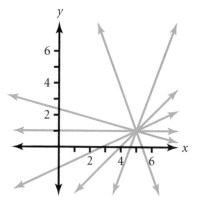

3. The diagrams for Questions 1 and 2 show some of the lines through (3, 4) and some of the lines through (5, 1). There is one line, not shown in either diagram, that goes through both points.

   a. Use the equations involving a and b from Questions 1a and 2a to find a line of the form $y = ax + b$ that goes through both (3, 4) and (5, 1).

   b. Verify that your answer is correct.

A Line Through (4, −1) and (−2, 7)

4. Use the method of Questions 1 to 3 to find a line of the form $y = ax + b$ that goes through both (4, −1) and (−2, 7).

Ages, Coins, and Fund-Raising

1. Paige is half as old as Quiana. Quiana is three years younger than Ryan. Ryan is nine years older than Paige.

   How old are Paige, Quiana, and Ryan?

2. Uncle Ralph has 18 coins in his pocket. Each coin is a quarter, a dime, or a nickel. The number of quarters and dimes combined is the same as the number of nickels. He has $2.10 worth of coins in his pocket.

   How many of each type of coin does he have?

3. Sonya, Dan, and Jesse were raising money for sports programs at their school. They had a pie sale, held a car wash, and sold raffle tickets.

   They charged $8 for each pie, charged $4 for each car wash, and sold the raffle tickets for $1 each. Altogether they collected $760.

   They spent $\frac{1}{2}$ hour on each car they washed and 2 hours making each pie they sold. These two activities required a total of 65 hours. They made twice as much money from raffle tickets as from car washes.

   How many pies did they sell? How many car washes did they do? How many raffle tickets did they sell?

Saved by the Matrices!

You've seen that solving a linear programming problem requires solving many systems of linear equations. And the unit problem has six variables! As you saw in the activity *Grind It Out,* even a four-variable system can require a huge amount of work.

Fortunately, your graphing calculator can assist you. Before you use the calculator, though, you will learn about matrices. A matrix is a notational shorthand for organizing a whole bunch of numbers.

Giovanni Guzman uses a graphing calculator to address a system of linear equations with many variables.

Matrix Basics

A **matrix** is a rectangular array of numbers. Here are three examples

$$\begin{bmatrix} 1 & -8 & 3 & -1 & -4 \\ 5 & 3 & 4 & -1 & -6 \end{bmatrix} \qquad \begin{bmatrix} 1 & 1 & 1 \\ 2 & 1 & -1 \\ 3 & 2 & 2 \end{bmatrix} \qquad \begin{bmatrix} 6 & 17 & \frac{1}{8} & -368 \end{bmatrix}$$

The plural of matrix is *matrices*. Matrices are often written using parentheses instead of brackets. Either method is correct.

The matrix $\begin{bmatrix} 1 & -8 & 3 & -1 & -4 \\ 5 & 3 & 4 & -1 & -6 \end{bmatrix}$ has two rows and five columns, so it is called a *2-by-5 matrix*. A row is horizontal; a column is vertical. The pair of numbers -4 and -6 form one column of this matrix.

The numbers 2 and 5 are called the **dimensions of the matrix.** The phrase "2-by-5" is usually represented in writing as 2×5, just as we refer to a rectangle that is 3 inches wide and 4 inches long as a "3×4 rectangle." The first dimension of a matrix tells how many rows the matrix has. The second dimension tells how many columns it has.

The matrix $\begin{bmatrix} 1 & 1 & 1 \\ 2 & 1 & -1 \\ 3 & 2 & 2 \end{bmatrix}$ has three rows and three columns, so it is a 3×3 matrix. The matrix $\begin{bmatrix} 6 & 17 & \frac{1}{8} & -368 \end{bmatrix}$ has one row and four columns, so it is a 1×4 matrix.

A matrix with the same number of rows as columns, such as a 3×3 matrix, is called a **square matrix.** A matrix with only one row is often called a **row vector,** and a matrix with only one column is often called a **column vector.** Each individual number in a matrix is called an **entry.**

Inventing an Algebra

Matrix Basics defines what a matrix is and introduces you to the standard notation and terminology of matrices. There is also an *algebra* of matrices, which means there are rules for adding and multiplying them.

This activity will help you discover some of those rules by using matrices in meaningful contexts.

1. A matrix could be used to keep track of students' points in a class. Each row could stand for a different student, such as Ana, Ben, Cass, and Devon. The first column might be for homework, the second for oral reports, and the third for POWs.

   Suppose this table represents the results for the first grading period.

	Homework	Reports	POWs
Ana	18	54	30
Ben	35	23	52
Cass	46	15	60
Devon	60	60	60

   A matrix representation of this information might look like this.

   $$\begin{bmatrix} 18 & 54 & 30 \\ 35 & 23 & 52 \\ 46 & 15 & 60 \\ 60 & 60 & 60 \end{bmatrix}$$

continued

Here, in table form, are the students' points in each category for the second grading period.

	Homework	Reports	POWs
Ana	10	60	0
Ben	52	35	58
Cass	42	20	48
Devon	60	60	60

a. Write these second-grading-period scores in a matrix.

b. Compute each student's total points *in each assignment category* for the two grading periods combined. Write the totals in matrix form.

c. Congratulations! If you completed part b, you have added two matrices. Based on your work, write an equation showing two matrices being added to give your matrix from part b.

2. The Woos' bakery is open six days a week.

Last week, for chocolate chip cookies, the Woos sold 30 dozen cookies on Monday, 25 dozen on Tuesday, 27 dozen on Wednesday, 23 dozen on Thursday, 38 dozen on Friday, and 52 dozen on Saturday.

For plain cookies, they sold 30 dozen on Monday, 28 dozen on Tuesday, 20 dozen on Wednesday, 25 dozen on Thursday, 35 dozen on Friday, and 45 dozen on Saturday.

continued ▶

For iced cookies, they sold 45 dozen on Monday, 32 dozen on Tuesday, 40 dozen on Wednesday, 38 dozen on Thursday, 48 dozen on Friday, and 70 dozen on Saturday.

a. Use a matrix to represent the Woos' sales. Let each row represent a different kind of cookie and each column represent a different day of the week.

b. Make up sales numbers for the Woos for a second week. Show your sales in a matrix similar to that for part a.

c. Add the Woos' sales for the two weeks. Show the totals in a matrix similar to those for parts a and b.

d. Write the matrix addition equation that corresponds to your work.

3. Which of the matrix sums shown here do you think make sense? Find those sums, and explain why you think the other sums don't make sense.

a. $\begin{bmatrix} 1 & 5 & 0 & -6 \\ 2 & -2 & 4 & 1 \\ 0 & 1 & -3 & 1 \end{bmatrix} + \begin{bmatrix} 8 & -4 & 0 & 3 \\ 3 & 2 & 4 & 5 \\ 1 & -3 & 3 & 6 \end{bmatrix}$

b. $\begin{bmatrix} 1 & 5 & 0 & -6 \\ 2 & -2 & 4 & 1 \end{bmatrix} + \begin{bmatrix} 8 & -4 & 0 \\ 3 & 3 & 2 \\ 7 & 5 & 1 \end{bmatrix}$

c. $\begin{bmatrix} -3 & 7 & 9 \end{bmatrix} + \begin{bmatrix} 7 & -3 & 5 \end{bmatrix}$

d. $\begin{bmatrix} 5 & -4 & 2 & 1 \end{bmatrix} + \begin{bmatrix} 4 \\ -2 \\ 7 \\ 1 \end{bmatrix}$

4. What has to be true of two matrices for it to make sense to add them together?

5. Describe a rule for adding any matrices that fit your condition from Question 4.

Fitting Quadratics

In *Fitting a Line* and *Fitting More Lines,* your task was to find a linear function through a particular pair of points. That is, you were asked to find coefficients a and b so that the line $y = ax + b$ would go through the given points.

In this activity, you move from linear functions to another important category: the family of **quadratic** functions. A quadratic function is often written in the form $y = ax^2 + bx + c$. In this equation, the coefficients a, b, and c can be any three numbers, not necessarily different, except that a cannot be zero. If $a = 0$, the function is linear. (*Reminder:* The graph of a quadratic equation is a shape called a *parabola.*)

As you might suspect, because a quadratic function has three coefficients, it generally takes three points on its graph to determine the function. In Questions 1 to 3, you will consider all the parabolas going through a particular point. Question 4 asks you to put the information from those questions together.

1. The diagram shows some of the parabolas that go through the point $(1, 6)$.

   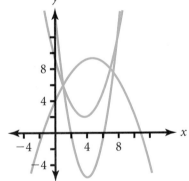

   a. Verify that the parabola defined by the equation $y = 3x^2 + 2x + 1$ goes through $(1, 6)$.

   b. Find at least two other possible choices of values for a, b, and c so that the parabola $y = ax^2 + bx + c$ goes through $(1, 6)$.

   c. Find an equation involving a, b, and c that holds true for every parabola $y = ax^2 + bx + c$ that goes through $(1, 6)$.

2. Now consider the set of parabolas that go through the point $(3, 8)$. Find an equation involving a, b, and c that holds true for every parabola $y = ax^2 + bx + c$ that goes through $(3, 8)$.

3. Find an equation involving a, b, and c that holds true for every parabola $y = ax^2 + bx + c$ that goes through $(5, 2)$.

continued ▶

4. a. Use the equations you found in Questions 1, 2, and 3 to find a parabola that goes through all three points: (1, 6), (3, 8), and (5, 2). That is, find values for a, b, and c so that the parabola $y = ax^2 + bx + c$ goes through all three points.

   b. Is your solution to Question 4a unique? Explain.

Flying Matrices

You've seen that there is a natural way to add matrices. Namely, if the matrices have the same dimensions, you simply add the corresponding entries. (If the matrices have different dimensions, you can't add them.)

Defining multiplication of matrices is harder, and the definition is somewhat arbitrary. The arithmetic in these questions will be the basis for deciding what might make sense when defining how matrices are multiplied.

1. In *Heavy Flying,* you were given these facts about the materials that Lindsay transports.

   • Charley's Chicken Feed packages its product in containers that weigh 40 pounds and are 2 cubic feet in volume.

   • Careful Calculators packages its materials in boxes that weigh 50 pounds and are 3 cubic feet in volume.

     Organize this information into a matrix. Label the rows and columns to show what the numbers represent.

2. Suppose that on Monday, Lindsay transports 500 containers of chicken feed and 200 boxes of calculators. Put those facts into a matrix.

3. Use the information in your two matrices to find the total weight and the total volume Lindsay transported on Monday. Put those two answers into a matrix.

4. Explain how you used the information in the matrices you created in Questions 1 and 2 to calculate the numbers for Question 3.

5. Suppose that on Tuesday, Lindsay transports 400 containers of chicken feed and 300 boxes of calculators. Combine this information with the data from Question 2 to form a 2 $\times$ 2 matrix showing exactly what she carried on Monday and on Tuesday.

continued ▶

6. Combine the information in your answers to Questions 1 and 5 to find the total weight and the total volume transported on Monday and on Tuesday. Find separate totals for each day. Put all of that information into a matrix.

7. Explain how you calculated the numbers for your matrix in Question 6.

Matrices in the Oven

The Woos' bakery provides another example for multiplying matrices. The questions in this activity are similar to those in *Flying Matrices*. Pay careful attention to the arithmetic they involve.

For this activity, you can ignore the constraints from the *More Cookies* problem. The facts about the ingredients remain the same.

- One dozen plain cookies requires 1 pound of cookie dough (and no icing or chocolate chips).
- One dozen iced cookies requires 0.7 pound of cookie dough and 0.4 pound of icing (and no chocolate chips).
- One dozen chocolate chip cookies requires 0.9 pound of cookie dough and 0.15 pound of chocolate chips (and no icing).

1. Put all of this information into a matrix. Be sure to label your rows and columns.

2. Suppose that on Wednesday, the Woos made 30 dozen plain cookies, 45 dozen iced cookies, and 30 dozen chocolate chip cookies. On Thursday, they made 28 dozen plain cookies, 32 dozen iced cookies, and 25 dozen chocolate chip cookies.

   Put all of this information into a matrix.

3. Combine the information in your answers to Questions 1 and 2 to create a matrix that shows the total amount *of each ingredient* used on Wednesday and on Thursday.

4. Describe how you calculated the numbers for your matrix in Question 3.

Fresh Ingredients

The Woos buy their ingredients fresh each day. They shop at two markets, and the prices are slightly different at each.

It takes too much time for them to go to both markets. Each day they have to decide where to shop, depending on what they are baking that day.

The Woos' baking plan for Wednesday and Thursday is the one described in *Matrices in the Oven*. It can be represented by this matrix.

$$
\begin{array}{c}
 \\
 \\
\text{Wed} \\
\text{Thurs}
\end{array}
\begin{array}{ccc}
 & & \text{choc} \\
\text{plain} & \text{iced} & \text{chip} \\
\end{array}
\left[\begin{array}{ccc}
30 & 45 & 30 \\
28 & 32 & 25
\end{array}\right]
$$

The first 30 in the matrix, for example, means they will make 30 dozen plain cookies on Wednesday.

You also need the information in this ingredient matrix.

$$
\begin{array}{c}
 \\
 \\
\text{plain} \\
\text{iced} \\
\text{choc chip}
\end{array}
\begin{array}{ccc}
 & & \text{choc} \\
\text{dough} & \text{icing} & \text{chips} \\
\end{array}
\left[\begin{array}{ccc}
1 & 0 & 0 \\
0.7 & 0.4 & 0 \\
0.9 & 0 & 0.15
\end{array}\right]
$$

The entry 0.7, for example, means the Woos need 0.7 pound of cookie dough for each dozen iced cookies.

Now, if the Woos shop at Farmer's Market, their ingredient costs are

- dough: 30¢ per pound
- icing: 20¢ per pound
- chocolate chips: 32¢ per pound

If they shop at Downtown Grocery, their costs are

- dough: 29¢ per pound
- icing: 28¢ per pound
- chocolate chips: 22¢ per pound

continued ▶

The prices at the stores don't change from Wednesday to Thursday. The Woos want to know what it would cost to do all of their Wednesday shopping at Farmer's Market or all of it at Downtown Grocery. They want similar information for Thursday.

1. Put all the pricing information for the two markets into a single matrix. Set up your matrix in a way that will allow you to multiply matrices to get the cost information the Woos need.

2. Use matrices to help the Woos decide which market to shop at on Wednesday and which to shop at on Thursday.

Calculators to the Rescue

You've seen that multiplying matrices can involve a lot of cumbersome arithmetic. Even without matrices, you would still have to do the same arithmetic to solve problems like those in *Fresh Ingredients*. And this type of computation is done in businesses every day.

Fortunately you can avoid all this arithmetic by entering the information as matrices into a graphing calculator and letting the calculator do the work.

1. The Woos' baking plan is given by this matrix.

$$
\begin{array}{c}
 & \text{plain} & \text{iced} & \text{choc} \\
 & & & \text{chip} \\
\text{Wed} & \begin{bmatrix} 30 & 45 & 30 \\ \text{Thurs} & 28 & 32 & 25 \end{bmatrix}
\end{array}
$$

Give this matrix a name and enter it into your calculator.

2. The amount of each ingredient for each type of cookie is given by this matix.

$$
\begin{array}{c}
 & \text{dough} & \text{icing} & \text{choc} \\
 & & & \text{chips} \\
\text{plain} & \begin{bmatrix} 1 & 0 & 0 \\ \text{iced} & 0.7 & 0.4 & 0 \\ \text{choc chip} & 0.9 & 0 & 0.15 \end{bmatrix}
\end{array}
$$

Enter this matrix into your calculator. Give it a different name from the one you used in Question 1.

3. The costs of the ingredients at each market are given by this matrix

$$
\begin{array}{c}
 & \text{Frmr} & \text{Dntn} \\
 & \text{Mkt} & \text{Groc} \\
\text{dough} & \begin{bmatrix} 30 & 29 \\ \text{icing} & 20 & 28 \\ \text{choc chips} & 32 & 22 \end{bmatrix}
\end{array}
$$

Enter this matrix into your calculator, giving it a third name.

continued ▶

4. In *Fresh Ingredients,* you found a matrix showing how much all the ingredients would cost the Woos at each market on each day—Wednesday and Thursday. Check that result using your calculator.

Make It Simple

1. Write instructions explaining how to multiply two 3 × 3 matrices (using pencil and paper, not a calculator). Make your instructions very clear.

2. Give your instructions to someone who has not learned how to multiply matrices. See whether he or she can use your instructions to multiply two 3 × 3 matrices that are different from those in your instructions.

3. Describe any difficulties the person may have had in following your instructions. Indicate what may have been wrong with the instructions.

4. Revise your instructions as necessary.

Back and Forth

You have seen that a single linear equation can be written as a matrix equation. More specifically, the equation can be represented as a statement that the product of two matrices is a certain number. (Technically, the product is a 1×1 matrix, but we usually think of it as just a number.)

For example, the equation

$$5x + 3y + 7z = 10$$

states that the product of the row matrix $[5\ 3\ 7]$ and the

column matrix $\begin{bmatrix} x \\ y \\ z \end{bmatrix}$ is equal to 10. So the original equation

$5x + 3y + 7z = 10$ says the same as the matrix equation

$$[5\ 3\ 7] = \begin{bmatrix} x \\ y \\ z \end{bmatrix}$$

Now consider this system of linear equations.

$$5x + 3y + 7z = 10$$
$$2x + y - z = 1$$
$$3x + 2y + z = 4$$

1. Develop a way to write this system of equations as a single matrix equation. Think of the numbers on the right of the equal signs as forming a column vector.

2. Now turn the process around by writing this matrix equation as a pair of linear equations.

$$\begin{bmatrix} 3 & -2 \\ 1 & -6 \end{bmatrix} \begin{bmatrix} u \\ v \end{bmatrix} = \begin{bmatrix} 2 \\ 1 \end{bmatrix}$$

continued ▶

For the rest of these questions, either turn the system of linear equations into a single matrix equation or write the matrix equation as a system of linear equations. You do not have to solve any of these equations.

3. $3a - 2b = 7$

   $-4a + 5b = 9$

4. $\begin{bmatrix} 1 & 0 \\ -2 & 3 \end{bmatrix} \begin{bmatrix} r \\ s \end{bmatrix} = \begin{bmatrix} 2 \\ -3 \end{bmatrix}$

5. $3c = 4$

   $-c + 2d = -5$

6. $\begin{bmatrix} 1 & -1 & 2 \\ 0 & 3 & 0 \\ 3 & -3 & 1 \end{bmatrix} \begin{bmatrix} e \\ f \\ g \end{bmatrix} = \begin{bmatrix} 2 \\ -4 \\ 1 \end{bmatrix}$

7. $3x + 2y - z = 4$

   $3y + 2z = 0$

   $5x - 3z = 1$

Matrices and Linear Systems

A system of linear equations can be expressed as a single matrix equation, which will look like

$$[A][X] = [B]$$

In this equation, $[A]$ is the **coefficient matrix** of the system of linear equations and $[B]$ is a column matrix made up of the numbers on the right of the equal signs in the linear equations. (This column matrix is sometimes called the **constant term matrix.**) The matrix $[X]$ is a column matrix made up of the individual variables in the system of linear equations.

For example, consider this pair of equations.

$$3a - 2b = 7$$
$$-4a + 5b = 9$$

The coefficient matrix $[A]$ is $\begin{bmatrix} 3 & -2 \\ -4 & 5 \end{bmatrix}$, the constant term matrix $[B]$

is $\begin{bmatrix} 7 \\ 9 \end{bmatrix}$, and $[X]$ is the column matrix $\begin{bmatrix} a \\ b \end{bmatrix}$.

Solving the pair of equations is the same as finding values for a and b so that

$$\begin{bmatrix} 3 & -2 \\ -4 & 5 \end{bmatrix} \begin{bmatrix} a \\ b \end{bmatrix} = \begin{bmatrix} 7 \\ 9 \end{bmatrix}$$

Any system of linear equations can be expressed as a matrix equation. Similarly, an appropriate matrix equation $[A][X] = [B]$, where $[X]$ is a matrix of variables, can be interpreted as a system of linear equations.

Solving the Simplest

1. Solve these matrix equations. You will probably want to turn each one into a system of linear equations.

   a. $\begin{bmatrix} 1 & 2 \\ 3 & 4 \end{bmatrix} \begin{bmatrix} w \\ z \end{bmatrix} = \begin{bmatrix} 6 \\ 16 \end{bmatrix}$

   b. $\begin{bmatrix} 1 & 3 \\ 0 & 2 \end{bmatrix} \begin{bmatrix} r \\ s \end{bmatrix} = \begin{bmatrix} 7 \\ 2 \end{bmatrix}$

   c. $\begin{bmatrix} 2 & 0 \\ 0 & 3 \end{bmatrix} \begin{bmatrix} u \\ v \end{bmatrix} = \begin{bmatrix} 8 \\ 15 \end{bmatrix}$

2. Compare the three matrix equations in Question 1. Which coefficient matrix led to the most easily solved system of linear equations?

3. Find the 2 × 2 coefficient matrix that will give the system of linear equations that is the absolute easiest to solve. Explain your choice.

Things We Take for Granted

We often take for granted all sorts of details about mathematics. For instance, properties like $8 \cdot 5 = 5 \cdot 8$ seem so natural and obvious that we may not even think about them.

In this activity, you will consider two properties that are true for numbers and explore whether similar properties hold true for 2×2 matrices.

1. The Commutative Property of Multiplication

The **commutative** property of multiplication for numbers is illustrated by the example $8 \cdot 5 = 5 \cdot 8$. More generally, according to this property, when you change the order of the quantities you are multiplying, you get the same answer. We can express this property in symbols as $ab = ba$.

Does a similar property hold true for multiplication of 2×2 matrices? See if you can find a counterexample.

2. The Associative Property of Multiplication

The **associative** property of multiplication for numbers applies when three numbers are multiplied together. This property says that regrouping the factors to change which multiplication is performed first does not change the result. An example is $(3 \cdot 4) \cdot 5 = 3 \cdot (4 \cdot 5)$. The left side is $12 \cdot 5$, and the right side is $3 \cdot 20$, and both sides equal 60.

Does a similar property hold true for multiplication of 2×2 matrices? See if you can find a counterexample.

Finding an Inverse

You have seen that you can solve a matrix equation like

$$\begin{bmatrix} 1 & 2 \\ 3 & 5 \end{bmatrix} \begin{bmatrix} w \\ z \end{bmatrix} = \begin{bmatrix} 2 \\ 1 \end{bmatrix}$$

by first finding a matrix C that fits the equation

$$[C] \begin{bmatrix} 1 & 2 \\ 3 & 5 \end{bmatrix} = \begin{bmatrix} 1 & 0 \\ 0 & 1 \end{bmatrix}$$

If there is such a matrix [C], it is called the

multiplicative inverse of $\begin{bmatrix} 1 & 2 \\ 3 & 5 \end{bmatrix}$.

To look for this inverse, suppose that [C] is the matrix $\begin{bmatrix} r & s \\ t & u \end{bmatrix}$. The equation defining [C] then becomes

$$\begin{bmatrix} r & s \\ t & u \end{bmatrix} \begin{bmatrix} 1 & 2 \\ 3 & 5 \end{bmatrix} = \begin{bmatrix} 1 & 0 \\ 0 & 1 \end{bmatrix}$$

1. Multiply out the product $\begin{bmatrix} r & s \\ t & u \end{bmatrix} \begin{bmatrix} 1 & 2 \\ 3 & 5 \end{bmatrix}$ to get a matrix with entries in terms of r, s, t, and u.

2. Use the fact that the product in Question 1 is equal to $\begin{bmatrix} 1 & 0 \\ 0 & 1 \end{bmatrix}$ to get a system of linear equations involving r, s, t, and u.

3. Solve the equations from Question 2 to find the values of r, s, t, and u.

4. a. Use your results from Question 3 to write the matrix [C].
   b. Check your work by finding the product $[C] \begin{bmatrix} 1 & 2 \\ 3 & 5 \end{bmatrix}$.

Inverses and Equations

1. You know that some systems of linear equations have unique solutions, some have no solutions, and some have infinitely many solutions. For each of these systems, find the unique solution or explain why there is not a unique solution.

   a. $x + 2y = 4$
   $3x + 4y = 8$

   b. $x + 2y = 2$
   $3x + 4y = 1$

   c. $x + 2y = 4$
   $2x + 4y = 8$

   d. $x + 2y = 2$
   $2x + 4y = 1$

2. The matrices in parts a and b here are each the coefficient matrix for two of the systems of equations in Question 1. For each matrix, either find the **inverse** or explain why there is no inverse.

   a. $\begin{bmatrix} 1 & 2 \\ 3 & 4 \end{bmatrix}$

   b. $\begin{bmatrix} 1 & 2 \\ 2 & 4 \end{bmatrix}$

3. Explain how your results in Question 2 are related to those in Question 1.

4. In general, which 2×2 matrices have inverses and which do not? What is the connection between a system of equations and whether a matrix has an inverse?

Calculators Again

You know that you can use a graphing calculator to multiply matrices. Graphing calculators have another wonderful use. They can calculate the multiplicative inverse of a matrix when the matrix is invertible (as long as the matrix dimensions are not too large for the calculator's capacity). And this is easy once you have entered a matrix into the calculator's memory.

Try to solve the following linear systems without doing any arithmetic, letting the calculator do all the hard work for you. Check your solutions, at least for the first system, to make sure you are doing the process correctly.

1. $5d + 2e = 11$

   $d + e = 4$

2. $2r + 3s - t = 3$

   $r - 2s + 4t = 2$

   $4r - s + 7t = 8$

3. $4w + x + 2y - 3z = -16$

   $-3w + x - y + 4z = 20$

   $-w + 2x + 5y + z = -4$

   $5w + 4x + 3y - z = -10$

4. $a + b + c + d + e + f = 30$

   $2a + 3b - 6c + 4d - e + f = 8$

   $5a + 4b + 3c - d + 5e - 2f = 34$

   $2a - 3b + 8c - 6d + e + 4f = 38$

   $6a + 2b + 7c - 5d - 3e - 2f = -42$

   $-5a + 8b - 5c + 3d - 9e + 4f = -18$

Fitting Mia's Birdhouses

Mia and her friends spent the semester building birdhouses, and now they are painting them. (You may remember Mia and her birdhouses from the Year 1 unit *The Pit and the Pendulum.*) After one hour, they had painted two birdhouses. After three hours, they had painted six birdhouses. And after five hours, they had painted nine birdhouses.

1. Plot the data about birdhouse painting. Use *number of hours* for the *x*-axis and *number of birdhouses* for the *y*-axis.

2. Explain why there is no linear function that fits the data perfectly.

3. Find a quadratic function that does fit the data perfectly. That is, find values for *a*, *b*, and *c* so that all three data points from the birdhouse situation fit the equation $y = ax^2 + bx + c$.

4. What do you think about the usefulness of the function from Question 3 in this situation?

Solving *Meadows or Malls?*

Congratulations! You are now ready to solve the unit problem.

With so many constraints and so many variables, it won't be easy—but careful work and a few shortcuts will help you complete the task.

You will also be preparing your unit portfolio in this final portion of the unit. Because this unit involves so many ideas, your portfolio work will be spread out over several activities.

Jon Honn and Rodolfo Contreras make sure the list of combinations each developed is complete before they begin to solve the unit problem.

Getting Ready for *Meadows or Malls?*

A while back (it may seem like a year ago!), you started working on the *Meadows or Malls?* problem. You now have all the tools you need to solve that problem, although it still will take some work to answer the main question in that problem.

As you have seen, the *Meadows or Malls?* problem has 12 constraints, of which four are equations and eight are inequalities. Here are those constraints.

$$\text{I} \qquad G_R + G_D = 300$$

$$\text{II} \qquad A_R + A_D = 100$$

$$\text{III} \qquad M_R + M_D = 150$$

$$\text{IV} \quad G_D + A_D + M_D \geq 300$$

$$\text{V} \qquad A_R + M_R \leq 200$$

$$\text{VI} \qquad A_R + G_D = 100$$

$$\text{VII} \qquad G_R \geq 0$$

$$\text{VIII} \qquad A_R \geq 0$$

$$\text{IX} \qquad M_R \geq 0$$

$$\text{X} \qquad G_D \geq 0$$

$$\text{XI} \qquad A_D \geq 0$$

$$\text{XII} \qquad M_D \geq 0$$

These constraints give you a lot of combinations to check to find corner points of the feasible region. Your task now is to list all the combinations you need to check. Refer to the constraints by number in your list of combinations.

continued

As you work, keep these things in mind.

- The four equations must be part of every combination.

- Look for ways to reduce your list (without actually solving any of the systems). For instance, it is possible to prove from the constraints that certain variables can't be zero. Once you do that, you can eliminate some of constraints VII through XII from consideration.

Meadows or Malls? Revisited

River City has three parcels of land to work with.

- 300 acres of farmland willed to the city by Mr. Goodfellow
- 100 acres from the U.S. government from a closed army base
- 150 acres of land formerly leased for mining

The city needs to decide how much of each parcel to use for recreation and how much to use for development, based on several constraints.

Your Task

Remember that your group is a consulting team that the city manager has come to for help. Not only should you give her an answer, but you should also try to convince her that yours is the best possible answer. You'd like her to use your group in the future when the city needs help again.

Prepare a group report for the city manager. Your report should include three parts.

- An answer to the city's dilemma
- An explanation that will convince the city manager that your solution will cost the least
- Any graphs, charts, equations, or diagrams that are needed to support your explanation

You will probably want to review what you already know about the problem based on your notes and the previous activities.

Beginning Portfolios—Part I

This unit involves several closely related ideas.

- Graphing linear equations in three variables
- Solving systems of linear equations in three variables
- Finding intersections of planes in 3-space

1. Summarize how these ideas are related. In particular, focus on these two questions and how they are connected.

   - What are the possible results from solving a system of three linear equations in three variables?

   - What are the possible results of the intersection of three planes in 3-space?

2. Select activities from the unit that were important in developing your understanding of the ideas you discussed in Question 1. Explain why you made the selections you did.

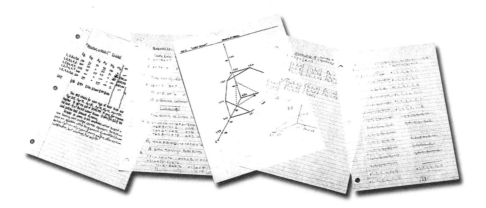

Beginning Portfolios—Part II

In this unit, you have used matrices both to represent information and to solve linear equations.

1. Summarize what you have learned about matrices. Answer these questions in your summary.

   • What is a matrix?

   • How are matrices used to solve linear equations?

2. Select activities from the unit that were important in developing your understanding of the ideas you discussed in Question 1. Explain why you made the selections you did.

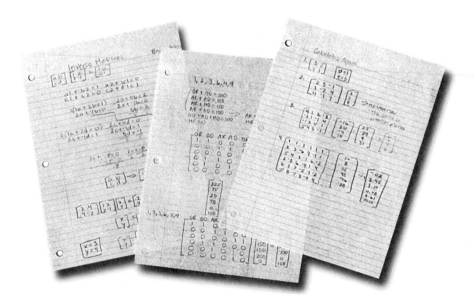

Meadows or Malls? Portfolio

Now that *Meadows or Malls?* is completed, it is time to assemble your portfolio for the unit. This process has three steps.

• Write a cover letter that summarizes the unit.

• Choose papers to include from your work in the unit.

• Discuss your personal mathematical growth during the unit.

Cover Letter

Look back over *Meadows or Malls?* and describe the central problem of the unit and the key mathematical ideas. Your description should give an overview of how the key ideas were developed and how they were used to solve the central problem.

In compiling your portfolio, you will select some activities you think were important in developing the unit's key ideas. Your cover letter should include an explanation of why you selected each item. For ideas discussed in *Beginning Portfolios—Part I* and *Beginning Portfolios—Part II,* you can simply refer to your work on those activities.

continued ▶

Selecting Papers

Your portfolio for *Meadows or Malls?* should contain these items.

- *Meadows or Malls? Revisited*
- *Beginning Portfolios—Part I* and *Beginning Portfolios—Part II*

  Include these two earlier portfolio assignments and the activities you discussed in them as part of your cover letter.

- *Just the Plane Facts*
- An activity on solving systems of linear equations that does not use matrices
- An activity in which you learned concepts that allowed you to solve linear programming problems in more than two variables
- A Problem of the Week

  Select one of the POWs you completed in this unit: *That's Entertainment!, SubDivvy,* or *Crack the Code.*

Personal Growth

Your cover letter for *Meadows or Malls?* describes how the mathematical ideas develop in the unit. In addition, write about your personal development during this unit. You may want to address this question.

> *How did your experiences in the Year 2 unit* Cookies *affect your work in* Meadows or Malls?

Include any thoughts about your experiences that you wish to share with a reader of your portfolio.

SUPPLEMENTAL ACTIVITIES

The supplemental activities in *Meadows or Malls?* touch on algebraic and geometric ideas, as well as principles of linear programming. Here are some examples.

- *Embellishing the Plane Facts* asks you to find equations to illustrate some of your conclusions from *Just the Plane Facts.*

- *Producing Programming Problems—More Variables* asks you to create a linear programming problem involving at least four variables.

- *Determining the Determinant* asks you to investigate the concept of a determinant, which is a useful tool in deciding whether a matrix is invertible.

How Many Regions?

Any line in the coordinate plane will divide the plane into two regions, one on either side of the line. (The line itself is not considered a region.) Each of these regions can be represented by an inequality.

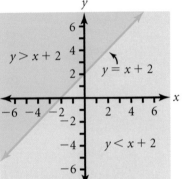

For example, the diagram shows the line defined by the equation $y = x + 2$. The line itself contains all the points that fit the equation, such as $(-3, -1)$ and $(2, 4)$.

The darkly shaded region above the line consists of points that fit the inequality $y > x + 2$, such as $(0, 3)$ and $(-4, 1)$. The lightly shaded region below the line consists of points that fit the inequality $y < x + 2$, such as $(3, 4)$ and $(-2, -2)$.

Your task is to investigate what happens if you start with more than one line. Specifically, how many regions might you get, and how can you describe the different regions using inequalities?

1. Begin with the case of two lines.

   a. What are the possibilities for the number of regions you get when you draw two lines in the plane?

   b. For each possibility in part a, give a specific pair of equations you could use for the lines, and describe how to represent each resulting region using inequalities. Some regions may require more than one inequality.

   c. Explain why you think your answer to part a includes all the possibilities.

continued

2. Do the same thing for the case of three lines and then for the case of four lines. Give specific examples for each possibility you describe, and explain why you think you have covered all the possibilities.

The Eternal Triangle

Krys, Greg, and Juranso are creating a musical love story based on the life of Pythagoras. Krys will design the sets, Greg will compose the music, and Juranso will write the script. Greg and Juranso will both perform in the musical.

The three have agreed that the play will be a mixture of straight acting scenes and musical scenes. They need to decide how many of each type of scene to include.

Krys, Greg, and Juranso have a limited amount of time for the project. Krys can design at most 16 sets. There will be one set per scene, no matter what kind of scene it is. Greg and Juranso can each spend at most 36 hours on the play. Greg figures it will take him an hour for each acting scene but, because he has to write the music, three hours for each musical scene. For Juranso, it's the opposite. Because he's developing the script, he figures the acting scenes will take him three hours each and the musical scenes will require only one hour each.

Of course, the trio wants to maximize the number of people who will attend their performance. Juranso does a lot of acting, and they figure Greg's musical scenes will be a special draw. They estimate that 20 people will attend for each musical scene they include and 10 people will attend for each acting scene they include.

How many of each type of scene should they include in their play to maximize the number of attendees?

Note: You can interpret an answer with fractions as representing a scene that is partly music and partly straight acting, so don't limit yourself to whole numbers.

The Jewelry Business

Rebecca, Noel, and Keenzia have decided to start a jewelry business. They will buy hand-crafted jewelry in bulk at a discount and sell it at craft fairs and art shows.

To purchase jewelry at the special bulk price, they need to spend at least $3,000. The earrings will cost them $5 per pair. The necklaces will cost them $9 apiece.

They have different opinions about what portion of their purchase should be for earrings and what portion should be for necklaces. At this point, all they've decided is that the number of necklaces they buy should be at least half but at most three times the number of pairs of earrings they buy.

Aside from the time spent planning and purchasing, the partners estimate it will take an average of 15 minutes to sell each pair of earrings and 20 minutes to sell each necklace. Together, the group can devote a total of up to 240 hours to the endeavor.

After all their costs are considered, they make $4 profit on each necklace and $3 on each pair of earrings.

Assuming they sell everything they buy (and they will, because they are shrewd businesspeople), how many necklaces and how many pairs of earrings should they buy to maximize their profit?

Special Planes

You know that the graph of a linear equation in three variables is a plane. Now you will find equations for planes that fit some specific conditions.

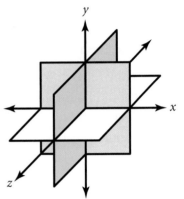

1. a. Find a linear equation whose graph is a plane that includes the *z*-axis. (Consider what's true about the coordinates of all points on the *z*-axis.)

   b. Find a linear equation whose graph differs from the graph of your equation from part a but still includes the *z*-axis.

2. a. Find a linear equation whose graph includes the points $(0, 0, 0)$ and $(1, 1, 0)$.

   b. Find a linear equation whose graph differs from the graph of your equation from part a but still includes the points $(0, 0, 0)$ and $(1, 1, 0)$.

3. There are many planes whose graph includes both $(0, 0, 0)$ and $(1, 1, 0)$.

   a. In what kind of set do all these planes intersect?

   b. What points in addition to $(0, 0, 0)$ and $(1, 1, 0)$ must be in the set where all these planes intersect?

4. a. Find a linear equation whose graph includes the point $(2, -1, 4)$.

   b. Find a linear equation whose graph includes both $(2, -1, 4)$ and $(1, 1, 0)$.

Embellishing the Plane Facts

In the activity *Just the Plane Facts,* you described the possible ways in which two or more planes might intersect. You explained each case using a diagram or model.

Now you will describe each case by giving equations of specific planes that create the given type of intersection.

1. First consider the case of two planes.

    a. Describe the different ways in which two planes can intersect. (This is Question 2 of *Just the Plane Facts.*)

    b. For each kind of intersection, give the equations of two planes that intersect in that way. Do not use the coordinate planes for either of the two planes.

    c. How can you tell by looking at the equations for two planes how the planes will intersect?

2. Now consider the case of three planes.

    a. Describe the different ways in which three planes can intersect.

    b. For each kind of intersection, give the equations of three planes that intersect in that way. Do not use the coordinate planes for any of the three planes.

A Linear Medley

Linear equations and systems of equations arise in many types of situations. Examine the situations given here. Express each situation in terms of linear equations, and then try to answer the questions by solving the equations.

If a problem does not have a solution, or does not give enough information to answer the questions, propose a way to change the problem so that it will have a unique solution.

1. Hound Dog Busline charges passengers $50 to ride to Nashville plus $5 for each piece of luggage. King Busline charges $70 for the trip and only $3 per piece of luggage.

    a. Write an expression for how much Hound Dog Busline charges if a passenger brings b pieces of luggage.

    b. Write an expression for how much King Busline charges if a passenger brings b pieces of luggage.

    c. For what number of pieces of luggage carried by a passenger do the two companies charge the same amount? What is the charge?

2. The length of a certain rectangle is 9 times its width. The perimeter of the rectangle is 200 meters. What are the dimensions of the rectangle?

3. When Nicole sold 8 pounds of tomatoes and 5 pounds of apples, she made $12.10. When she sold 12 pounds of tomatoes and 9 pounds of apples, she made $20.10. How much does Nicole charge per pound for tomatoes and for apples?

4. Six hundred people attended the city basketball championship. Two types of tickets were sold: adult tickets and student tickets. A total of $2,200 was collected at the gate. How much did each type of ticket cost?

continued ▶

5. Rancher Gonzales hired some workers to put up a fence around her ranch. On the first day, she hired four experienced carpenters and six apprentices, and they completed 420 feet of fencing. The next day, she hired five experienced carpenters and three apprentices, and they completed 390 feet of fencing.

For simplicity, assume the workers all work independently, so the amount of fencing completed is simply the sum of the amounts completed by each individual. Also assume that each experienced carpenter does the same amount of work and that each apprentice does the same amount of work.

Based on these assumptions, how much fencing does each experienced carpenter finish per day? How much fencing does each apprentice finish per day?

The General Two-Variable System

You have seen that every linear equation in one variable can be solved using basic ideas about equivalent equations.

The standard linear equation has the form $ax + b = c$. You can get from $ax + b = c$ to a solution for x in terms of the other variables using this sequence of equations.

$$ax + b = c$$

$$ax = c - b$$

$$x = \frac{c - b}{a}$$

Your task is to develop a similar solution to the general system of two linear equations in two variables.

Such a system is shown here. The coefficients and constant terms are represented by the variables a, b, c, d, e, and f. Treat the variables x and y as the "unknowns."

$$ax + by = c$$
$$dx + ey = f$$

1. Find a general solution to this system of linear equations. That is, solve for x and y in terms of a, b, c, d, e, and f.

2. Discuss whether your solution makes sense for all values of the variables a, b, c, d, e, and f. Explain how this is related to the concepts of **inconsistent** and **dependent systems.**

Playing Forever

1. The high school baseball team has seven excellent outfielders: Andrew, Brett, Carl, Duane, Ethan, Felipe, and Griswold. Only three can start a given game.

   What is the most games the team can play before they have to repeat the same starting group of three outfielders? It doesn't matter which player is at which outfield position—simply consider which three are chosen and list all possible combinations.

2. The basketball team has nine excellent players: Hanna, Isabella, Jacinda, Katherine, Lana, Madeleine, Nikki, Oriana, and Paulette. Only five can start a given game.

   What is the most games the team can play before they have to repeat the same starting group? List all possible combinations.

The Shortest Game

In the game SubDivvy (from the POW *SubDivvy*), there are often many ways to get from the starting number to 1.

For example, if the starting number is 10, the game can proceed in several ways, including the two shown below. The first path takes four steps, while the second takes five steps.

$$
\begin{array}{cc}
10 & 10 \\
\underline{-5} & \underline{-1} \\
5 & 9 \\
\underline{-1} & \underline{-3} \\
4 & 6 \\
\underline{-2} & \underline{-3} \\
2 & 3 \\
\underline{-1} & \underline{-1} \\
1 & 2 \\
 & \underline{-1} \\
 & 1
\end{array}
$$

Examine whether the shortest path to 1 is always achieved by subtracting the greatest possible divisor at each step. Then see what else you can find out about shortest paths in SubDivvy.

Producing Programming Problems— More Variables

In the Year 2 unit *Cookies,* you invented your own linear programming problem involving two variables. Your task now is to invent a linear programming problem involving four or more variables.

Here are the key items your problem must have.

- Four or more variables
- Something to be maximized or minimized that is a linear function of those variables
- Some linear constraints involving your variables (Some of these constraints can be equations instead of inequalities.)

Write your problem, and then solve it.

Your Own Three-Variable Problem

In the activity *Ages, Coins, and Fund-Raising,* you examined three problems. Each of them could be represented by a system of three linear equations in three variables.

Make up a problem of your own that can be represented that way, and solve your problem.

Fitting a Plane

In the activities *Fitting a Line* and *Fitting More Lines,* your task was to find a linear function through a particular pair of points. That is, you were asked to find coefficients a and b so that the line $y = ax + b$ would go through the given points.

This activity adds another dimension to this task—literally. Instead of finding the equation of a line through two points, you're asked to find the equation of a plane through three points.

Consider functions in which z is written as a linear expression in terms of x and y. That is, consider functions defined by equations of the form $z = ax + by + c$, where a, b, and c are any three numbers. The graph of any such equation is a plane.

Comment: A linear equation involving only x and y, such as $2x - 3y = 7$, can be graphed in 3-space, and its graph is a plane (just as an equation like $x = 3$ can be graphed in the xy-plane, and its graph is a line). Thus, the form $z = ax + by + c$ does not represent the most general plane.

1. Suppose you want a plane that goes through the point $(3, 2, 1)$.
   a. Show that the graph of the equation $z = 2x - 4y + 3$ goes through this point.
   b. Find a condition on a, b, and c that guarantees the graph of the equation $z = ax + by + c$ goes through $(3, 2, 1)$.

2. Find a condition on a, b, and c that guarantees the graph of the equation $z = ax + by + c$ goes through $(1, -2, 5)$.

3. Find a condition on a, b, and c that guarantees the graph of the equation $z = ax + by + c$ goes through $(2, -1, 6)$.

4. Find values of a, b, and c so that the graph of the equation $z = ax + by + c$ goes through all three points: $(3, 2, 1)$, $(1, -2, 5)$, and $(2, -1, 6)$.

5. Can you pick any three points and then find an equation of the form $z = ax + by + c$ whose graph goes through all three points?

Surfer's Shirts

1. Anna is ordering special T-shirts for the annual Cross Town Race. T-shirts come in two sizes: small and large. A small T-shirt costs $8 for the shirt itself and $2 to print the design. A large T-shirt costs $10, and it costs $2.50 to print the design. Anna needs to itemize the printing costs separately from the cost of the blank shirts.

   Suppose Anna orders *S* small shirts and *L* large shirts, with designs. Set up matrices with all of the necessary information. Write an expression using the matrices that will give Anna the total cost for the T-shirts and the total cost for printing (in terms of *S* and *L*).

2. Ming's latest surfing competition is conducted in three heats. Ming is using her three classic moves: the off-the-lip, the cutback, and the tube ride.

   In this competition, off-the-lips are worth 4 points each, cutbacks are worth 6 points each, and tube rides are worth 10 points each.

   - In heat 1, Ming did 5 off-the-lips, 3 cutbacks, and 2 tube rides.
   - In heat 2, Ming did 7 off-the-lips, 2 cutbacks, and 1 tube ride.
   - In heat 3, Ming did 3 off-the-lips, 4 cutbacks, and 3 tube rides.

continued ◗

a. Suppose Ming wants to know how many points she scored in each heat. Set up matrices and write a matrix expression that will give her this information.

b. Suppose instead Ming wants to know the total number of points she scored (in the three heats combined) for each type of move. Set up matrices and write a matrix expression that will give her this information.

An Associative Proof

In the activity *Things We Take for Granted,* you investigated whether matrix multiplication is commutative or associative. This activity follows up on that work.

1. Prove that multiplication of 2×2 matrices is associative.

2. a. Is matrix addition commutative?

   b. Is matrix addition associative?

   Justify your answers.

When Can You Find an Inverse?

In the activity *Inverses and Equations,* you saw that some 2 × 2 matrices have an inverse for multiplication and others do not. You will now investigate the existence of matrix inverses more fully.

1. Think about the connection between whether a matrix has an inverse and the graphs of certain equations related to the matrix. Use the geometry of these graphs to find out which 2 × 2 matrices have inverses. Explain your answer.

2. Which of these 3 × 3 matrices have inverses? Explain your answers.

   a. $\begin{bmatrix} 1 & 2 & 1 \\ 0 & 2 & -1 \\ 2 & 4 & 2 \end{bmatrix}$

   b. $\begin{bmatrix} 1 & -1 & 2 \\ 0 & 3 & 0 \\ 3 & -3 & 1 \end{bmatrix}$

   c. $\begin{bmatrix} 1 & -1 & 2 \\ 0 & 3 & 0 \\ 1 & 2 & 2 \end{bmatrix}$

   d. $\begin{bmatrix} 1 & 2 & 1 \\ 0 & 2 & -1 \\ 2 & 6 & 2 \end{bmatrix}$

3. Based on your work in Question 2 and other examples of your own, what can you say about when a 3 × 3 matrix has an inverse and when it does not?

Determining the Determinant

If a system of linear equations has the same number of equations as variables, it will usually have a unique solution. In some cases, the system will have no solution (an inconsistent system) or infinitely many solutions (a dependent system).

Whether a system has a unique solution depends on the coefficients of the variables. As you may have seen in the activity *The General Two-Variable System,* the system

$$ax + by = c$$
$$dx + ey = f$$

will have a unique solution whenever a certain expression involving a, b, d, and e is not zero. When that expression is zero, the system will be either dependent or inconsistent, depending on the values of c and f.

This special expression involving the coefficients is called the *determinant* of the matrix $\begin{bmatrix} a & b \\ d & e \end{bmatrix}$.

In fact, determinants are defined for square matrices of all sizes and can be used to solve systems of linear equations.

Your Task

Your task is to learn more about determinants and to write a report about what you learn.

Begin your report with the definition of the determinant for 2×2 matrices. Explain how determinants can be used to solve two-variable systems of equations like the one shown in this activity.

Then discuss how determinants are used in general to solve systems of linear equations and what the relationship is between the determinant of a matrix and the invertibility of the matrix. Go beyond the 2×2 case and include the definition of the determinant for at least the case of a 3×3 matrix.

Cracking Another Code

$$
\begin{array}{r}
A\,B \\
\times\ \ C \\
\hline
D\,E
\end{array}
\qquad
\begin{array}{r}
D\,E \\
+\,F\,G \\
\hline
H\,I
\end{array}
$$

These two arithmetic problems use a single code in which letters have been substituted for numbers, as in the POW *Crack the Code*.

As in that POW, any solution must follow these rules.

- If a letter is used more than once, it stands for the same number each time it is used.
- Different letters always stand for different single-digit numbers.
- A letter standing for 0 never starts a number with more than one digit. For example, the expression 03 cannot be used, but 507 and 80 and just plain 0 are all allowed.

Your job is to crack the code. Keep in mind that the multiplication problem and the addition problem use the same code.

You must not only find all the solutions, if there are any, but also prove your answer.

Adapted from a problem in *Oregon Mathematics Teacher*, January–February 1989.

Small World, Isn't It?

Slope, Derivatives, and Exponential Growth

Small World, Isn't It?—Slope, Derivatives, and Exponential Growth

As the World Grows

How many people are there in the world today? What about a century or two ago? What about in the future?

The central problem of this unit involves analyzing world population trends. You will begin by studying population data since 1650, with the goal of determining how long it will take until people are "squashed up against one another."

Lisa Newton rephrases the unit's central problem in her own words.

A Crowded Place

Everyone knows the world's population is increasing. The table shows the estimated world population over the past several centuries.

Suppose this pattern of data continues. How long do you think it will take until we are all squashed up against one another?

You may find these facts useful.

- The total surface area of the earth is approximately 197,000,000 square miles.
- Approximately 29.2% of the earth's total surface area is land.

As you consider this question, make note of any difficulties you encounter or any issues you think need clarification.

Year	Estimated Population
1650	470,000,000
1750	629,000,000
1850	1,030,000,000
1900	1,550,000,000
1950	2,560,000,000
1960	3,040,000,000
1970	3,710,000,000
1980	4,450,000,000
1990	5,280,000,000
2000	6,090,000,000
2005	6,480,000,000

Source: U.S. Census Bureau.

The More, the Merrier?

Isn't life more interesting when there are lots of people around? Then why should people worry about a population explosion? Your task in this POW is to study some aspect of our world's rapid population growth and to find out why some people are concerned.

Write a report on your findings, which may include your own opinions and conjectures about why things are the way they are. Graphs, drawings, and tables may help you communicate your ideas.

Choose from these topics, or think of your own topic for your report.

- Population growth and the food supply
- Pros and cons of limiting family size
- Comparison of population growth in different countries
- Population growth and the environment
- Ways to cope with increasing population
- Traffic congestion

How Many of Us Can Fit?

The activity *A Crowded Place* asks you when we will all get "squashed up against one another." That probably won't ever happen, but you may be curious about how many people that would require.

1. How many square miles of land surface area are there on the earth? Use the information in *A Crowded Place* to answer this question.

2. How many square feet of land area are there on the earth? Use the fact that 1 mile is equal to 5280 feet, so 1 square mile is 5280^2 square feet, which is 27,878,400 square feet.

3. In 2005, the world population was about 6.48 billion people. If this population were spread evenly over the earth's land area, about how many square feet of area would each person have, on average?

4. Suppose we interpret the phrase "squashed up against one another" to mean that each person has about 1 square foot of area to call his or her own. How many people would there need to be for us to really be squashed up against one another?

How Many More People?

Part I: The Graph

Making a graph can help you get some ideas about how the world population has grown over the centuries.

1. Choose an appropriate scale and plot the data from *A Crowded Place*. On your graph, show all the data points given in that activity. Label the data points with their coordinates.

Part II: Average Increases

2. a. Find the increase in population between the years 1650 and 1900.

   b. Explain how the increase you found shows up on the graph.

   c. Find the average increase in population *per year* between 1650 and 1900.

   d. What would the portion of the graph from 1650 to 1900 look like if the population had increased by the same number of people each year of this time period?

3. a. Find the increase in population between 1900 and 1950.

   b. Explain how the increase you found shows up on the graph.

   c. Find the average increase in population per year between 1900 and 1950.

   d. What would the portion of the graph from 1900 to 1950 look like if the population had increased by the same number of people each year of this time period?

Part III: Making Comparisons

4. Which interval—1650 to 1900, or 1900 to 1950—has the greater average increase in population per year? How could you answer this question simply by looking at your graph?

Growing Up

The graph shows the average height for boys ages 0 to 6 in the United States around the middle of the twentieth century.

1. Suppose the average amount of growth shown during the first year after birth were to continue during the second year. What would be the average height for boys on their second birthdays?

2. The section of the graph for ages 3 to 6 is nearly straight. What does that mean in terms of the average growth for boys during those years?

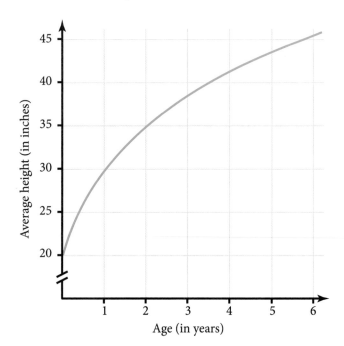

3. a. How much does the average height for boys increase between ages 3 and 4?

   b. Express your answer to part a as a percentage of the average height for boys at age 3.

4. a. How much does the average height for boys increase between ages 5 and 6?

   b. Express your answer to part a as a percentage of the average height for boys at age 5.

   c. Compare your answers for Questions 4a and 4b to your answers for Questions 3a and 3b.

Data source: Department of Pediatrics, State University of Iowa, 1943.

Average Growth

Most growth—such as the growth of living things, the economy, or organizations—is uneven. Population growth is no exception. Over the next few days, you'll look at some examples of growth and rates of change. You will focus your attention on how you can use graphs to understand what's going on.

When a rate of growth is changing, it sometimes helps to examine the *average* rate of growth. When a growth rate is constant, the graph of the situation is a straight line. The slope of that line is the standard numeric method for measuring the steepness of the graph. In these activities, you'll learn a new way to think about slope.

Leilani Juan and Liana DeGracia begin their investigation of growth and rates of change.

Story Sketches

1. This graph describes a wagon train's progress along the Overland Trail.

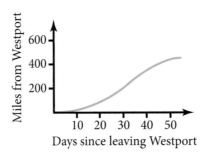

a. About how many miles per day did the wagon train travel for the first 20 days? Explain how you got your answer.

b. What was the fastest pace the wagon train achieved? Explain how you got your answer.

2. Tyler Dunkalot and his elementary school friends want to get basketball uniforms. They are saving money so they can contribute to the purchase. One Friday afternoon, right after getting their weekly allowances, they each put some of the allowance into their piggy banks and count the savings so far.

Here's how much Tyler and his friends have that Friday (including the amount they just added) and how much each will add to savings every Friday from then on.

- Tyler has $2 now and will add 50¢ each week.
- Robin has $2 now and will add 70¢ each week.
- Max has $4 now and will add 70¢ each week.
- Daniel has $4 now and will add 30¢ each week.

Draw graphs showing accumulated savings versus time elapsed for Tyler and each of his friends for a 10-week period. Assume they add their savings to their piggy banks each Friday and do not spend any of the saved money.

Draw all four graphs on the same set of axes, using a different color to represent each friend.

continued ▸

3. Compare your four graphs. Describe how they are the same and how they are different.

4. For each friend, develop a formula or an equation that shows how much money is in the piggy bank *n* weeks after they first counted their savings.

What a Mess!

Part I: The Mess

An oil tanker has suffered an explosion out at sea. Thousands of gallons of oil are spreading across the ocean. Lindsay, who is flying over in her airplane, sees that the oil slick appears to be in the shape of a circle.

When Lindsay first sees the oil slick, the radius of the circle is 70 meters. She flies overhead for a while and estimates that the radius is increasing at a rate of 6 meters per hour.

1. Make an In-Out table in which the *In* is the number of hours since Lindsay first observed the oil slick and the *Out* is the radius of the oil slick after that many hours.

2. Draw a graph based on your In-Out table.

3. Find a rule for your graph and table.

Part II: The Cleanup

Seven hours after Lindsay first sees the oil spill with a radius of 70 meters, a cleanup operation begins. Rescue workers pump a special detergent into the center of the spill. As the detergent spreads, a circle of clean water develops inside the oil spill. The radius of this circle increases at 10 meters per hour.

4. What was the radius of the oil spill when the cleanup operation began? Did the rescue team start soon enough and pump fast enough to eventually counteract the oil spill? If not, why not? If so, how many hours will it take until the spill is neutralized?

Traveling Time

Abida has packed her bags and is ready to leave for college. She needs to catch an early train because she has a long way to travel.

Abida lives in Cincinnati, Ohio, and will be going to school in Philadelphia, Pennsylvania, 550 miles away. She is hoping to reach Philadelphia in time to see some historical landmarks. She figures that if she gets to Philadelphia by 3:00 p.m., she will have enough time to visit the Liberty Bell Center and Independence Hall before they close for the evening.

1. Abida's train leaves at 5:00 a.m. Assume the train ride is exactly 550 miles. How many miles per hour must the train average for her to get to Philadelphia by 3:00 p.m.? (Cincinnati and Philadelphia are in the same time zone.)

2. The 5:00 a.m. train averages 40 miles per hour for the first hour and a half. What speed must it average for the rest of the trip for Abida to reach Philadelphia by 3:00 p.m.?

3. Suppose the train actually averaged 50 miles per hour for the whole trip (which means the trip took 11 hours altogether). That doesn't necessarily mean the train traveled at a constant rate of 50 mph.

   Make up a scenario in which the train averaged 50 mph for the trip but traveled at least two different speeds along the way. Be specific about speeds, times, and distances.

continued ▶

4. Abida's train left on time at 5:00 a.m. This graph shows one possibility for how far the train traveled as a function of the time elapsed.

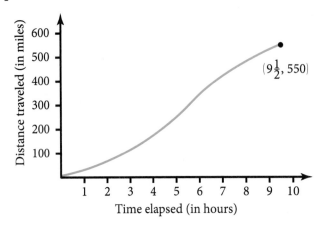

Use the graph to answer these questions

a. Was the train's average speed faster during the first 2 hours of the trip or the last 2 hours?

b. During what 1-hour period was the train's average speed the fastest?

c. If you had to pick the precise instant the train was going the fastest, what point would you choose and why?

Comparative Growth

Josh is doing a study comparing the population growth of his hometown in the early twentieth century with its population growth in the early 1980s.

When he comes across the two graphs shown here, Josh notices that the first graph appears to be steeper than the second. He concludes that the population was growing faster at the beginning of the century than in the early 1980s.

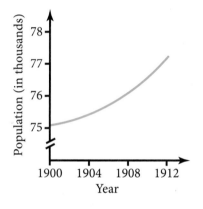
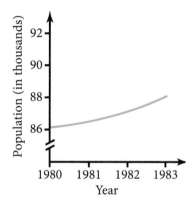

1. Use the first graph to calculate the average increase in population per year for the interval from 1900 to 1912. The graph shows the coordinates of the starting and ending points of this period.

2. Use the second graph to calculate the average increase in population per year for the interval from 1980 to 1983. The graph shows the coordinates of the starting and ending points of this period.

3. Do your results support Josh's conclusion? What does this suggest about using graphs to compare rates of change? If Josh's conclusion is incorrect, what should he do instead?

If Looks Don't Matter, What Does?

In the activity *Comparative Growth,* you saw that you can't necessarily compare rates of growth in two graphs solely from the appearance of the graphs. Now you will examine some specific situations to decide what really matters.

1. The first graph shows only two of the data points from the activity *A Crowded Place.*

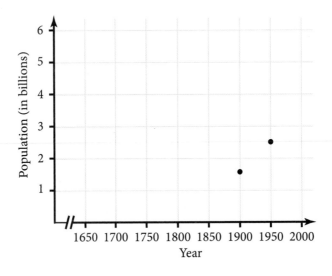

   a. Use the two points to find the average population growth per year from 1900 to 1950. Explain the process you use.

   b. What would this portion of the graph look like if the population had grown by the same number of people each year?

2. The graph at the right shows two points from the graph in Question 1 of *Story Sketches.* Use the graph to find the average distance traveled per day from Day 20 to Day 30. Explain the process you use.

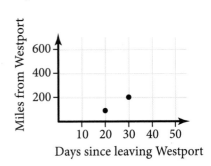

continued ▶

3. Lani is a bit older than Tyler Dunkalot and his friends. The graph below shows the amount of money Lani has in her savings account at various times over the course of several weeks.

   At what rate did the amount in Lani's savings account change per week? Explain how you found your answer from the graph.

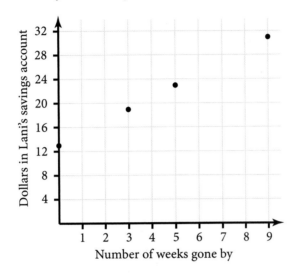

4. Find the rate of change of the function whose graph is shown below. Explain your work.

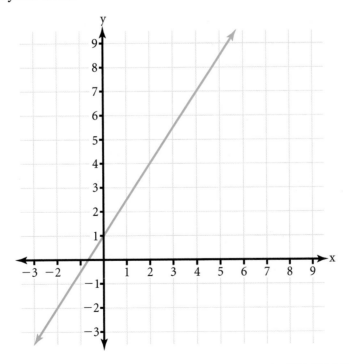

All in a Row

The simplest type of growth to study is constant growth, and that leads to work with linear functions. In the next several activities, you will develop the important concept of slope. Slope is the primary tool for describing the rate of change for a linear function.

You'll use this concept to develop equations for straight lines. You'll also see whether a linear model for population growth can accurately predict future trends.

Niall McNamara and Melyssa Brixner explore connections between graphs and formulas.

Formulating the Rate

In each situation in *If Looks Don't Matter, What Does?*, you used coordinates of points on a graph to find a rate of change. You were given specific numbers for the coordinates, or you could at least estimate the values of the coordinates from the graph.

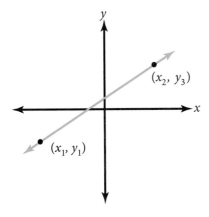

Now suppose you have a function whose graph is a straight line and that (x_1, y_1) and (x_2, y_2) are two points on the graph. That is, instead of numeric values, variables represent each of the coordinates.

Find an expression for the rate of change of the function in terms of x_1, y_1, x_2, and y_2.

Rates, Graphs, Slopes, and Equations

The concept of **slope** comes from the idea of a constant rate of change. Formally, the slope of the line connecting two points (x_1, y_1) and (x_2, y_2) is defined as the ratio

$$\frac{y_2 - y_1}{x_2 - x_1}$$

The numerator of this fraction is sometimes referred to as the *change in y* or the *rise*. The denominator is called the *change in x* or the *run*.

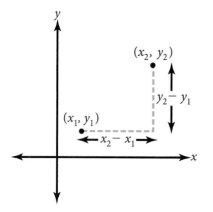

In this activity, you will work with rates and slopes, exploring their connections to graphs and formulas.

1. A jogger is moving at a rate of 500 feet per minute. That's about 6 miles per hour.

   a. Plot a graph showing the distance the jogger has traveled (in feet) as a function of t (in minutes). Use $t = 0$ as the time when the jogger starts.

   b. Find an equation for this function.

   c. Choose two points on your graph and use their coordinates to compute the slope of the graph.

2. A reservoir that is partly filled contains 200,000 cubic feet of water. Water is then added to the reservoir at a rate of 7000 cubic feet per hour.

   a. Plot a graph showing the amount of water in the reservoir as a function of t. Use $t = 0$ as the time when the water begins to be added. You may want to "skip" part of the vertical axis as was done in the graph in *Growing Up*.

   b. Find an equation for this function.

   c. Choose two points on your graph and use their coordinates to compute the slope of the graph.

continued ▶

3. a. Plot the data in this In-Out table.

In	Out
3	18
5	26
10	46
16	70

b. Choose two points on your graph and use their coordinates to compute the slope of the line connecting them.

c. Find an equation to describe your graph.

4. a. Choose two points on the line shown here and use their coordinates to compute the slope of the line.

b. Find an equation for the line.

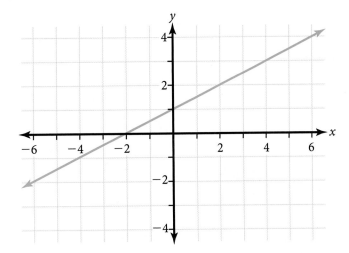

More About Tyler's Friends

In *Story Sketches,* you met Tyler Dunkalot and his friends, who were saving money to help buy basketball uniforms.

You may recall that two of Tyler's friends, Robin and Max, both saved 70¢ per week. At the start of their savings program, Robin had $2 and Max had $4.

1. Graph both Robin's and Max's savings as functions of the time elapsed. Treat these as *continuous* functions, as if Robin and Max were each saving their allowances gradually throughout the week at a constant rate. Use $t = 0$ to represent the moment when they started saving, and use the same set of axes for both graphs.

2. Find the slope of each of your graphs. Explain what you notice about the slopes.

3. Will the two graphs ever intersect? Explain your answer.

4. a. Find a formula for the amount of money each of the friends has at time t.

   b. How are these formulas related to your answers to Question 2?

Wake Up!

Getting going in the morning was probably hard for folks on the Overland Trail (just as it may be for you today), so coffee was a highly valued commodity.

The Cazneau family starts their journey with a supply of 30 pounds of coffee. When they arrive at Sutter's Fort in California, 188 days later, they have only 3 pounds left.

1. Draw a graph showing the amount of coffee remaining as a function of the time elapsed since the start of the journey. For simplicity, assume the Cazneaus consume coffee at a constant rate.

2. Find the average amount of coffee consumed per day.

3. Develop an equation for the function represented by your graph.

4. Find the slope of your graph.

5. Suppose that at the beginning of their 188-day journey, the Cazneaus are 1600 miles from Sutter's Fort.

   a. How many miles per day do they travel? For simplicity, assume they travel the same distance each day.

   b. Of course, as the Cazneaus travel, their distance from Sutter's Fort decreases. Write a formula expressing the distance remaining as a function of the number of days they have been traveling.

   c. Make a graph of your function from part b.

   d. Find the slope of your graph.

California, Here I Come!

According to the U.S. census, the population of California in 1850 was about 92,600. During the 1850s, with the great westward migration, the population grew substantially. In 1860, the census population was 380,000.

1. What was the average annual population increase during the 1850s (that is, from 1850 to 1860)?

2. Suppose California's population had continued to increase after 1860 by the same annual amount as it averaged during the 1850s. What would the population have been in each of these years?

   a. 1900

   b. 1950

   c. 2000

3. Generalize your results from Question 2. That is, develop a formula for California's population in year X. Base your formula on the assumption that the population continued to increase after 1860 by the same annual amount as it averaged during the 1850s.

4. According to the U.S. census, California's population in 2000 was 33,871,648. How does this amount compare to the figure you found in Question 2c? What do you think accounts for the difference between your prediction and the actual population in 2000?

continued ▶

Historical note: At the time of the gold rush (the 1850s), the U.S. Constitution stated that taxes and representation in Congress would be apportioned among the states "according to their respective numbers, which shall be determined by adding to the whole number of free persons, including those bound to service for a term of years, and excluding Indians not taxed, three-fifths of all other persons." Thus, Native Americans were not counted at all unless they were taxed, and slaves were counted as three-fifths of a person each. The Fourteenth Amendment (1868) changed the Constitution to count everyone except "Indians not taxed."

○ The Platform Display

River City is getting ready for the big Fourth of July band concert that precedes the fireworks. The concert is always a major event, but this year the bandleader, Kevin, plans to make it better than ever.

Kevin wants each of the baton twirlers to stand on an individual platform, as shown here.

The twirlers will toss batons up and down to one another. Kevin wants the difference in height from one platform to the next to be the same in each case.

○ Kevin's Decisions

Kevin has several decisions to make.

- He needs to decide on the number of platforms. He isn't sure how many of his baton twirlers will be good enough to perform by the Fourth of July.

- He needs to decide on the height of the first platform. This will depend on how tall the baton twirler on the first platform is, and Kevin hasn't decided who the first twirler will be.

- He needs to decide on the difference in height from one platform to the next. Kevin doesn't know yet how high the twirlers will be able to toss their batons.

continued ▸

○ Camilla's Dilemma

Camilla is in charge of building and decorating the structure. She needs a permit from the city to build the structure, so she needs to know how high the tallest platform will be.

She plans to hang a colorful strip of material from the front of each platform. Each strip will reach from the top of the platform to the ground. The width of the material is the same as the width of each platform, so she needs only one strip per platform.

Camilla needs to know the total length of material she should buy, but she can't determine that until Kevin makes his decisions.

○ Your Task

You are Camilla's assistant. She has asked you to be ready to give her the information she needs as soon as Kevin makes his decisions.

Your task in this POW is to create two formulas that will allow you to compute the total length instantly. One formula should tell you the height of the tallest platform. The other should tell you the total length of material Camilla will need. Your formulas should give these results in terms of the number of platforms, the height of the first platform, and the difference in height between adjacent platforms.

○ Write-up

1. *Problem Statement:* State the problem mathematically, independent of the context of the platforms, batons twirlers, and so on.

2. *Process:* Give details of any specific examples you worked out. Explain how those examples helped you develop the formulas.

3. *Solution:* Give the two formulas and explain why they work.

4. *Self-assessment*

Points, Slopes, and Equations

In *California, Here I Come!*, you saw that knowing two data points allows you to develop a linear model for population growth. This makes geometric sense, because two points determine a straight line.

When you actually wrote the equation, you may have worked primarily with the slope (the rate of growth) and one of those points. This also makes geometric sense, because a line can also be determined by knowing one point and the "steepness" of the line (the slope).

The questions in this activity are similar to your work in *California, Here I Come!*, except they do not involve population. Each question in Part I gives you the slope and one point of a line. Each question in Part II gives you two points in a line. For Part II, you may want to find the slope as a first step in writing the equation. Part III examines the special cases of horizontal and vertical lines.

Part I: Point-Slope Equations

1. Find an equation for the line with slope 5 that goes through the point (3, 2).

2. Find an equation for the line with slope 10 that goes through the point (−4, 7).

3. Find an equation for the line with slope −3 that goes through the point (5, −4).

4. Find an equation for the line with slope $\frac{2}{3}$ that goes through the point (4, 6).

Part II: Two-Point Equations

5. Find an equation for the line that goes through the points (6, 2) and (8, 8).

6. Find an equation for the line that goes through the points (1, 5) and (3, −1).

7. Find an equation for the line that goes through the points (−7, 2) and (−2, 5).

continued

Part III: Horizontal and Vertical Lines

8. Find an equation for the horizontal line that goes through the point (5, 1). What is the slope of this line?

9. Find an equation for the vertical line that goes through the point (2, −6). What is the slope of this line?

The Why of the Line

You've seen that the slope between any pair of points on a given line will be the same. But why is this so?

Consider this diagram, which shows four points—*A*, *B*, *C*, and *D*—on the same line. The diagram also shows right triangles with segments $\overline{AB}$ and $\overline{CD}$ as their hypotenuses. The lengths of the legs of these right triangles are represented with the variables *r*, *s*, *t*, and *u*.

Use ideas from geometry to explain why the slope for the pair of points *A* and *B* must be the same as the slope for the pair of points *C* and *D*. That is, explain why the ratio $\frac{r}{s}$ must equal the ratio $\frac{t}{u}$.

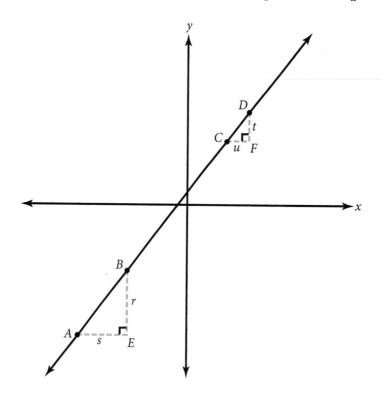

To the Rescue

A helicopter is flying to drop a supply bundle to a group of firefighters who are behind the fire lines. At the moment the helicopter crew makes the drop, the helicopter is hovering 400 feet above the ground.

The principles of physics that describe the behavior of falling objects state that when an object is falling freely, it goes faster and faster as it falls. In fact, these principles provide a specific formula describing the object's fall, which can be expressed this way.

If an object is dropped from a height of N feet, then $h(t)$, its height (in feet) off the ground t seconds after it is dropped, is given by the equation $h(t) = N - 16t^2$.

In the case of the falling supplies, the formula is $h(t) = 400 - 16t^2$, because the supply bundle is 400 feet off the ground when it starts to fall.

1. What is $h(3)$? That is, what is the height of the supply bundle 3 seconds after it is dropped?

2. How far has the supply bundle fallen during those 3 seconds?

3. What is the supply bundle's average speed during those 3 seconds?

4. How long does it take the supply bundle to reach the ground?

Beyond Linearity

Slope is an excellent concept for working with straight-line graphs. But what about rates of change that are not constant?

With the activity *The Instant of Impact,* you will begin an exploration of the meaning of an **instantaneous rate of change.** You will then refine this idea and explore it from several different perspectives.

Andrew Hawn uses the slope of a tangent line to determine an instantaneous rate of change.

The Instant of Impact

In *To the Rescue,* a supply bundle is dropped from a helicopter. The bundle's height off the ground t seconds after it is dropped is given by the equation

$$h(t) = 400 - 16t^2$$

with $h(t)$ measured in feet.

Suppose the bundle can withstand the impact of hitting the ground only for speeds up to 165 feet per second. To determine whether the bundle will survive the fall, you need to find out how fast it is traveling when it hits the ground.

Keep careful track of your computations in this activity so you can compare results from question to question.

1. a. How far does the bundle fall during its last 2 seconds (that is, during the time from $t = 3$ to $t = 5$)?

    b. What is the bundle's average speed during that 2-second interval?

2. a. How far does the bundle fall during the last second before it hits the ground?

    b. What is the bundle's average speed during that last second?

3. What is the bundle's average speed during the last half-second before it hits the ground?

4. What is the bundle's average speed during the last tenth of a second before it hits the ground?

5. What is the bundle's speed at the exact moment it hits the ground?

Doctor's Orders

Clayton is a stunt diver. His most famous dive is off a cliff into the ocean near the town of Poco Loco.

Unfortunately, Clayton has injured his wrist. The impact of hitting the water at a high speed could do further damage. His doctor recommends that he do no dives in which the speed of his entry into the water is greater than 60 feet per second.

The cliff at Poco Loco is 62 feet high. Clayton always begins his dive with a jump, so he actually starts his fall from a height of 64 feet. Therefore, his height above the ocean is given by the formula

$$h(t) = 64 - 16t^2$$

where t is the time (in seconds) from when he begins his fall and $h(t)$ is his height (in feet) above the ocean.

1. How high above the ocean is Clayton 1 second after he begins his fall?

2. What is the value of t when Clayton hits the water?

3. What is Clayton's average speed during the final second of his dive?

4. What is Clayton's average speed during the final half-second of his dive?

5. Can Clayton perform his famous dive without violating his doctor's instructions? Explain.

Photo Finish

Speedy is the star runner of her country's track team. Among other events, she runs the last 400 meters of the 1600-meter relay race.

A sports analyst studied the video of one of Speedy's races. The analyst came up with this formula to describe the distance Speedy had run at a given time in the race.

$$m(t) = 0.1t^2 + 3t$$

In this formula, $m(t)$ gives the number of meters Speedy had run after t seconds, with time and distance measured from the beginning of her 400-meter segment of the race. (Although this formula might not be very accurate, treat it as if it were completely correct.)

1. How long did it take Speedy to finish the race? That is, how long did it take her to run 400 meters? Explain how you found your answer.

2. The analyst photographed Speedy at the instant she crossed the finish line. The photo is slightly blurred, so you know Speedy was going pretty fast, but you can't tell her exact speed at the instant the photo was taken.

   Find Speedy's speed at that instant.

3. a. Find Speedy's speed at three other instants during the race.

   b. Was there an instant when Speedy was going exactly 10 meters per second? If so, when was that instant?

Speed and Slope

Part I: An Instantaneous Summary

You know that average speed can be defined by the simple formula

$$\text{average speed} = \frac{\text{distance traveled}}{\text{time elapsed}}$$

You've also realized that instantaneous speed is a more complicated idea.

Summarize what you have learned about how to calculate instantaneous speed from *The Instant of Impact, Doctor's Orders,* and *Photo Finish.*

Part II: A Linear Review

You have recently investigated how rate of change might be calculated for nonlinear situations. But you shouldn't forget how to use constant rates and the slope of a straight line, whether in the context of a real-life situation or in terms of a graph. Here is one problem of each type.

1. Zoe likes to keep track of rainfall in her area by watching the level of water in a barrel outside her house. A steady rainstorm starts one morning. At one point, Zoe observes that the water level is 420 millimeters. Three hours later, the level has increased to 438 millimeters.

   Assume the rain continues steadily, so that the water level rises at the same rate throughout that 3-hour period. Use t to represent the time elapsed (in hours) from Zoe's first measurement, and write a function expressing the water level in terms of t.

2. Find an equation for the line that goes through the points $(5, -8)$ and $(13, 4)$.

ZOOOOOOOOM

In *Photo Finish,* the function $m(t) = 0.1t^2 + 3t$ describes the distance Speedy had run in terms of time elapsed. Graph this function, and adjust the viewing window so your graph includes the point (50, 400).

Because Speedy completed her 400-meter run in 50 seconds, this point is on the graph. Zoom in on the point (50, 400) until the graph on your screen looks pretty much like a straight line.

1. a. Trace the graph to find the coordinates of two points on this apparent straight line. Write down those two coordinate pairs.

   b. Find the slope of the line connecting those points.

2. What does the slope you found mean in terms of Speedy's race?

The Growth of the Oil Slick

The idea of an instantaneous rate of change applies to more than speed. This activity concerns the rate of growth of the area of the oil slick from *What a Mess!*

When Lindsay first spotted the circular oil slick, the radius of the circle was 70 meters. She noticed that the radius was increasing by 6 meters per hour. This means the radius can be described by the formula $r = 70 + 6t$, where t is the number of hours since Lindsay first saw the oil slick. So the area in square meters of the oil slick after t hours is given by the function

$$A(t) = \pi(70 + 6t)^2$$

1. What was the area covered by the oil slick when Lindsay first saw it (at $t = 0$)?

In the remaining questions, express the rate of growth of the oil slick in square meters per hour.

2. a. At what average rate did the oil slick grow during the first 2 hours after Lindsay's initial observation?

   b. At what average rate did the oil slick grow during the first half-hour after Lindsay's initial observation?

   c. At what average rate did the oil slick grow during the 15 minutes before Lindsay's initial observation?

3. At what rate was the oil slick growing at the instant when Lindsay first saw it?

Speeds, Rates, and Derivatives

The derivative of a function at a point is one of the basic concepts of calculus. If a function is defined by the equation $y = f(x)$ and (a, b) is a point on the graph, then the **derivative** of f at (a, b) can be thought of in at least two ways.

- It is the slope of the line that is tangent to the curve at (a, b).

- It is the instantaneous rate at which the y-value of the function is changing as the x-value increases through $x = a$. We often call this the derivative at $x = a$ rather than the derivative at (a, b).

In this activity, you will work with this new idea in connection with some familiar situations. Keep in mind that you can find derivatives by using smaller and smaller intervals around a particular value of a.

1. The function $h(t) = 400 - 16t^2$ gives the height of the supply bundle (in feet) t seconds after it is dropped from a height of 400 feet.

   a. Find the derivative of this function at the point $(3, 256)$.

   b. What does your answer tell you about the speed at which the supply bundle is falling?

2. The function $A(t) = \pi(70 + 6t)^2$ gives the area of the oil slick (in square meters) t hours after Lindsay first spots it.

   a. Find the rate at which the area is growing exactly one hour after Lindsay first saw it.

   b. Express your answer as a derivative.

continued ▶

3. The activity *Wake Up!* described the Cazneau family's consumption of coffee. The function $f(d) = 30 - 0.14d$ gives a good approximation of the amount of coffee (in pounds) the Cazneau family had left after d days.

For this question, treat this as a continuous function, rather than as a discrete function. That is, assume d need not be a whole number.

a. Because $f(5) = 29.3$, the graph of this function goes through the point (5, 29.3). What is the derivative of the function at this point?

b. What does your answer tell you about the rate at which the Cazneaus drank coffee?

c. Pick a point on the graph of the function other than (5, 29.3). Find the derivative at that point.

Zooming Free-for-All

You saw in *ZOOOOOOOOM* that if you zoom in on the graph of the function $m(t) = 0.1t^2 + 3t$, the graph quickly begins to look like a straight line. (Of course, you have to take into account that on a calculator screen, even the graph of a linear function might not look perfectly straight.)

Now you will investigate whether this phenomenon occurs for other functions as well.

1. Start with a graph of the function $h(t) = 400 - 16t^2$, which represents the height of the falling supply bundle. Choose a point on the graph and zoom in on that point.

   a. Does the graph begin to appear straight?

   b. If the graph does appear straight, what does the slope of that apparent straight line mean in terms of the falling supply bundle?

2. Experiment with other functions and other points. Pick a function, choose a point on its graph, and zoom in on that point. Don't worry about whether you can find a meaningful real-life situation for the function.

   a. Does the graph begin to appear straight?

   b. If the graph does appear straight, what does a straight line with that slope through your given point represent in terms of the graph?

3. Can you find a graph and a point on the graph so that, no matter how much you zoom in on that point, the graph will still not appear straight? You might try to sketch such a graph by hand, even if you can't find a formula for it.

On a Tangent

A **secant line** for the graph of a function is the line (or line segment) connecting two points on the graph. A **tangent line** is a line that "just touches" the graph at a point. In this activity, you will explore these two geometric concepts and their connections with derivatives.

1. Consider the function f defined by th e equation $f(x) = 0.5x^2$.

   a. Sketch the graph of this function, with the scale on your x-axis going from -1 to 3. Use a full-size sheet of graph paper so you will be able to get enough detail in part c.

   b. Label the point $(2, 2)$ on your graph.

   c. The points listed here are also on your graph. In each case, draw the secant line connecting the point to $(2, 2)$ and find the slope of that secant.

      i. $(0, 0)$ ii. $(1, 0.5)$ iii. $(1.5, 1.125)$ iv. $(1.9, 1.805)$

   d. Draw the line that is tangent to your graph at $(2, 2)$. Estimate the slope of that tangent line and explain your reasoning.

   e. Find the derivative of the function f at the point $(2, 2)$.

2. Consider this graph of a function.

   a. Make a copy of this graph.

   b. Draw the tangent lines to the graph at each of points A, B, and C.

   c. Use your tangent lines to estimate the derivative of the function at each of points A, B, and C.

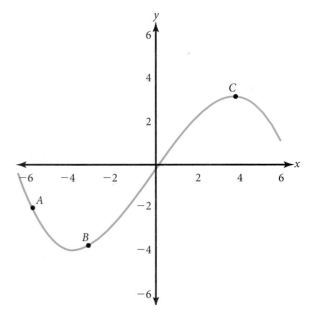

Around King Arthur's Table

King Arthur, the ruler of Camelot, loves inviting his knights over for parties around his round table.

If there is something pleasant the king can give to only one knight—like an extra dessert or a dragon to chase—he has them play a game to determine who will get it.

The game goes like this.

First, King Arthur puts numbers on the chairs, beginning with 1 and continuing around the table, with one chair for each knight. He has the knights sit down so every chair is occupied.

The king then stands behind the knight in chair 1 and says, "You're in." He moves to the knight in chair 2 and says, "You're out," and that knight leaves his seat and goes to stand at the side of the room to watch the rest of the game. The king next moves to the knight in chair 3 and says, "You're in." Then he says, "You're out" to the knight in chair 4, and that knight leaves his seat to stand at the side of the room.

The king continues around the table in this manner. When he comes back around to the knight in chair 1, he says either "You're in" or "You're out," depending on what he said to the previous knight. If the previous knight was "in," the knight in chair 1 is now "out," and vice versa.

The king keeps moving around and around the table, alternately saying, "You're in" or "You're out" to the knights who remain at the table. If a chair is now empty, he simply skips it. He continues until only one knight is left sitting at the table. That knight is the winner.

continued

○ *Your Task*

The number of knights varies from day to day, depending on who is sick and who is out chasing dragons. Sometimes there are only a few, and sometimes there are over a hundred!

Here's the big question of this POW.

If you know how many knights are going to be at the table, how can you quickly determine which chair to sit in so that you will win?

Your task is to develop a general rule, formula, or procedure that will predict the winning seat in terms of the number of knights present. Be sure to explain why your rule works.

○ *Write-up*

1. *Problem Statement*
2. *Process*
3. *Solution*
4. *Self-assessment*

What's It All About?

The idea of "the derivative of a function at a point" is important in mathematics. In fact, it plays a key role in calculus.

You will be using this idea more in the unit. Thus, it would be a good idea for you to pull together what you know about it now, so you will be ready to build on that knowledge.

Write down what you have learned so far about the idea of a derivative. Focus on these issues.

- What it means
- How you calculate it
- How it relates to other important ideas

Be sure to include specific examples.

A Model for Population Growth

You've learned that linear functions are not necessarily good for modeling population growth. So what kind of function should you use?

In the upcoming activities, you'll discover that for a certain family of functions, the derivative has a special property that makes it an excellent candidate for modeling population growth.

Erika Cohen and Alex Ryane are writing equations based upon patterns they observed from the tables they completed for Slippery Slopes.

How Much for Broken Eggs?!!?

Do you remember a POW from Year 1 called *The Broken Eggs*? It involved a farmer whose cart was hit as she was taking her eggs to market. She wasn't injured, but her eggs were broken. You spent a while figuring out how many eggs there were.

The cost of replacing 301 eggs may not have amounted to much then, but as prices rise, it could get expensive. In this activity, you'll investigate what would happen if prices went up by the same percentage each year.

Assume that at the end of 2000, a dozen eggs cost 89¢. Also assume that prices rise 5% every year. In a situation like this, the figure of 5% is called the *rate of inflation*.

In the first two questions, you will begin to analyze the situation.

1. a. How much did a dozen eggs cost at the end of 2001?

    b. How much did the price go up during 2001?

2. a. How much did a dozen eggs cost at the end of 2002?

    b. How much did the price go up during 2002?

Gather similar information for other years, until you think you understand what's happening. Then answer these questions, assuming the 5% inflation rate continues.

3. How much will a dozen eggs cost at the end of 2100? Explain your answer.

4. In what year will a dozen eggs first cost over $100?

Small but Plentiful

The activity *How Much for Broken Eggs?!!?* involves growth in prices. This activity involves a type of population growth and is somewhat like the POW *Growth of Rat Populations* in Year 2.

As you might recall, that POW was pretty complicated. You had to keep track of males and females, of different generations of rats, of when the females were ready to give birth, and so on. The situation in this activity is much simpler.

Imagine a microscopic creature like an amoeba. Suppose that whenever one of these creatures reaches a certain size, it splits into two. Then these two amoebas each grow. When they get big enough, they each split into two, making four altogether, and so on.

Suppose that at 12:01 a.m. on January 1 (just after midnight), there is one such tiny creature. And suppose it takes exactly 12 hours for such a creature to grow large enough to split into two, with the first split taking place at 12:01 p.m. (just after noon) on January 1.

Your task is to find a general rule for figuring out the number of creatures at a given time. (*Note:* In this model, these creatures never die—they simply split into two.)

1. Begin with specific examples by figuring out how many creatures there are at each of these times.

   a. 12:01 p.m. on January 1

   b. 12:01 a.m. on January 2

   c. 12:01 a.m. on January 5

   d. 12:01 a.m. on January 31

2. Find a general formula that tells how many creatures there are at 12:01 a.m., d days after the start of the experiment. (At 12:01 a.m. on January 1, $d = 0$.)

3. What will be the first day when there are more than one million creatures?

The Return of Alice

In the Year 2 unit *All About Alice*, Lewis Carroll's fictional character could change her height by eating special cake.

Each ounce Alice eats of a given type of cake multiplies her height by a particular factor. Alice names the different kinds of cake to match their effects. For example, if the cake multiplies her height by a factor of 3, she calls it "base 3 cake."

1. What would Alice's height be multiplied by if she eats each of these amounts of the given types of cake? Write your answers using **exponential** expressions.

    a. 4 ounces of base 3 cake

    b. 5 ounces of base 2 cake

    c. x ounces of base 7 cake

2. Suppose Alice eats 4 ounces of base 2 cake and then 3 more ounces of the same type of cake.

    a. Use this situation to explain the equation $2^4 \cdot 2^3 = 2^7$.

    b. Explain the equation $2^4 \cdot 2^3 = 2^7$ in terms of repeated multiplication.

3. Explain the equation $(4^6)^7 = 4^{6 \cdot 7}$ in each of these ways.

    a. In a situation involving Alice

    b. In terms of repeated multiplication

Alice realizes that she can express "cake questions" using exponential equations. For example, if she wants to know how much base 2 cake to eat to multiply her height by 32, she asks herself, "What's the solution to the equation $2^x = 32$?" She also realizes that the solution to this equation can be expressed as a logarithm: $\log_2 32$.

4. Find the value of $\log_2 32$ by solving the equation $2^x = 32$.

continued ⯈

5. For each of these questions, write an exponential equation to represent the situation. Then find the numeric solution to the equation, and write the solution as a logarithm.

   a. How much base 3 cake should Alice eat to multiply her height by 81?

   b. How much base 2 cake should Alice eat to multiply her height by 128?

   c. How much base 5 cake should Alice eat to multiply her height by 93? For this example, give your numeric solution to the nearest tenth.

Slippery Slopes

The derivatives of exponential functions show an interesting pattern. In this activity, you will find that pattern.

1. Start with the exponential function defined by the equation $y = 2^x$.

   a. Create an In-Out table like the one below. Follow these two steps to fill in several rows of your table.

   - Pick a whole-number value for x and find the y-value that goes with it.

   - Get a good approximation for the derivative of the function at the point on the graph of $y = 2^x$ that is represented by your x- and y-values.

x-value	y-value	Derivative

   b. Study the data in your table. Write an equation expressing the derivative in terms of the y-value. If necessary, add more rows of data to your table.

2. Repeat the process from Question 1, this time using the function $y = 10^x$.

3. Repeat the process from Question 1 for a third exponential function of your choice.

The Forgotten Account

Tyler and his friends (from *Story Sketches* and *More About Tyler's Friends*) had $50 left over after buying uniforms. They put the money into a bank account to give next year's team a head start.

Well, next year's team forgot about the account, and so did the following year's team. Pretty soon, the account was completely forgotten.

Suppose the account earned 4.5% interest at the end of each year. (For simplicity, assume the account was opened on January 1.) The interest is added to the amount already in the account, so each year's interest is on a larger amount than the year before. (This is called *compound interest*. More specifically, the interest for this account is said to be *compounded annually* because interest is added to the account at the end of each year.)

1. How much money was in the account 5 years after Tyler and his friends started it?

2. Find a formula that describes the amount of money in the account after *t* years.

3. Write an equation that could be used to figure out how many years it would take for the account to grow to $500.

4. Solve your equation.

5. Express the solution to your equation as a logarithm.

How Does It Grow?

To solve the central unit problem, you will need to find a function that grows in the same way that populations grow.

In Question 1, you will look at a simple situation to get an intuitive sense of what to expect from population growth.

1. Suppose a town has a population of 5000 and the population grows by 40 people in a single year. How much growth would you expect for a similar town with a population of 10,000? Explain your reasoning.

Questions 2 to 5 present two functions as possible models to describe population as a function of time. You will begin by getting some data for each function and its derivative.

2. Consider the linear function $f(x) = 3x + 4$.

   a. Choose three values for x. Find $f(x)$ for each value.

   b. Find the derivative of the function at each of your three x-values.

3. Now consider the quadratic function $g(x) = x^2 - 9$.

   a. Choose three values for x. Find $g(x)$ for each value.

   b. Find the derivative of the function at each of your three x-values.

In Questions 4 and 5, remember that the derivative describes a rate of growth.

4. Return to the function $f(x) = 3x + 4$ from Question 2.

   a. Describe any relationships you notice between the derivative and either x or $f(x)$.

   b. Explain why the relationships you found are or are not appropriate to use in a mathematical representation of population growth. Consider whether those relationships seem to hold true for the situation in Question 1.

continued ▶

5. Now look at the function $g(x) = x^2 - 9$ from Question 3.

   a. Describe any relationships you notice between the derivative and either x or $g(x)$.

   b. Explain why the relationships you found are or are not appropriate to use in a mathematical representation of population growth. Consider whether those relationships seem to hold true for the situation in Question 1.

The Significance of a Sign

When you are graphing a function, knowing the signs of the coordinates of the points can be helpful. For instance, those signs tell you which quadrant a point is in. And if a coordinate is 0, you know that the point is on a coordinate axis.

In this activity, you'll explore similar issues concerning the sign of the derivative of a function.

1. Make a copy of the graph. Then identify where on the graph the function's derivative is positive, where the derivative is negative, and where the derivative is 0. Remember that the derivative at a point on the function's graph can be thought of as the slope of the tangent line at that point.

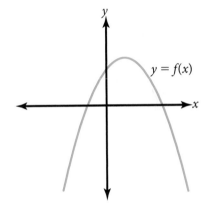

2. Sketch the graph of a function for which the derivative is positive for all values of x.

3. Sketch the graph of a function for which there are exactly two points where the derivative is 0.

The Sound of a Logarithm

Logarithms are a convenient concept for talking about exponents. For instance, the expression $\log_{10} 564$ represents the solution to the equation $10^x = 564$. Logarithms are also used as the basis for certain units of measurement in science.

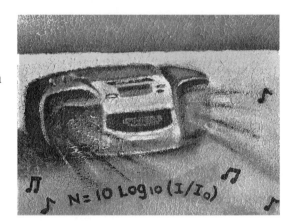

One such application concerns the measurement of noise levels. The *decibel scale* uses logarithms to describe the intensity of a sound in comparison to a particular reference value. The symbol I_0 is used to represent the intensity of a sound at the threshold of human hearing—that is, the quietest sound that humans can hear.

If I is the intensity of some other sound, the ratio of this intensity to I_0 is called the *relative intensity* of that other sound. We will represent the ratio $\frac{I}{I_0}$ by the letter R. Using this ratio, the *noise level* of that other sound, represented by N, is given by the equation

$$N = 10 \log_{10} R$$

The value of N is given in *decibels,* abbreviated as dB.

Suppose a sound has an intensity I that is 100 times the intensity of a sound at the threshold of human hearing. That is, suppose the relative intensity R is 100. Because $\log_{10} 100 = 2$, this means the sound has a noise level of $10 \cdot 2$, or 20 decibels.

A sound at the threshold of human hearing, for which I is equal to I_0, has a noise level of 0 decibels, because $R = 1$ and $10 \cdot \log_{10} 1 = 10 \cdot 0 = 0$.

continued ▶

1. A normal conversation has a relative intensity of approximately 100,000. What is its noise level in decibels?

2. A loud police whistle has a noise level of approximately 90 decibels.

   a. How does the whistle's sound intensity compare to the threshold of human hearing?

   b. How does the whistle's sound intensity compare to ordinary conversation?

3. A sound intensity of approximately 10^{13} times the threshold level will cause a person's ears to hurt. What is the noise level of such a sound?

4. a. If one sound measures 42 decibels, and the relative intensity of a second sound is 3 times the relative intensity of the first, what is the noise level of the second sound?

   b. If one sound measures 60 decibels and another measures 68 decibels, how does the relative intensity of the second sound compare to the relative intensity of the first sound?

Adapted with permission from *College Algebra: A Preliminary Edition,* by Linda Kime and Judy Clark ©1996 by John Wiley and Sons. Reprinted by permission of John Wiley & Sons, Inc.

The Power of Powers

You saw in *Slippery Slopes* that certain functions have the special property that the derivative at each point is proportional to the y-value at that point.

For instance, for the function $f(x) = 2^x$, you found that an equation very much like

$$f'(x) = 0.69 \cdot f(x)$$

appears to hold true for all values of x. For the function $g(x) = 10^x$, the equation is approximately

$$g'(x) = 2.30 \cdot g(x)$$

The Proportionality Property

When such a relationship between the derivative and the y-value holds true, we say the function has the **proportionality property.** (This is not standard terminology, but is used as shorthand for a complex idea.)

When a function has the proportionality property, the ratio between the derivative and the y-value is called the *proportionality constant.* For instance, the numbers 0.69 and 2.30 are (approximately) the proportionality constants for the functions f and g.

Because the growth of a population is often proportional to the population itself, the proportionality property of functions like f and g makes them excellent candidates for a mathematical model of population growth.

In this activity, you will begin an exploration of which functions have the proportionality property.

continued ▶

The Examples

For each of the two functions below, go through these steps.

- Estimate the value of the derivative for at least three points on the graph.
- Based on your results, state whether you think the function has the proportionality property.
- If you think the function has the proportionality property, give an approximate value for the proportionality constant.

1. $h(x) = 2^x + 3^x$

2. $p(x) = 4.6 \cdot 2^x$

The Power of Powers, Continued

In *The Power of Powers,* you examined whether two particular functions had the proportionality property. Now you will continue your investigation of this property.

1. For each of the three functions below, go through these steps. Estimate the value of the derivative for at least three points on the graph.

   • Based on your results, state whether you think the function has the proportionality property.

   • If you think the function has the proportionality property, give an approximate value for the proportionality constant.

   a. $m(x) = 100 + 2^x$

   b. $k(x) = 0.83^x$

   c. $n(x) = 2^{3x}$

2. Based on your answers in Question 1 and your results from *The Power of Powers,* make some conjectures about the general form of functions with this special property.

The Best Base

You've learned that exponential functions seem to be an excellent choice for modeling population growth. But what base should you use? 2? 10? Does it matter?

This part of the unit begins with an activity in which you'll investigate whether bases are interchangeable. Eventually you'll discover that with regard to derivatives, one base is clearly the best choice. And you'll see that this special base has a connection with a concept that at first seems completely unrelated.

In their work with bases and exponents, Nikki Robinson and Ameilia Mitcalf discuss which might be the "best" base.

A Basis for Disguise

You've seen that the derivative of an exponential function is a fixed multiple of the function's y-value.

Another useful fact is that exponential expressions can sometimes "disguise" themselves in other number bases. For example, 81^5 can also be written as 3^{20}. Here, a power of 81 is "disguised" as a power of 3. In this activity, you will explore this change-of-base idea.

1. How can you show that 81^5 and 3^{20} are equal without finding the value of either expression?

2. Find a general rule for writing powers of 81 as powers of 3. That is, imagine that you want to put something in the box to make the equation $81^x = 3^{\square}$ true. Explain how the number that goes in the box depends on x. You might think about how much base 3 cake would have the same effect on Alice as x ounces of base 81 cake.

3. Reverse the roles of the two bases, 81 and 3, and find a general rule for writing powers of 3 as powers of 81. The Alice metaphor may help here, too.

4. Questions 1 to 3 may seem like special cases, because 81 is a whole-number power of 3.

   a. Suppose the two bases are 7 and 5. Can you find a general rule for writing 7^x as a power of 5?

   b. Examine whether there is always a general rule for writing b^x as a power of a, no matter what numbers are used for a and b. (Of course, the rule itself would have to depend on a and b.)

   Give the rule in the cases for which such a rule exists. Also describe the values for a or b for which such a rule does not exist.

Blue Book

Car dealers sometimes use the rule of thumb that a car loses about 30% of its value each year. Use this rule to answer Questions 1 and 2.

1. Suppose you bought a new car in December 2010 for $15,000.

    a. According to the rule of thumb, what would the car be worth at each of these times?

       i. December 2011

       ii. December 2015

       iii. December 2020

    b. Develop a general formula for the value of the car t years after its purchase.

2. Tara notices that a $20,000 car will lose about $6,000 of its value the first year, while a $10,000 car will lose about $3,000 of its value the first year. She reasons that because the more expensive car loses more value each year, it will eventually be worth less than the cheaper car.

    How long do you think it will take until this happens? Explain.

California and Exponents

In 1850, the population of California was about 92,600. In 1860, it was about 380,000. In *California, Here I Come!* you found a linear function that went through the points (1850, 92,600) and (1860, 380,000).

Now you will find an exponential function for the same population data and then examine its accuracy for making predictions. To make the arithmetic much simpler, treat the year 1850 as $x = 0$ and the year 1860 as $x = 10$.

1. Find two numbers a and b so that the exponential function $y = a \cdot b^x$ goes through the points (0, 92,600) and (10, 380,000). To do this, substitute the coordinates of the first point for x and y to get an equation that involves only a. Solve that equation, and then use the second point and the value you found for a to find b.

2. Use your answer to Question 1 to determine what California's population would have been in 2000 if population growth had continued at the same growth rate as during the gold rush period.

3. Based on this exponential model, do you think the population growth rate in California has decreased or increased since the gold rush period?

Find That Base!

You know that the derivative of the exponential function $y = b^x$ is a particular constant multiplied by the y-value. As long as the base b is fixed, this proportionality constant is the same at every point on the graph. However, the proportionality constant does depend on the value of b.

Scientists prefer to use a standard base to make it easier to compare one function to another. Because any exponential function can be expressed in any base (as long as you stick to positive bases other than 1), scientists are free to pick any number for this standard base.

Because scientific work often involves derivatives, scientists have chosen for this standard base the number that makes the proportionality constant equal to 1.

Your job is to estimate this special base. In other words, estimate the value of b for which, at every point on the graph of the function $f(x) = b^x$, the derivative is equal to b^x.

Double Trouble

In inflation situations like that of *How Much for Broken Eggs?!!?*, the length of time it takes for the price to double is called the *doubling time*.

Of course, the doubling time depends on the rate of inflation. In this activity, you will investigate the relationship between these two values.

1. Consider the case of an inflation rate of 5% per year, and find the related doubling time. For simplicity, start with a price of $1 and see how long it takes until the price gets to $2. Give your answer to the nearest hundredth of a year.

2. Choose a different inflation rate, and find the related doubling time.

3. Find the doubling times for several other inflation rates. Put your results in an In-Out table in which the *In* is the inflation rate and the *Out* is the doubling time.

4. a. Look for a pattern or rule that describes your In-Out table.

   b. Try to explain why your pattern works.

5. a. For each inflation rate in your table, also compute the *quadrupling time*—the length of time it takes for the price to be multiplied by a factor of 4. If you started with $1, this would be the time required to reach $4.

   b. How does the quadrupling time compare with the doubling time? Explain your answer.

The Generous Banker

"Double Your Money in 20 Years!" read the bank's advertisement. Adam thinks this sounds like a pretty good deal, but he also thinks he might be able to talk his way into something even better. So he goes in to speak with the banker.

"Doubling your money is like increasing it by 100%, I think," he said with a practiced uncertainty. "But what if I need my money before 20 years? Can I get a proportional part of the interest each year, just in case?"

Never having studied much mathematics, the banker hesitates. "Well, that seems fair, Mr. Smith," she finally replies. "How much should you get each year?"

Adam takes out his calculator. "100% for 20 years . . . let's see . . . 100 divided by 20 . . . I guess that's 5% each year. Can you increase my account by 5% each year instead?"

The banker agrees, and Adam deposits $1,000 in an account.

1. How much will be in the account 20 years later?

2. How much will be in the account if Adam instead convinces the bank to give him a proportional amount of interest compounded every 6 months instead of once a year?

3. If Adam gets a proportional amount of interest compounded every 3 months, then how much will be in the account 20 years later?

Comparing Derivatives

Part I: Shared Points

Here are the equations for three functions whose graphs all pass through the point $(0, 0)$. The three graphs also all passthrough $(1, 1)$.

$$f(x) = x$$
$$g(x) = x^2$$
$$h(x) = x^3$$

Do you think all three functions will have the same derivative at $(0, 0)$? What about at $(1, 1)$? These questions will help you decide.

1. Draw graphs of all three functions on the same set of axes for x-values from -1 to 2. Plot enough points for each function (including noninteger values of x) to get accurate graphs. Take particular care in plotting x-values between 0 and 1.

2. Based on your graphs, answer each of these questions and explain your reasoning.

   a. Which of the three functions has the greatest derivative at the point $(0, 0)$?

   b. Which of the three functions has the greatest derivative at the point $(1, 1)$?

3. Find the actual derivative of each function at each of the two common points. Compare your results with your answers to Question 2.

continued ◗

Part II: Derivative Sketch

Suppose this is the graph of the function defined by the equation $y = f(x)$.

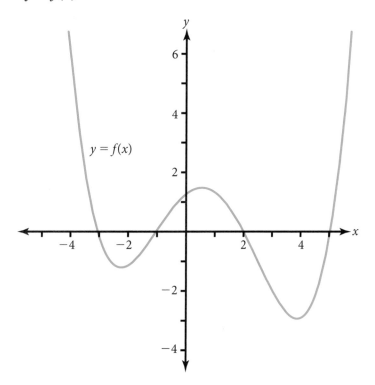

$y = f(x)$

4. Make a copy of the graph. Show where on the graph the derivative of this function is positive, where the derivative is negative, and where the derivative is 0. Make your answers as complete as possible.

5. Sketch the graph of f', which is the derivative function of f. Use the same scale for the x-axis as you used for the graph of f.

The Limit of Their Generosity

In *The Generous Banker,* Adam deposits $1,000 in a bank. The bank advertised that it would double his money in 20 years. But Adam persuades the banker to increase his deposit by 5% for each of the 20 years instead of increasing it by 100% all at once at the end of the 20-year term.

Thinking he might be able to get rich because of the banker's generosity, Adam talks to the banker some more and persuades her to give him an appropriate fraction of the interest every 6 months. Then he persuades her to calculate the interest every month.

Once he has gotten this far, Adam is ready to spring his ultimate request. He asks the banker to give him proportional interest *every day* and add it to his account.

1. Without doing any calculations, about how much money do you think will be in Adam's account in 20 years?

2. Use your calculator to compute Adam's wealth after 20 years. Figure 365.25 days per year.

3. What will Adam end up with if the bank gives him proportional interest *every hour*?

California Population with e's

In the activity *California and Exponents*, you used a function of the form $y = a \cdot b^x$ to get a model of California's population growth between 1850 and 1860.

Using $x = 0$ to represent 1850 and $x = 10$ to represent 1860, you found the values of a and b so that the function $y = a \cdot b^x$ went through the points (0, 92,600) and (10, 380,000).

This activity is similar, but now you will use e as the base of the exponential function.

1. Find values for k and c so that the exponential function $y = k \cdot e^{cx}$ goes through those two points. As in the previous activity, use the first point to get an equation involving only one of the two unknown values.

2. Express the value you get for c in terms of a **natural logarithm.** A natural logarithm is a logarithm that uses the base e.

3. How are the coefficients k and c in this activity related to the coefficients a and b in *California and Exponents*? If necessary, redo Question 1 of that activity to find a and b.

Back to the Data

You're now ready to reexamine the population data from the beginning of this unit. As a first step, you'll explore how to "tweak" a function—how to make little changes in the function so its graph is closer to what you want.

You'll conclude the unit by looking for a function that comes close to the initial data, and by using that function to predict when we will all be squashed up against one another.

Kimberly Lao uses a function to predict population growth.

Tweaking the Function

Suppose you have some data points, and you need to fit them with a function. Also suppose you know more or less what type of function should fit the data and that your first guess comes pretty close to fitting, but not as close as you would like.

You then need to change the function a bit—to adjust it somehow to make it fit the data better.

How do you adjust the function to better fit the data? This activity will help you answer that question.

Begin with the function $y = e^x$. Change it in different ways and watch how the graph is affected. For instance, you might try multiplying e^x by various coefficients, or you might adjust the exponent in some way.

As you explore how the graph changes, here are some things to watch for.

- What makes the graph "more curvy" or "less curvy"?
- What changes the horizontal or vertical position of the graph?

Begin with these questions, and then investigate some others. Find out whatever you can and keep track of what you learn.

Beginning Portfolios—Part I

Think about the examples of growth and change you have studied in this unit. Focus on two particular kinds of functions.

- Linear functions, which have the form $y = a + bx$
- Exponential functions, which have the form $y = k \cdot e^{cx}$

Compare the two types of functions, addressing these issues.

- How does each function represent rates of growth or change?
- How does each function represent starting points or initial values?
- What kinds of situations is each function appropriate for describing or modeling? Be more specific than simply saying "linear growth" or "exponential growth."

Return to *A Crowded Place*

Here are the data, from the beginning of the unit, of the estimated world population over the past several centuries.

Year	Estimated Population
1650	470,000,000
1750	629,000,000
1850	1,030,000,000
1900	1,550,000,000
1950	2,560,000,000
1960	3,040,000,000
1970	3,710,000,000
1980	4,450,000,000
1990	5,280,000,000
2000	6,090,000,000
2005	6,480,000,000

As initially stated, your task is to determine, based on these data, how long it will take until people are "squashed up against one another." In this unit, that phrase is interpreted to mean that each person has exactly 1 square foot to call her or his own. Based on estimates of the earth's surface area, this means the population would have to reach approximately $1.6 \cdot 10^{15}$ people.

Here are your tasks in this final activity.

1. Plot the population data.

2. a. Find a function that approximates the data. Begin by looking for a function of the form $y = k \cdot e^{cx}$. This first approximation need not be very accurate.

continued ▶

b. Assuming the population grows according to your function, determine when each person will have only 1 square foot to call his or her own. That is, based on your function, how long will it take for the population to reach $1.6 \cdot 10^{15}$ people?

3. Repeat the process in Question 2 as often as you think is useful, looking for a better approximation. Use ideas from the activity *Tweaking the Function* to try to make whatever adjustments you think are needed.

State your best approximating function and its estimate for how long it will take the population to reach $1.6 \cdot 10^{15}$ people.

4. Discuss whether you think the population data in the table are really exponential and whether you think the data will be exponential in the future. Give reasons for your conclusions.

Beginning Portfolios—Part II

1. The beginning of this unit concentrated on linear functions. Summarize what you have learned about finding equations of straight lines, and select one or two activities that were particularly helpful to you in this area.

2. Much of this unit focused on exponential functions, a topic that leads naturally into working with compound interest.

   Pick an activity from the unit that helped develop your understanding of compound interest, and describe what you learned from the activity.

Annie Tam, Ryan Tran, and Carlos Catly spend time reviewing activities for their portfolios.

Small World, Isn't It? Portfolio

You will now put together your portfolio for *Small World, Isn't It?*
This process has three steps.

- Write a cover letter that summarizes the unit.
- Choose papers to include from your work in the unit.
- Discuss your personal growth during the unit.

Cover Letter for *Small World, Isn't It?*

Look back over *Small World, Isn't It?* and describe the central problem
of the unit and the key mathematical ideas. Your description should
give an overview of how the key ideas were developed and how they
were used to solve the central problem.

In compiling your portfolio, you will select some activities you think
were important in developing the unit's key ideas. Your cover letter
should include an explanation of why you selected each item.

Selecting Papers from *Small World, Isn't It?*

Your portfolio for *Small World, Isn't It?*
should contain these items.

- *What's It All About?*
- *Beginning Portfolios—Part I*
- *Beginning Portfolios—Part II*
  Include the activities from the unit you
  selected as part of this assignment.
- A Problem of the Week
  Select any one of the three POWs you
  completed in this unit: *The More the
  Merrier?, Planning the Platforms,* or
  Around King Arthur's Table.

continued ◗

Personal Growth

Small World, Isn't It? focused on various kinds of growth. Your cover letter describes how the mathematical ideas developed in the unit. In addition, write about your own personal development during this unit. You may want to specifically address this question.

What changes or growth have you noticed during Year 3 in your ability to work well in groups?

Include any thoughts about your experiences that you wish to share with a reader of your portfolio.

Supplemental Activities

The supplemental activities for *Small World, Isn't It?* continue the unit's areas of emphasis—rates of change and linear and exponential functions—along with a few other topics. Here are some examples.

- *Solving for Slope* and *The Slope's the Thing* give additional perspectives on how to find the slope for a linear equation.

- *Summing the Sequences*—Parts I and II are follow-ups to the POW *Planning the Platforms*.

- *Deriving Derivatives* looks at developing general formulas for derivatives.

- *Dr. Doubleday's Base* and *Investigating Constants* examine the role of the parameters in two different forms of the general exponential function.

Solving for Slope

You've seen that in an equation like $y = 3x + 5$, the coefficient of x (in this case, 3) is the slope of the graph. Now you will examine linear equations that do not have this form.

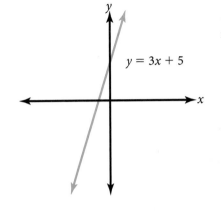

$y = 3x + 5$

1. Begin by examining these specific examples. In each case, solve the equation for y in terms of x to determine the slope of the graph.

   a. $3y - 2x = 12$

   b. $x + 4y = -8$

   c. $5x - 2y = 10$

   d. $-6y + 7x = -2$

2. Now consider the general linear equation in the standard form.

$$ax + by = c$$

   a. Develop an expression for the slope in terms of a, b, and c.

   b. Based on examples, describe how to answer each of these questions simply by looking at a, b, and c.

   - Is the line rising or falling as it goes to the right?
   - For lines rising to the right, is the line steeper than $y = x$?
   - For lines falling to the right, is the line steeper than $y = -x$? Explain not only how your method works, but also why it works.

Slope and Slant

One way to describe the "steepness" or "slant" of a line is to measure the angle formed between that line and a horizontal line. This angle is called the *angle of inclination* of the line.

For instance, this diagram shows a line *l* and a horizontal line *h*. The angle labeled θ (the Greek letter *theta*) is the angle of inclination of line *l*.

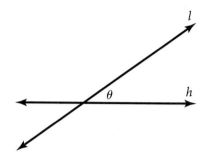

You've been working with lines that are the graphs of linear equations. In the context of the coordinate system, the angle of inclination of a line is the angle formed between that line and the positive direction of the *x*-axis. You might expect to find some relationship between the slope of such a line and its angle of inclination.

Finding such a relationship is complicated by the fact that the scales on the axes affect the steepness of the graph. In this activity, you will eliminate that complication by assuming that the vertical and horizontal axes have the same scale.

1. This diagram shows the graph of the equation $y = 2x - 1$ and two points, $(-1, -3)$ and $(3, 5)$, that fit this equation. The diagram also shows an angle of inclination θ for the line and a right triangle with $(-1, -3)$ and $(3, 5)$ as two of its vertices.

   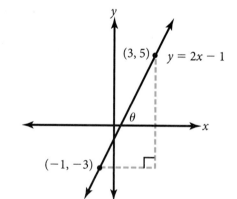

   a. Find the slope of the line $y = 2x - 1$.

   b. Use trigonometry and the right triangle to find a relationship between the slope of this line and its angle of inclination.

   c. Use your work from part b to find the measure of angle θ.

   d. Carefully draw the line through $(-1, -3)$ and $(3, 5)$ on graph paper, using the same scale for the vertical and horizontal axes. Then measure the angle of inclination and check whether it matches your result from part c.

continued ▶

2. Use the ideas from Question 1 to answer these questions. Again, assume the vertical and horizontal axes have the same scale.

   a. What is the angle of inclination for a line with a slope of 1?

   b. What is the slope of a line with an angle of inclination of 30 degrees?

3. State a general principle, using trigonometry, relating the slope of a line to its angle of inclination. (*Note:* So far, we have defined the trigonometric functions only for acute angles in right triangles. Therefore, assume the line has an angle of inclination between 0 and 90 degrees.)

Predicting Parallels

When a linear equation is written to express y in terms of x, the coefficient of x is equal to the slope of the graph. For example, the graph of $y = 3x + 5$ has slope 3. This makes it easy to recognize when two distinct (that is, not equivalent) equations have graphs that are parallel, because they have the same coefficient for x.

According to this principle, the graphs of $y = 3x + 5$ and $y = 3x + 9$ should be parallel. That is, they should not have any points in common. The first task in this activity is to prove this fact.

1. Show that the equations $y = 3x + 5$ and $y = 3x + 9$ cannot have any common solutions. That is, show there is no point that is on the graphs of both equations.

What about lines that are not in "$y =$" form? Is there a simple way to recognize that two lines in the standard form $ax + by = c$ are parallel? Answer Questions 2, 3, and 4, and then try to generalize your results in Question 5.

2. a. Draw the graph of the equation $4x - 3y = 24$.

   b. Choose a point *not* on the graph. Draw a line through that point that is parallel to your graph.

   c. Find the equation of the line you drew in part b.

3. Graph the equation $8x - 6y = 24$, and compare it with the graphs from Question 2.

4. Graph the equation $20x - 15y = 120$, and compare it with the graphs from Question 2.

5. Based on Questions 2, 3, and 4, and on other equations you might examine, what general principles can you state for determining at a glance whether two linear equations in standard form have parallel graphs?

The Slope's the Thing

You know that two points determine a straight line. That means knowing the coordinates of two points on a line is enough information to get an equation for that line. You will now explore a systematic way to get the equation from that information, based on slope.

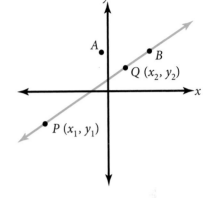

Let's call the two given points P and Q. The method is based on these two statements.

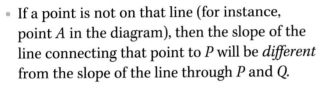

- If a point is not on that line (for instance, point A in the diagram), then the slope of the line connecting that point to P will be *different* from the slope of the line through P and Q.

- If a point is on that line (for instance, point B), then the slope of the line connecting that point to P will be the same as the slope of the line through P and Q.

1. Suppose P has coordinates (x_1, y_1), Q has coordinates (x_2, y_2), and R is another point in the plane, with coordinates (x, y).

    a. Write an expression for the slope of the line through P and Q.

    b. Write an expression for the slope of the line through P and R.

    c. Combine your expressions to get an equation stating that these two slopes are equal.

2. Apply this method to find the equation of the line through $(1, 5)$ and $(-2, -1)$.

3. Use similar triangles to prove the two statements on which this method is based.

Speedy's Speed by Algebra

In the activity *Photo Finish*, Speedy the track star runs the last 400 meters of a 1600-meter relay race.

Based on a video of her race, an analyst came up with the function $m(t) = 0.1t^2 + 3t$ to describe how many meters Speedy had run after t seconds of her segment of the race. The equation $m(50) = 400$ shows that Speedy crosses the finish line after exactly 50 seconds.

In *Photo Finish*, you found Speedy's average speed for small time intervals near the end of the race. You used those average speeds to estimate her speed at the instant she crossed the finish line. You may wonder how accurate or reliable your estimate is. That is, you may be wondering this.

> *How fast was Speedy* really *going at the instant she crossed the finish line?*

In this activity, you will explore an algebraic approach to answering this question.

1. First, write out in detail the computation for finding Speedy's average speed for the last tenth of a second of the race.

   a. Find out how far Speedy had run after 49.9 seconds. That is, compute $m(49.9)$.

   b. Find out how far Speedy ran during the last tenth of a second. That is, find the difference between $m(49.9)$ and 400.

   c. Find Speedy's average speed during the last tenth of a second. That is, divide the distance you found in part b by the length of the time interval, which is 0.1 second.

continued ◗

2. Now use the process from Question 1, substituting the last h seconds for the last tenth of a second. That is, instead of working with the time interval from $t = 49.9$ to $t = 50$, work with the interval from $t = 50 - h$ to $t = 50$. Parts a to c will guide you through this process.

   a. Find out how far Speedy had run after $50 - h$ seconds. That is, find $m(50 - h)$. Your answer should be an expression in terms of h.

   b. Find out how far Speedy ran during the last h seconds. That is, write an expression (in terms of h) for the difference between $m(50 - h)$ and 400.

   c. Divide the distance you found in part b by the length of the time interval, which is h seconds.

   d. Confirm your expression in part c by substituting 0.1 for h. Does that give the same answer you found in Question 1c?

3. Your result for Question 2c should be an algebraic expression in terms of h. This expression gives Speedy's average speed during the last h seconds of the race.

   a. Simplify this expression as much as you can.

   b. What happens to your simplified expression as h gets smaller and smaller?

   c. What does your result in part b mean in terms of Speedy's instantaneous speed?

4. Does your work in Questions 1 to 3 give you further confidence in your results from *Photo Finish*? Explain.

Potential Disaster

Construction workers have partially ruptured a natural gas pipeline in a research building. The pipe's protective inner membrane has been forced out through the opening, forming a sphere-shaped balloon on the outside of the pipe.

Emergency crews are confident they can patch the hole but see no way to push the balloon back into the pipe. They decide they must cut off the balloon and then quickly patch the hole.

An electrical wire nearby poses a serious danger. If the wire and balloon come in contact with each other, the gas in the balloon will ignite and the balloon will explode, causing massive damage.

Gas is flowing into the balloon so that its volume is growing at a constant rate. The balloon was discovered 30 minutes after the rupture. In those 30 minutes, the balloon had grown to a diameter of 1 foot. The balloon will come in contact with the wire if its diameter reaches 2 feet.

It is now 20 minutes since the balloon was discovered, and the building's manager is in a panic. He thinks the balloon will explode in only 10 more minutes. But the engineer in charge of the emergency crew seems rather calm.

1. a. Why do you suppose the manager thinks they have only 10 minutes left before the balloon explodes?

   b. What is wrong with the manager's reasoning?

2. How much time does the crew really have? (The volume of a sphere of diameter d is given by the expression $\frac{1}{6}\pi d^3$.)

Proving the Tangent

In the activity *On a Tangent,* you examined the graph of the function $f(x) = 0.5x^2$ near the point $(2, 2)$. You were asked to use a series of secant lines through $(2, 2)$ to estimate the slope of the tangent line at that point, which seemed to be equal to 2.

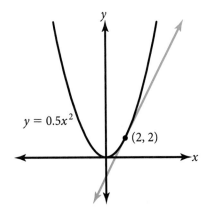

1. Use this estimate of the derivative to write the equation of the tangent line. That is, write the equation of the line that goes through the point $(2, 2)$ and has a slope of 2.

2. Prove that your estimate of the derivative is correct by showing that $(2, 2)$ is the only point where the line you found in Question 1 meets the graph of the function $f(x) = 0.5x^2$. To do this, you will need to show that your equation from Question 1 and the equation $y = 0.5x^2$ have only one solution in common.

Summing the Sequences—Part I

In the POW *Planning the Platforms,* Camilla needs to find the sum of a sequence of numbers in which each term differs from the previous term by the same amount.

For instance, suppose the first platform is 28 inches tall, the difference in height between adjacent platforms is 8 inches, and there are 5 platforms altogether. Camilla would need to find the sum

$$28 + 36 + 44 + 52 + 60$$

A sequence such as 28, 36, 44, and so on, in which the *difference* between terms is constant, is called an **arithmetic sequence.** (In this context, the word *arithmetic* is an adjective and is pronounced ar-ith-*met*-ic, with the emphasis on the third syllable.)

The first number in an arithmetic sequence is called the *initial term.* The amount added to get each successive term is called the *difference.* In the example, the initial term is 28 and the difference is 8.

1. a. Find an expression in terms of *n* for the *n*th term of the arithmetic sequence with an initial term of 28 and a difference of 8.

   b. Find an expression in terms of *n* for the sum of the first *n* terms of this sequence.

continued ▶

If we use *a* to represent the initial term and *d* to represent the difference, then the general arithmetic sequence has the terms a, $a + d$, $a + 2d$, $a + 3d$, and so on.

2. Find an expression in terms of *a*, *d*, and *n* for the *n*th term of the general arithmetic sequence.

3. Find an expression in terms of *a*, *d*, and *n* for the sum of the first *n* terms of the general arithmetic sequence. Give your answer as an algebraic expression in closed form—that is, without using summation or ellipsis (. . .) notation.

4. Apply your expression from Question 3 to find the sum of the first 50 terms of the arithmetic sequence 15, 21, 27, 33, and so on.

Summing the Sequences—Part II

In *Summing the Sequences—Part I,* you examined arithmetic sequences, which have a constant difference between terms.

Sequences with a constant ratio between terms are called **geometric sequences.** For instance, the sequence 8, 24, 72, 216, and so on, in which each term is 3 times the previous term, is a geometric sequence. Here, 8 is the initial term and 3 is the ratio.

1. a. Find an expression in terms of n for the nth term of the geometric sequence with an initial term of 8 and a ratio of 3.

   b. Find an expression in terms of n for the sum of the first n terms of this sequence.

   To do this, compare the sum of the first n terms of this sequence with the sum of the first n terms of the sequence 24, 72, 216, and so on. The second sum is 3 times the first (because each term is 3 times the corresponding term in the original sequence). What do you get if you subtract the first sum from the second? Think about terms that cancel out. You may want to look at specific values of n.

Using a to represent the initial term and r to represent the ratio, the general geometric sequence has the terms a, ar, ar^2, ar^3, and so on.

2. Find an expression in terms of a, r, and n for the nth term of the general geometric sequence.

3. Find an expression in terms of a, r, and n for the sum of the first n terms of the general geometric sequence. Give your answer as an algebraic expression in closed form—that is, without using summation or ellipsis (. . .) notation.

4. Apply your expression from Question 3 to find the sum of the first 20 terms of the sequence 3, 6, 12, 24, and so on.

continued ▶

5. Consider the case of the geometric sequence with $a = 1$ and $r = \frac{1}{2}$.

   a. Write an expression (in terms of n) for the sum of the first n terms of this sequence. Use your work from Question 3.

   b. Find the sum of the first 10 terms of this sequence by actually adding the terms. Use it to verify your expression from part a.

   c. What happens to your expression as n increases? Does that fit your intuitive idea? Explain.

6. (Challenge) How can you generalize Question 5 to the case in which the ratio r is any number between 0 and 1?

Looking at Logarithms

Logarithms are defined in terms of exponential equations. For instance, $\log_b a$ is defined as the value of x that fits the equation $b^x = a$.

Because of this relationship between logarithms and exponents, there is a principle about logarithms corresponding to every principle about exponents.

In this activity, you will develop principles for logarithms. Throughout the activity, b represents a positive number other than 1.

1. The additive law of exponents states

$$b^x \cdot b^y = b^{x+y}$$

Your first task is to find a corresponding principle for logarithms. Start with the specific examples in parts a and b.

a. What is $\log_2 2^5$? What is $\log_2 2^9$? What is $\log_2 (2^5 \cdot 2^9)$?

b. Find approximate values for $\log_3 8$, $\log_3 7$, and $\log_3 56$. What relationship do you see among these three logarithms?

c. Generalize your results from parts a and b to get a formula for $\log_b rs$ in terms of $\log_b r$ and $\log_b s$.

d. Use the additive law of exponents to prove your general result. (Think of r as b^x and s as b^y.)

continued▸

2. Another principle for exponents states

$$(b^x)^n = b^{xn}$$

Your task is to find a corresponding principle for logarithms by first looking at specific examples.

a. How does $\log_5 (5^7)^6$ compare to $\log_5 5^7$?

b. Find approximate values for $\log_3 17$ and $\log_3 17^4$. What relationship do you see between these two logarithms?

c. Generalize your results from parts a and b to get a formula for $\log_b r^n$ in terms of $\log_b r$ and n.

d. Use the principle $(b^x)^n = b^{xn}$ to prove your general result. (Again, think of r as b^x.)

3. The range, or set of possible outputs, for the function $y = b^x$ consists of all positive numbers. That is, as x varies over all possible values, y can be any positive number. What does this say about the domain, or set of possible inputs, of the function $f(u) = \log_b u$? That is, what numbers can be used for u in this function?

4. a. What is the domain of the function $y = b^x$?

b. What does your answer say about the range of the function $g(v) = \log_b v$?

Finding a Function

In the activity *The Significance of a Sign,* you were asked to sketch the graph of one function for which the derivative is positive for all values of x and another function for which the derivative is zero at exactly two points. Now you will continue that exploration.

1. Sketch the graph of a function f that fits these two conditions.
   - $f'(x)$ is positive for all values of x between -2 and 3.
   - $f'(x)$ is negative if $x < -2$ or $x > 3$.

2. Sketch the graph of a function $g(x)$ that fits these three conditions.
   - $g'(x)$ is zero for exactly three values of x.
   - $g(x)$ is positive between $x = -1$ and $x = 4$.
   - $g(x)$ is negative if $x > 4$ or $x < -1$.

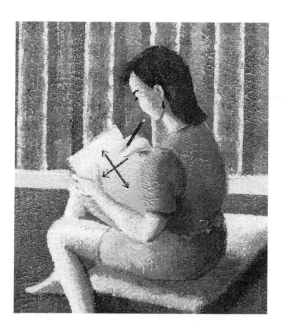

Deriving Derivatives

By looking at the derivative of a function at many of its points, you can sometimes find a rule for its derivative at any point.

In this activity, you will look for a rule that allows you to quickly find the derivative of a function of the form $y = ax^n$. The functions defined by the equations $y = 2x^2$, $y = x^3$, and $y = -3x^6$ are examples of this type of function.

Start with a specific function of this form. Make a table of values for the function's derivative, and find a rule for your table. You might then try other functions that use the same exponent and look for a generalization for functions with that exponent. This exponent, you may recall, is called the *degree* of the function.

Once you have a rule for functions of a particular degree, try a different degree and then try to generalize your results.

The Reality of Compounding

You saw in the activity *The Generous Banker* that getting 5% annual interest, compounded each year for 20 years, is not the same as doubling your money in 20 years.

1. Suppose the bank compounds interest annually. What yearly rate of interest should the bank give for money to double in 20 years?

2. Suppose the bank compounds interest quarterly. What quarterly rate of interest will double the value of an account in 20 years?

Transcendental Numbers

In the unit *Orchard Hideout,* you worked with the number π. The number π can be defined as the ratio between the circumference and the diameter of a circle. In this unit, you were introduced to the number e. Both π and e are examples of *transcendental numbers*.

What is a transcendental number? Your task is to investigate this category of numbers. Then write a report explaining what you learned about transcendental numbers and their history.

Dr. Doubleday's Base

You have seen that for any positive number b, the derivative of the exponential function $y = b^x$ is a proportionality constant multiplied by the y-value.

For example, you found that if the base b is 2, then the proportionality constant is approximately 0.69. In other words, for the function $y = 2^x$, the derivative at a point $(x, 2^x)$ on the graph is approximately $0.69 \cdot 2^x$.

You have also seen that there is a special base, called e, for which this proportionality constant is 1. In other words, for the function $y = e^x$, the derivative at any point on the graph is equal to the y-value at that point.

While it is convenient for scientists to use e as the base, Dr. Doubleday would like a base for which the proportionality constant is 2. (We don't know why.) In other words, the doctor would like to find an exponential function whose derivative at every point on its graph is equal to twice its y-value at that point.

1. Determine what base Dr. Doubleday should use. That is, find a number b such that for every point (x, b^x) on the graph of the function $f(x) = b^x$, the derivative is equal to $2 \cdot b^x$. You will only be able to estimate b. Try to get its value to the nearest hundredth.

2. Look for a relationship between your answer and the number e.

Investigating Constants

1. You've seen that the general exponential function can be written in the form $y = k \cdot e^{cx}$, where k and c are any two nonzero numbers. (What happens if k or c is zero?)

   You also know that any such function has the proportionality property. That is, the derivative at any point on the graph is proportional to the y-value at that point.

   Investigate how the value of the proportionality constant depends on the value of the parameters k and c.

2. The general exponential function can also be written in the form $y = k \cdot b^x$, where k is some nonzero number and b is a positive number other than 1. (What happens if b is equal to 1?) In this form, too, the function has the proportionality property.

   Investigate how the value of the proportionality constant depends on the value of the parameters k and b.

Pennant Fever

Permutations, Combinations, and the Binomial Distribution

Pennant Fever—Permutations, Combinations, and the Binomial Distribution

Play Ball!

In this unit, the central problem involves two baseball teams in a pennant race. Your main task will be to find each team's probability of winning the pennant.

In the first few activities, you will have a chance to speculate about the problem. Over the course of the unit, you will occasionally leave the central problem to explore a variety of other situations, including the chance of finding two people in a room with the same birthday.

Gabi Reyes and Brandon Yi determine the baseball teams' probabilities.

Race for the Pennant!

It's almost the end of the baseball season, and only two teams still have a chance to win the pennant: the Good Guys and the Bad Guys. Here are their records for the season so far.

Team	Games won	Games lost	Games left
Good Guys	96	59	7
Bad Guys	93	62	7

The Good Guys and the Bad Guys will not play against each other in any of their remaining games.

The central problem of this unit is to find the probability that the Good Guys will win the pennant.

1. Study the possibilities for each team.

   a. What is the best record the Good Guys could have at the end of the season? That is, what is the most wins and fewest losses they could end up with?

   b. What is the worst record the Good Guys could have at the end of the season?

   c. What is the best record the Bad Guys could have at the end of the season?

   d. What is the worst record the Bad Guys could have at the end of the season?

2. a. Discuss with your group what you think is the most likely outcome for each team in its remaining seven games.

   b. Make your own decision about part a, and give reasons to support your conclusion.

continued ▸

3. a. Discuss with your group the Good Guys' probability of winning the pennant. Try to come to agreement on the likelihood that they will win.

    b. Give your best guess right now of this probability, and explain your thinking. Be sure to state any assumptions you make.

Happy Birthday!

The seven-day week is used throughout the world. Many cultures have sayings about how the day of the week on which a person is born might affect that individual's personality.

People sometimes use as role models individuals born on the same day of the week they were born. Here are some famous people born on each day of the week

Sunday: Louis Armstrong (Aug. 4, 1901)
Whoopi Goldberg (Nov. 13, 1955)
Katharine Hepburn (May 12, 1907)
Michael Jordan (Feb. 17, 1963)
Elizabeth Cady Stanton (Nov. 12, 1815)

Monday: Henry "Hank" Aaron (Feb. 5, 1934)
Michelangelo Buonarroti (Mar. 6, 1475)
Bill Clinton (Aug. 19, 1946)
Natalie Coughlin (Aug. 23, 1982)
Jodie Foster (Nov. 19, 1962)

Tuesday: Dr. Martin Luther King Jr. (Jan. 15, 1929)
Mao Tse-tung (Dec. 26, 1893)
Golda Meir (May 3, 1898)
Michelle Pfeiffer (Apr. 29, 1958)
Tiger Woods (Dec. 30, 1975)

Wednesday: Maya Angelou (Apr. 4, 1928)
Roald Dahl (Sep. 13, 1916)
Dr. Seuss (Mar. 2, 1904)
Steven Spielberg (Dec. 18, 1946)
Desmond Tutu (Oct. 7, 1931)

Thursday: Louisa May Alcott (Nov. 29, 1832)
Marie Curie (Nov. 7, 1867)
Nelson Mandela (July 18, 1918)
John Steinbeck (Feb. 27, 1902)
Laura Ingalls Wilder (Feb. 7, 1867)

continued

Friday: Madeleine L'Engle (Nov. 29, 1918)
Michelle Obama (Jan. 17, 1964)
Jesse Owens (Sep. 12, 1913)
Mother Teresa (Aug. 26, 1910)
Oprah Winfrey (Jan. 29, 1954)

Saturday: Amelia Earhart (July 24, 1897)
Mahatma Gandhi (Oct. 2, 1869)
Eleanor Roosevelt (Oct. 11, 1884)
J. K. Rowling (July 31, 1965)
Booker T. Washington (Apr. 5, 1856)

This raises an interesting question:

Do you know what day of the week you were born on? How would you figure it out if you didn't know?

Your POW task is to develop a system for determining the day of the week on which someone was born, based on the date that person was born.

1. Use only a calendar for the current month and the "Basic Information About Calendars" provided here to figure out on which day of the week you were born. Do not look at calendars for any other month of this year or for other years.

2. Develop general directions so that someone else could apply the method you used in Question 1 to determine the day of the week on which he or she was born.

3. Have someone try to use the directions you created and then tell you how well your directions worked. Based on this feedback, make changes to correct or clarify your directions.

continued ▸

Basic Information About Calendars

The number of days in each month, except February, is the same every year. February gets an extra day in leap years. For the period from 1901 through 1999, leap years are those years that are multiples of 4: 1904, 1908, 1912, and so on. (For this POW, only consider birth dates from 1901 through 1999. There are special rules for years that are multiples of 100.)

Here is a list of the number of days in each month.

- January: 31 days
- February: 28 days (but 29 in leap years)
- March: 31 days
- April: 30 days
- May: 31 days
- June: 30 days
- July: 31 days
- August: 31 days
- September: 30 days
- October: 31 days
- November: 30 days
- December: 31 days

○ *Write-up*

1. *Problem Statement*

2. *Process*

3. *Solution:* Describe how you determined the day of the week on which you were born, and give the general directions you created. Also write about the experience of having someone else use your directions. If you modified the directions based on that person's feedback, describe the changes you made.

4. *Self-assessment*

Playing with Probabilities

1. Suppose someone throws a dart at this target. Assume the dart will hit the target, with all points equally likely to be hit.

   What is the probability that a given dart will land in the black area? In the white area? In the green area? Explain your answers.

2. Draw an area model that represents a situation with three outcomes. One outcome should have a probability of $\frac{1}{5}$, the second should have a probability of .7, and the third should have a probability of—well, you figure out the probability of the third outcome.

   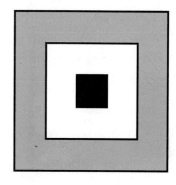

   Explain how you found the third probability and how your area model represents these probabilities.

3. Make up a situation with three outcomes that would have the probabilities in Question 2.

4. Ms. Hernandez and her twins are in front of a gumball machine that contains red, blue, and purple gumballs. Nine gumballs are purple, 25% of the gumballs are red, and the remaining 60% are blue.

   How many of the gumballs are red and how many are blue? Explain how you know your answer is correct.

Special Days

This activity will help you get started on your POW. It asks you to determine what day of the week three special events fell on during the calendar year *previous* to the current year.

Remember to take into account whether either the current year or the previous year was a leap year.

Explain each of your answers. As in the POW, determine these days of the week without consulting any calendar except one for the current month.

1. New Year's Day (January 1)

2. Valentine's Day (February 14)

3. Your birthday

Trees and Baseball

One of the best techniques for analyzing situations like the baseball problem is the tree diagram. You may recall using tree diagrams in the Year 1 unit *The Game of Pig*.

Over the next several days, you'll apply this technique to several situations. You'll also get your first definitive probability results for particular possible outcomes of the baseball pennant race.

Alexander Reyes uses a tree diagram to help solve a probability problem.

Choosing for Chores

Part I: Wash or Dry?

Scott and Letitia are brother and sister. After dinner, they have to do the dishes, with one washing and the other drying. They are having trouble deciding who will do which task, so they come up with a method based on probability.

Letitia grabs some spoons and puts them in a bag. Some have purple handles and others have green handles. Scott has to pick two of the spoons. If their handles are the same color, Scott will wash. If they are different colors, he will dry.

It turns out that there are two purple spoons and three green ones. What is the probability that Scott will wash the dishes? Explain your answer.

Part II: Allowance Choices

Scott and Letitia's parents want to encourage them to learn more about probability. They gave Scott and Letitia two choices for how to get paid for their chores.

- **Choice 1:** They get $4.
- **Choice 2:** They pick two bills out of a bag that contains four $1 bills and one $5 bill.

Which choice would you take? Explain your reasoning carefully.

Baseball Probabilities

Willie is one of the star hitters for the Good Guys. Every time he comes up to bat, he has one chance in three of getting a hit. In standard baseball terminology, we would say his batting average is .333.

1. Suppose Willie comes up to bat twice in a certain game.

    a. What is the probability that he'll get a hit both times?

    b. What is the probability that he won't get a hit either time?

    c. Use your answers to find the probability that he will get exactly one hit.

2. Suppose that in another game, Willie comes up to bat three times.

    a. What is the probability that he'll get a hit all three times?

    b. What is the probability that he won't get any hits?

    c. Use your answers to find the probability that the number of hits will be either 1 or 2.

Possible Outcomes

The Good Guys and the Bad Guys can each achieve many different records for their final seven games. For instance, they could both win the rest of their games, or one team could win the rest of its games while the other team loses all of its games.

1. List the possible records the Good Guys could have for their final seven games.

2. List the possible records the Bad Guys could have for their final seven games.

3. a. How many combinations of records are there for the two teams? For instance, one combination is that the Good Guys win six games and lose one while the Bad Guys win three games and lose four.

   b. Make a table or other display showing all the possible combinations of records. Indicate in your display which team ends up winning the pennant in each case.

How Likely Is "All Wins"?

For the rest of this unit, use .62 as the probability that the Good Guys will win any given game. Use .6 as the probability that the Bad Guys will win any given game. These values come from the teams' current percentages of winning games. Remember that the two teams will not play against each other.

1. Find the probability that the Good Guys will win all seven of their remaining games. Justify your conclusion with a tree diagram or area model.

2. Find the probability that the Bad Guys will win all seven of their remaining games.

3. What is the probability that both teams will finish the season this way? That is, find the probability that both the Good Guys and the Bad Guys will win all seven of their remaining games.

Go for the Gold!

This is your lucky week. You received an invitation to be a contestant on the television game show *Go for the Gold!* You'll have a chance to win a lot of money if you accept the invitation. However, the *Go for the Gold!* producers require a nonrefundable fee of $100 for the opportunity to play.

Here's how the game works.

You are given a jar containing two white cubes and one gold cube. You choose a cube without looking (so each cube is an equally likely choice). If you get the gold cube, you are shown another jar. If you don't get the gold cube, you are out.

The second jar contains four white cubes and one gold cube. Again, you choose one cube from the jar without looking. If you get the gold cube, you win $1,000. If not, you get nothing.

1. a. What is the probability that you will pick the gold cubes from both jars and win the $1,000 prize? Use both an area model and a tree diagram to justify your results.

    b. Pick a section of your area model from part a, and explain what path of your tree diagram it corresponds to.

2. If you win the game (by picking the two gold cubes), you get $1,000. But you have to pay $100 just to play the game.

    Do you accept the show's offer to be a contestant? Explain your decision.

Diagrams, Baseball, and Losing 'em All

1. **a.** Compare the process of calculating probabilities using area models and tree diagrams. Describe the advantages and disadvantages of each method. Use specific examples to illustrate your ideas.

   b. When might you be better off using no diagram at all?

2. Where do you stand on solving the unit problem? That is, what parts of the problem have you solved and what remains to be figured out?

3. What is the probability that the season will end up with both the Good Guys and the Bad Guys losing all seven of their remaining games?

The Birthday Problem

In the first POW of this unit, you developed a method for finding the day of the week on which someone was born. Beginning with *Day-of-the-Week Matches,* you start a sequence of activities that continue this birthday theme. You may find the answer to the final activity in this sequence quite surprising.

First, though, you will work on an activity that relates to the new POW.

Sheila Roberts explains to her classmates what the probability is that there would be at least one birthday match in a group the size of their class.

Let's Make a Deal

Congratulations! You've been selected to be a contestant on the *Let's Make a Deal* television show! Let's review how the game works.

You are shown three doors, labeled A, B, and C. Behind one of the doors is a brand new sports car. Behind the other two doors are worthless prizes.

You select a door. The game-show host then opens one of the other doors. Because he knows where the car is hidden, he makes sure to open a door that reveals a worthless prize.

You now have a choice. You can either stay with the door you originally selected or switch to the remaining closed door.

You will win whatever is behind the door you choose this time.

Here's the big question for you (and for this POW).

Are your chances of winning the car better if you stay with your original choice, or are they better if you switch to the remaining closed door, or are they equally likely with the two strategies?

More precisely, your task is to find the probability of getting the car for each of the two strategies. Write a careful explanation of how you found these probabilities.

continued

Write-up

1. *Problem Statement*

2. *Process:* Include a description of how you and your partner did the simulation in the activity *Simulate a Deal*. Give the results of your simulation, and discuss how that activity contributed to your understanding of the problem.

3. *Solution:* Give the probability of winning for each strategy, including an explanation of how you found the probabilities.

4. *Self-assessment*

Adapted with permission from *Mathematics Teacher,* © April 1991 by the National Council of Teachers of Mathematics.

Simulate a Deal

In the POW *Let's Make a Deal,* you need to decide whether to switch to the remaining closed door or stay with your original choice.

In this activity, you and a partner will simulate the problem. That is, you will use each of the two strategies (switch or stay) a number of times and find out what happens.

1. First try the strategy in which the contestant always switches his or her guess after being shown the open door. One of you will play the game-show host and the other will play the contestant. Come up with some way to realistically act out the situation.

   Play the game ten times using this strategy, keeping track of how many times the contestant wins.

2. Switch roles with your partner and try the strategy in which the contestant always stays with the original door. Play the game ten times using this strategy, keeping track of how many times the contestant wins.

Day-of-the-Week Matches

The POW *Happy Birthday!* involves the day of the week on which a person is born. This activity is the first of several that connect that theme to probability.

In this activity, assume that each of the seven possibilities—Sunday through Saturday—is equally likely.

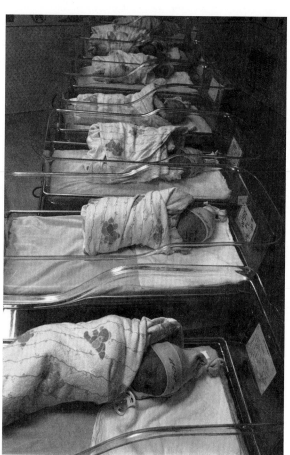

1. Imagine a random group of people. Is there a group size for which you would be certain that at least two people in the group were born on the same day of the week? What's the smallest such group size? Explain your answer.

2. If you pick two people at random, what is the probability that they were born on different days of the week? What is the probability that they were born on the same day of the week? Justify your answers.

3. If you pick three people at random, what is the probability that all three were born on different days of the week? What is the probability that at least two of the three people were born on the same day of the week? Justify your answers.

Day-of-the-Week Matches, Continued

In *Day-of-the-Week Matches,* you found the probability that two people chosen at random were born on the same day of the week and then the probability for three people.

You also found that if there were at least eight people, the probability would be 1, because you would be certain of a match.

Now you will investigate this question.

> *What is the minimum number of people needed so that the probability of having at least one day-of-the-week match is greater than $\frac{1}{2}$?*

As before, assume each day of the week is equally likely.

Be sure to explain your answer. (Because the probability for two people and the probability for three people are both less than $\frac{1}{2}$, you know that you need more than three people. You also know that the number can't be more than eight. It may be easier to figure out the probability that a group of people were all born on *different* days of the week than to figure out the probability that at least two were born on the *same* day of the week.)

Monthly Matches

You've been working on problems involving the probability that two people are born on the same day of the week. Now you move from days of the week to months of the year.

Although the months are not all the same length, make the simplifying assumption in this activity that each month is equally likely to be the birth month for a person chosen at random.

1. What is the smallest number of people needed for the probability to be 100% that at least two of them were born in the same month?

2. If you pick a person at random, what is the probability that you and that person were born in the same month?

3. If you have a group of three people chosen at random, what is the probability that at least two of them have the same birth month? What is the probability for a four-person group?

4. How many people would you need in a randomly chosen group for the probability of a month-of-birth match in the group to be greater than $\frac{1}{2}$?

The Real Birthday Problem

You've been working on day-of-the-week matches and month-of-the-year matches. Now you're ready to solve a very famous problem known simply as the "birthday problem."

What is the minimum number of people needed so that the probability of having at least one birthday match is greater than $\frac{1}{2}$?

For this problem, ignore leap years. That is, assume that a year has 365 days. Also assume that each of these 365 days is equally likely to be a person's birthday.

1. Before doing any computation or analysis, make a guess about the answer to the birthday problem and write it down.

2. Now do the necessary analysis to find the answer, and explain your work.

Six for the Defense

Mari wants to be a defense attorney. She is very excited because her civics teacher has just announced that the class will soon begin a four-day unit on the court system.

The class will act out a different famous court case each day. At the beginning of each class, the teacher will use a die to decide each student's role. If the die comes up 6, the student will be one of the defense attorneys for that case. If the die comes up 1 through 5, the student will play some other role.

1. Make a tree diagram or area model for the situation that will help Mari analyze how often she is likely to be a defense attorney over the four days.

2. What is the probability that Mari will be a defense attorney every day of the unit?

3. What is the probability that Mari will never be a defense attorney during the unit?

4. On the third day of the unit, the class will act out a case with which Mari is very familiar. What she'd like best is to be a defense attorney on that day and have other roles for the other three cases. What is the probability that she will get her wish?

5. What is the probability that Mari will be a defense attorney exactly once during the four days? Explain your answer.

Baseball and Counting

You will now return briefly to the central problem and find the probabilities for a few more cases.

Then you will investigate some sophisticated ways to count. Among other things, you'll count the number of different ways to create ice cream cones. You'll also apply your new counting techniques to some more baseball outcomes.

Mike Holcombe is clearly confident that the list method has resulted in his finding all possible combinations.

And If You Don't Win 'em All?

The Good Guys would like to win all of their remaining seven games, but winning six out of seven wouldn't be so bad. The Bad Guys would also be pretty happy to win six out of seven.

1. Find the probability that the Good Guys will win the first six of their remaining games and then lose the seventh game.

2. Question 1 involves only one of several ways the Good Guys can compile a record of six wins and one loss in their remaining games. Find the probability that the Good Guys will win exactly six of their seven remaining games.

3. Find the probability that the Bad Guys will win exactly six of their seven remaining games.

But Don't Lose 'em All, Either

The activity *And If You Don't Win 'em All?* involves the "next-to-best" scenario for each of the two teams: winning six games and losing just one. Now you will examine the "next-to-worst" scenario.

1. Find the probability that the Good Guys will win the first of their remaining games and then lose the remaining six.

2. Find the probability that the Good Guys will win exactly one of their seven remaining games.

3. Find the probability that the Bad Guys will win exactly one of their seven remaining games.

The Good and the Bad

You have discovered a great deal about the probability of the Good Guys and the Bad Guys getting certain records.

For instance, you know the probability that the Good Guys will win six games and lose one, and you know the probability that the Bad Guys will win six games and lose one. But what is the probability that both things will happen? And for what other combinations can you find the probability?

You have already begun a chart of all possible combinations of individual records for the Good Guys and the Bad Guys. Use the information you have so far on the probabilities of some of these records to fill in as much of your chart as possible.

Top That Pizza!

Jonathan delivers pizza several evenings a week. He doesn't earn a lot, but he does get a free pizza for dinner every night he works.

The pizza shop has five toppings that Jonathan likes: pineapple, olives, mushrooms, onions, and anchovies.

1. Jonathan likes variety. If he always has exactly two of these five toppings on his pizzas, how many nights can he work without repeating a combination? Explain your answer.

2. Jonathan's sister Johanna also delivers pizza. She likes the same five toppings as her brother, but she always wants exactly *three* of them on her pizzas. How many nights can she work without repeating a combination? Explain your answer.

3. How are your answers to Questions 1 and 2 related? Explain why this relationship holds true.

Double Scoops

After Jonathan finishes his deliveries, he always treats himself to a two-scoop bowl of ice cream at the shop next to the pizza store. The ice cream shop serves 24 flavors of ice cream.

1. Jonathan always gets two different flavors for his two scoops of ice cream. How many different combinations of two scoops can he create?

2. Johanna always visits the ice cream shop after her deliveries, too. She likes her ice cream on a cone, and it's important to her which scoop is on top. After all, she says, eating chocolate and then vanilla is a different taste experience from eating vanilla and then chocolate.

   Like her brother, Johanna always wants two different flavors. How many different two-scoop ice cream cones can she create?

Triple Scoops

Poor Johanna! She has had her tonsils out and is stuck at home with a sore throat. But fortunately, one of the things she can eat easily is ice cream.

Her friend Joshua is coming over, so she asks him to get her a three-scoop cone. She tells Joshua that he will probably find her brother Jonathan eating a bowl of ice cream at the shop. She asks Joshua to get her the same flavors that Jonathan has.

Sure enough, Jonathan is there—and he's actually having a three-scoop bowl of ice cream! He has one scoop each of pistachio, boysenberry, and chocolate, so Joshua knows to order those three flavors.

Unfortunately, neither Joshua nor Jonathan has any idea about the order in which Johanna will want her scoops. Joshua knows she is fussy about this, and he really wants her to get what she wants.

1. Joshua decides to get Johanna all possible cones with those three flavors. How many different cones does he buy?

2. Joshua realizes he is lucky that Johanna hadn't asked for a four-scoop cone. If she had requested a cone with pistachio, boysenberry, chocolate, and butter pecan without specifying the order of flavors, how many different cone possibilities would there be?

More Cones for Johanna

After Johanna recovers from her tonsillectomy, she continues to eat three-scoop ice cream cones. In fact, she thinks it would be fun to try every possible three-scoop cone the shop has to offer. Remember that the ice cream shop serves 24 flavors.

1. If Johanna has one three-scoop cone every day, how many days can she go before she will have to repeat?

2. Suppose instead that she has a different four-scoop cone each day. How long will it take for her to try them all?

3. Find a rule for determining the number of different cones in terms of the number of scoops on the cone. Base your work on the 24-flavor ice cream shop. Of course, your rule won't work for more than 24 scoops.

4. One day, while visiting relatives in another town, Johanna goes into a new ice cream shop. She figures out that there are 156 possible two-scoop cones that could be made from the flavors at this shop. How many different flavors does this shop serve?

Cones from Bowls, Bowls from Cones

In *Triple Scoops,* you saw that many different ice cream cones could be made from the scoops in a given bowl of ice cream. The number of cones depends on the number of scoops involved.

These questions continue that theme. (You do not need to figure out the number of flavors at each ice cream shop.)

1. At Francisco's Freeze, you can make 465 different two-scoop bowls of ice cream. How many different two-scoop ice cream cones can you make?

2. At Paige's Parlor, you can make 220 different three-scoop bowls of ice cream. How many different three-scoop ice cream cones can you make?

3. a. At Ashley's Ice Cream Shoppe, you can make 210 different four-scoop bowls of ice cream. How many different four-scoop ice cream cones can you make?

   b. At Carmen's Creamery, you can make 3024 different four-scoop ice cream cones. How many different four-scoop bowls of ice cream can you make? (*Careful:* This question and Question 4b reverse the situation presented in the other questions.)

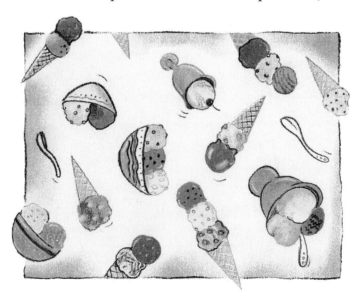

continued ▶

4. a. At Fiona's Flavors, you can make 792 different five-scoop bowls of ice cream. How many different five-scoop ice cream cones can you make?

    b. At Christopher's Cones, you can make 55,440 different five-scoop ice cream cones. How many different five-scoop bowls of ice cream can you make?

5. a. In general, if you know how many bowls of ice cream can be made with a given number of scoops, how do you find the number of different cones that can be made of that size?

    b. In general, if you know the number of cones that can be made with a given number of scoops, how do you find the number of different bowls that can be made?

Bowls for Jonathan

In *Cones from Bowls, Bowls from Cones,* you considered several ice cream shops. In some cases, you found the number of distinct bowls of ice cream of a particular size in terms of the number of distinct cones of that size. Apply the principles from that activity to these questions.

Johanna and Jonathan return to their favorite ice cream shop, which serves 24 flavors.

1. How many different three-scoop bowls of ice cream can they order?

2. How many different four-scoop bowls of ice cream can they order?

At the Olympics

1. The nation of Panacea will participate in the 400-meter race in the next Olympics. The nation has ten runners of equal ability. It must choose three of these runners to represent Panacea at the Olympics.

   How many different three-person teams are possible?

2. There will be ten finalists in the Olympics gymnastics competition. One of these ten will win the gold medal, one will win the silver, and one will win the bronze.

   After the competition, a plaque will be made listing the three winners in order. Use the fact that there are ten finalists to determine the number of possibilities for the sequence of names on this plaque.

3. Compare Questions 1 and 2.

   a. Which question is like an ice cream cone problem, and which is like an ice cream bowl problem?

   b. How can you find the answer to one of these two types of problems from the answer to the other?

Fair Spoons

○ The Original Problem

In the activity *Choosing for Chores*, Scott and Letitia determine who will wash the dishes and who will dry them by having Scott pull two spoons out of a bag.

The bag contains two spoons with purple handles and three with green ones. If the two spoons Scott pulls out are the same color, Scott will wash and Letitia will dry. If they are different colors, Letitia will wash and Scott will dry.

○ The New Problem

Letitia decides she doesn't like this method, because it turns out that she washes the dishes about 60% of the time. Scott thinks that if they find the right number of spoons of each color to put in the bag, they can make the probability of a match equal to 50%. But neither of them is sure what the right numbers would be.

What do you think? Find out as much about their choices as you can—don't merely find the simplest answer. Assume that plenty of spoons of both colors are available. As you work, keep track of the probability of a match in cases that do not come out to 50%.

continued

○ *Write-up*

1. *Problem Statement*

2. *Process*

3. *Solution:* Give the percentage of matches for all the specific examples you examined, and give all the combinations you found that led to matches exactly 50% of the time. Explain how you found the percentages in each case. Also describe any patterns you notice in the combinations that give matches 50% of the time.

4. *Self-assessment*

Which Is Which?

Permutations and Combinations

In recent activities, you have been carefully examining two types of counting problems. Mathematicians use the terms **permutations** and **combinations** to refer to these two types of problems.

We use the notation $_nP_r$ for permutation problems and the notation $_nC_r$ for combination problems. In both cases, the variable n stands for the size of the group you are choosing from. The variable r stands for the number of things you are picking from that group.

The numbers $_nC_r$ are called **combinatorial coefficients.** (There is no standard term for the numbers $_nP_r$.)

Your Task

In this activity, you will review the activities you have done so far in this unit.

1. Identify three specific problems you believe are combination problems and three specific problems you believe are permutation problems.

2. Explain why you think each problem is the type you say it is.

3. Express the answers to the questions in each problem you identified using the notations $_nP_r$ and $_nC_r$.

Formulas for $_nP_r$ and $_nC_r$

You have seen that many of the problems in this unit involve the concepts of combinations and permutations.

In *Which Is Which?*, you looked at how to apply these concepts and the notations $_nP_r$ and $_nC_r$ to problems in this unit. Now you will find formulas for $_nP_r$ and $_nC_r$.

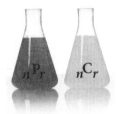

1. Find formulas for these specific cases of $_nP_r$. Give each answer as an expression in terms of n. You may want to think about specific situations to which these cases apply.

    a. $_nP_1$

    b. $_nP_2$

    c. $_nP_3$

2. Find a general formula for $_nP_r$ in terms of n and r.

Next, think about the relationship between permutations and combinations in specific situations. For example, for a given number of ice cream flavors, what is the relationship between the number of three-scoop bowls and the number of three-scoop cones?

3. Develop a general equation expressing the relationship between $_nP_r$ and $_nC_r$.

4. Combine your results from Questions 2 and 3 to get a formula for $_nC_r$ in terms of n and r.

Who's on First?

The Good Guys have a terrific team. In fact, the team's manager, Sammy Lagrange, is sure they will win the pennant and go on to play in the World Series.

In the World Series, the first team to win four games is declared the world champion. (American baseball has always assumed that its best team is the best in the world.)

Sammy is already planning ahead, but one drawback of having such a good team is that it's often hard to make decisions.

1. When the Good Guys get to the World Series, Sammy will have to pick four different pitchers, one for each of the first four games of the World Series. He isn't thinking beyond four games, because he expects the Good Guys to win four games in a row and be declared the champions.

   Sammy has seven excellent pitchers to choose from. To prepare properly, the pitchers need to know which game, if any, they will pitch. This means Sammy has to determine not only which four pitchers to use but who will pitch in which game.

   He decides to put all possible sequences of four pitchers on slips of paper. He'll then pick one of these slips out of a baseball cap to settle the pitching order.

   How many slips of paper does Sammy need? (The answer is not seven! Sammy isn't doing this the easy way. Remember that each slip of paper shows a sequence with the names of four pitchers in order.)

continued ▶

And that's only the pitchers! For the rest of the team, Sammy is thinking only as far as the first game, but he still has choices to make.

2. To begin with, Sammy needs to choose his outfield—a left fielder, a center fielder, and a right fielder. He has five good outfielders to choose from, and they can each play any of these positions. Sammy needs to decide which outfielder will play which position.

   How many ways are there for Sammy to fill these positions for the first game?

3. Then there's the infield. Sammy needs a first baseman, a second baseman, a shortstop, and a third baseman. He has six highly qualified infielders. They are all versatile and able to play any of these four positions.

   How many possibilities must Sammy consider in filling the infield positions for the first game?

4. Fortunately, Sammy knows who his best catcher is. That player will complete his nine-player team for the first game. The nine players are a pitcher, three outfielders, four infielders, and the catcher.

   Considering all that's going on, how many different possibilities are there altogether for who will play each position for the Good Guys in the first game?

5. Once Sammy has decided on his nine players, he has to choose a batting order. That is, he needs to decide which of the nine players bats first, bats second, bats third, and so on.

   How many ways are there to arrange his starting nine players in the batting order for the first game?

Five for Seven

It's time to return to the central unit problem about the Good Guys and Bad Guys. There are still many possible outcomes with probabilities you have not yet figured out.

You will look at a few of those cases in this activity. You may find that you can apply what you learned about pizza and ice cream to the race for the baseball pennant.

1. What is the probability that the Good Guys will win five and lose two of their remaining seven games? Explain your answer.

2. What is the probability that the Bad Guys will win two and lose five of their remaining seven games? Explain your answer.

3. What is the probability that the outcomes from Questions 1 and 2 will both happen? That is, what is the probability that the Good Guys will win five games and lose two *and* the Bad Guys will win two games and lose five?

More Five for Sevens

In *Five for Seven,* you found two probabilities that are important in solving the unit problem.

- The probability that the Good Guys will win five and lose two of their remaining seven games
- The probability that the Bad Guys will win two and lose five of their remaining seven games

1. Find each of these similar probabilities.

   a. The probability that the Good Guys will win two and lose five of their remaining seven games

   b. The probability that the Bad Guys will win five and lose two of their remaining seven games

In *Five for Seven,* you also found the probability of both events happening—that is, the probability that the Good Guys will win five and lose two *and* the Bad Guys will win two and lose five. This probability represents only one of the 64 cells in your chart of possible records for the two teams.

2. Enter the values from Question 1 in your chart. Then find and record the probabilities for the three other cells that involve either two wins or five wins for each team.

Combinatorial Reasoning

Combinatorial coefficients can be helpful in many situations besides baseball and ice cream. Because probability involves counting cases, these special numbers play a role in a wide variety of probability problems.

In the next activities, you'll see how to use both permutations and combinations—along with principles of statistical reasoning, such as the null hypothesis—to find probabilities and to make decisions.

Annie Tam computes the number of ways the baseball teams can win or lose their remaining games.

What's for Dinner?

Lai Yee wants to buy a motor scooter. His parents encourage him to take care of his own expenses, so they offer to pay him for providing the family's dinner four nights a week: Sunday, Tuesday, Thursday, and Saturday. They will pay him $20 a week for his work, in addition to reimbursing him for the cost of the food.

Lai Yee has never cooked before, and his parents want to make sure they won't get the same one or two meals over and over again. So they decide he must submit his planned menu for each week in advance, showing the four meals for that week. His menus must meet two rules.

- No weekly menu can contain two of the same meal.

- Each weekly menu must be different from all previous weekly menus.

Lai Yee is clever. After some research, he discovers that there are seven meals already prepared that he can buy from nearby restaurants. That way, he won't have to learn to cook. The seven meals are Chinese noodles, pasta, tacos, quiche, pizza, sushi, and roasted chicken.

1. How much money can Lai Yee earn before he has to learn to cook something? Express your answer using the notation $_nP_r$ or $_nC_r$ appropriately. Also find the actual numeric answer, and explain how you got your answer.

continued ▶

2. There was a misunderstanding between Lai Yee and his parents. He thought he could use the same set of four meals for more than one weekly menu if he simply presented them in a different order. To his parents, "different weekly menu" means "a different set of four meals."

   Whichever way you interpreted Question 1, now answer the question using the other interpretation. Again, express your answer using the notation $_nP_r$ or $_nC_r$ appropriately, and also find the actual answer.

3. What if Lai Yee were to cut back to three meals per week? How many weeks could he go under his interpretation before he has to cook something? Under his parents' interpretation?

All or Nothing

In most cases, the formulas for the combinatorial and permutation coefficients are pretty clear. In some special cases, though, it helps to have a situation to give concrete meaning to these numbers.

1. You found that there are 21 different sequences by which the Good Guys can win exactly five of their remaining seven games. In other words, the combinatorial coefficient $\binom{7}{5}$ is equal to 21. Remember that the notation $\binom{n}{r}$ means the same thing as $_nC_r$.

   Use the pennant race situation to determine the value of the combinatorial coefficient $\binom{7}{0}$. Explain your reasoning.

2. You found that there are ten different pizza combinations Johanna can create if she chooses three toppings for her pizza out of the five she likes. In other words, the combinatorial coefficient $\binom{5}{3}$ is equal to 10.

   Use the pizza situation to determine the value of the combinatorial coefficient $\binom{5}{5}$. Explain your reasoning.

3. Use either Jonathan's or Johanna's ice cream preferences to determine the values of $_{24}P_0$ and $\binom{24}{0}$. Explain your reasoning.

4. Use any of the situations in Questions 1 to 3, or another situation you make up, to determine the values of $_nP_1$ and $\binom{n}{1}$. Explain your reasoning.

The Perfect Group

At last, in his third year of high school, Julio has lucked out. He is finally part of what he considers the perfect four-person study group in his class. This is the group he would have chosen for himself on the first day of his first year of high school if he'd had a chance.

Each time new groups were formed, he hoped for this group. Sometimes he'd get one or two members of this ideal group, but never all three.

How lucky was Julio? Begin with these assumptions.

- There are 32 students in Julio's class.
- This 32-person class has been together throughout high school so far.
- New groups are created randomly every two weeks.
- Groups always have four students.

1. Guess the probability of Julio getting his perfect group sometime in three years. Resist the temptation to do any arithmetic yet—simply give your intuitive idea about what the chances are.

2. Now actually find this probability. You will need to make some further assumptions to do so. State those assumptions clearly.

And a Fortune, Too!

The King's New Scale

Do you remember the economical king from the Year 1 POWs *Eight Bags of Gold* and *Twelve Bags of Gold* (in the unit *The Pit and the Pendulum*)? Well, he's still around, and despite his economical nature, he has only five bags of gold now.

One reason he has less gold is that his old pan-balance scale broke down. His adviser found an antique scale to replace it—the kind in which you drop in a penny and are told your weight. This scale doesn't let the king compare weights, but it does give very precise measurements.

The king was very excited about another feature of the scale. With each weight, he also got a slip of paper that predicted his fortune. But he didn't pay attention to the fact that he was spending a penny every time he used the scale. He spent a lot of pennies before he realized his fortune had dwindled to five bags of gold.

The King's New Problem

Now, as before, the king has given one bag of gold to each of the five people he trusts the most in his kingdom. And, as before, rumors have drifted back to the king that one of these five caretakers is not to be trusted. According to rumor, this person is asking a counterfeiter to make phony gold.

The king has brought in the local counterfeiter for questioning. He wants to find out who hired her to double-cross him.

continued

She admits being involved, but refuses to name the traitor. She won't even say whether the counterfeit gold she is making is heavier or lighter than real gold. All the king learns from her is that one of the five bags is now filled with counterfeit gold and that this bag weighs a different amount from the others.

Your Challenge

The king wants to use his scale to determine two things.

* Which bag weighs a different amount
* Exactly how much that bag weighs

Of course, he wants to learn these things economically, using the fewest pennies possible. (He has suddenly started to economize—even with pennies!)

The court mathematician says it can be done by using only three pennies. No one else sees how it can be done with so few weighings. Anyone can do it with five pennies. Some say they can do it with four pennies. But three pennies? Can you figure it out?

Write-up

1. *Problem Statement*

2. *Process*

3. *Solution:* You might get only a partial solution to this problem. If so, explain what cases your solution covers and where you got stuck.

4. *Self-assessment*

Feasible Combinations

In the unit *Meadows or Malls?*, you generalized ideas about graphs and inequalities to solve linear programming problems in several variables.

One important principle from that unit is that you can find the corner points of a feasible region by examining certain systems of linear equations. If the set of constraints uses n variables, then each system you examine should contain n linear equations.

In this activity, you'll apply ideas from this unit to find how many linear systems you might have to consider to solve linear programming problems.

1. The central problem from *Meadows or Malls?* involves six variables. They are labeled G_R, A_R, M_R, G_D, A_D, and M_D. The situation is described by these 12 constraints.

I	$G_R + G_D = 300$	VII	$G_R \geq 0$
II	$A_R + A_D = 100$	VIII	$A_R \geq 0$
III	$M_R + M_D = 150$	IX	$M_R \geq 0$
IV	$G_D + A_D + M_D \geq 300$	X	$G_D \geq 0$
V	$A_R + M_R \leq 200$	XI	$A_D \geq 0$
VI	$A_R + G_D = 100$	XII	$M_D \geq 0$

Each inequality in this list has a corresponding linear equation. For instance, the inequality $G_D + A_D + M_D \geq 300$ corresponds to the linear equation $G_D + A_D + M_D = 300$.

So the 12 constraints lead to 12 linear equations. Because the *Meadows or Malls?* problem involves six variables, every corner point for the feasible region is the solution to a system that consists of six of these 12 equations.

a. How many six-equation systems can you form from the 12 equations? Of course, some of these systems do not actually lead to a corner point of the feasible region.

continued ▸

If any of the constraints in a linear programming problem are actually equations, then all corner points have to fit those equations. Therefore, in your search for corner points, you can restrict yourself to linear systems that include those equations.

b. In the *Meadows or Malls?* problem, four of the constraints are equations. Suppose you examine only six-equation systems that include these four equations. That is, you examine only systems consisting of the four constraint equations together with two of the eight equations that correspond to constraint inequalities.

How many systems will you need to consider?

2. Suppose a linear programming problem has eight variables and 20 constraints, and that three of the constraints are equations.

How many linear systems would you need to consider? Again, some of these systems might not actually lead to a corner point of the feasible region.

About Bias

At Bayside High, a 15-member committee handles many decisions. The school-wide committee consists of ten adults and five students. Principal Fifer has been asked to select a special subcommittee of six people out of this group of 15.

Students are furious because they just learned that the subcommittee consists entirely of adults. They feel that the principal stacked the subcommittee with adults and didn't consider students. Principal Fifer, however, claims the subcommittee was chosen randomly.

The students have decided to present their case to the school board.

1. As part of their presentation, they want to tell the school board the probability of getting only adults if the principal had selected six people at random from the committee of 15. Find this probability, giving your answer both as a number and as an expression using the notation $_nP_r$ or $_nC_r$ appropriately.

2. Do you think the principal stacked the committee? Explain your answer.

Binomial Powers

You've seen that combinatorial coefficients can be helpful in finding probabilities like those involved in the unit problem. As you know, these numbers are also called **binomial coefficients.**

(*Reminder:* A *binomial* is an expression that is the sum of two terms, each of which is a product of numbers and variables. For example, $3x + 2y$, $5 - z$, $-3xy + 15zw$, and $7x^3 + 3xy^2$ are binomials.)

A little later in this unit, you'll find out what binomials have to do with the combinatorial coefficients $_nC_r$. In preparation for that discussion, your task now is to simplify certain powers of binomials by writing each expression as a sum of terms, without parentheses.

The diagram illustrates Question 1. You may find similar diagrams helpful for Questions 2 through 6 (and perhaps even for Question 7).

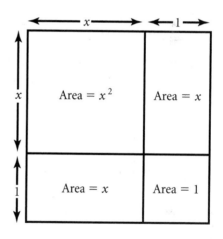

1. $(x + 1)^2$

2. $(a + b)^2$

3. $(r - 7)^2$

4. $(5g + 1)^2$

5. $(K + 4L)^2$

6. $(3y - 8)^2$

7. $(a + b)^3$

As long as you're simplifying algebraic expressions, go ahead and simplify these (which are not powers of binomials).

8. $x^2(2x^3 + 3x - 6)$

9. $(x^2 + 3)(x^2 - 2x + 4)$

Complete the square for each of these expressions. That is, find a value for c so that the expression is the square of a binomial.

10. $x^2 + 8x + c$

11. $x^2 - 13x + c$

Don't Stand for It

In a very small town is a small factory with ten workers. All ten workers go out for lunch every day, and they all go out at the same time. No one else in town goes out for lunch.

There are two restaurants in town. Every day, each worker randomly chooses to eat at one restaurant or the other. Both establishments have only counter seating (no tables).

One owner has ten stools at her counter just in case all ten workers visit her restaurant on the same day.

The other owner realizes it is unlikely all ten will come on the same day. He figures it's okay for business as long as he isn't short of stools more than an average of once a month. Because there are typically 20 workdays per month, he wants enough stools so that the chance of running short on any given day is less than 5%.

How many stools should he provide? Justify your answer.

Adapted from *Introduction to Finite Mathematics* by John G. Kemeny, J. Laurie Snell, and Gerald L. Thompson (Englewood Cliffs, NJ: Prentice-Hall, 1957).

Stop! Don't Walk!

Patience Walker always walks to school using the same route, although the time of day varies. She thinks one of the stoplights on the route to school has it in for her. It always seems to be red when she approaches the corner, no matter what time of day it is. She thinks it happens too often to be a coincidence.

Patience is actually not very patient, so she is anxious to get to the bottom of this.

She phones the Department of Public Works and is told that within the traffic light's timing cycle, the light is set to be red 60% of the time. Patience finds this difficult to believe and asks the DPW to investigate the light. The DPW representative tells her they have little time for such trivial matters and asks her to call back when she has some hard evidence.

1. Patience keeps track of the light for five days (one school week). Sure enough, the light is red on her way to school every one of those days.

    If the information from the DPW is correct, what is the probability of that happening? Explain your answer. Assume that Patience is equally likely to arrive at the light at any point during its cycle.

2. Patience is afraid the DPW won't be convinced by a five-day survey, so she keeps track for two more school weeks, for a total of 15 days. She finds the light to be red on 13 of those 15 days.

    She's ready to confront the DPW. If the light is really red exactly 60% of the time during each cycle, what is the probability that Patience would find it red 13 or more times out of 15?

Pascal's Triangle

Pascal's triangle is an array of numbers that contains many interesting patterns and relationships. The array is named for a French mathematician who did important work in the theory of probability, but this arrangement of numbers was studied long before his time.

In the upcoming activities, you'll investigate how the array is formed and see some of its many applications.

In creating Pascal's triangle, Maile Martin, Jeanette Austria, and Kahala Neil find many patterns.

Pascal's Triangle

The triangular arrangement shown here is the beginning of a pattern of numbers commonly called **Pascal's triangle.** Although only six rows are shown, the pattern can be extended indefinitely.

This number pattern is named in honor of the French mathematician Blaise Pascal (1623–1662), who developed the beginnings of the modern theory of probability.

Though Pascal was a distinguished mathematician, he was also famous as a physicist, geometer, and religious philosopher. Among other things, he invented the first digital calculator. A well-known computer language is named for him as well.

Pascal was not the first person to work with this numeric pattern. In fact, the pattern has been found in use as early as around 1300 CE, in a book of Chinese prints.

1. Find a pattern in Pascal's triangle that will allow you to extend it to more rows. Then use this pattern to extend Pascal's triangle to at least ten rows altogether. (Save this extended version of Pascal's triangle, because you will need it for the rest of the unit.)

2. Find other patterns in the triangle. Describe each new pattern you find in words and with examples.

Hi There!

The handshake problem is a classic mathematics problem. It goes like this.

There are n people in a room. Everyone shakes hands exactly once with everyone else. How many handshakes are there?

When two people shake hands, it counts as one handshake.

1. Find the answer to the handshake problem for the case $n = 3$. Also find the answers for $n = 5$, for $n = 10$, and for two other specific cases of your choice.

2. Look for a pattern in your answers, or find a general formula for n people.

3. Explain how this problem appears to be related to Pascal's triangle.

4. How is this problem related to combinatorial coefficients? Remember that the combinatorial coefficient $_nC_r$ tells how many different bowls of ice cream you can make with r scoops (of different flavors) if there are n flavors altogether.

Pascal and the Coefficients

The entries in Pascal's triangle, it turns out, are combinatorial coefficients. In fact, this is the main reason Pascal's triangle is important in mathematics.

It is standard practice to refer to the top row of Pascal's triangle as "row 0," the next row as "row 1," and so on. Similarly, the first number in each row is called "entry 0," the next number is "entry 1," and so on. This numbering system connects the position of a number to its meaning as a combinatorial coefficient.

For example, according to this system, the boxed number 10 shown here is entry 2 of row 5 of Pascal's triangle. This relates to the fact that 10 is equal to the combinatorial coefficient $\binom{5}{2}$, which tells how many different bowls of ice cream you can make with two scoops (of different flavors) if there are five flavors altogether.

```
                    1
                 1     1
              1     2     1
           1     3     3     1
        1     4     6     4     1
     1     5    [10]   10     5     1
   ?     ?     ?     ?     ?     ?     ?
 ?     ?     ?     ?     ?     ?     ?     ?
```

In general, it can be proved that entry r of row n is the combinatorial coefficient $\binom{n}{r}$. For instance, the row 1 4 6 4 1 is row 4 and consists of the combinatorial coefficients $\binom{4}{0}$, $\binom{4}{1}$, $\binom{4}{2}$, $\binom{4}{3}$, and $\binom{4}{4}$.

continued ▶

1. Check that $\binom{4}{0}$, $\binom{4}{1}$, $\binom{4}{2}$, $\binom{4}{3}$, and $\binom{4}{4}$ do have the values 1, 4, 6, 4, and 1, respectively. Explain the values in terms of bowls of ice cream.

2. Use the connection between Pascal's triangle and combinatorial coefficients to find these values.

   a. $\binom{6}{5}$

   b. $\binom{7}{4}$

   c. $\binom{9}{5}$

   d. $\binom{10}{6}$

3. One feature of Pascal's triangle is that each row begins and ends with the number 1. In terms of combinatorial coefficients, this means $\binom{n}{0}$ and $\binom{n}{n}$ are both equal to 1, for any value of n.

   Explain this feature of Pascal's triangle in terms of bowls of ice cream or using some other model for combinatorial coefficients.

Combinations, Pascal's Way

In the activity *Pascal's Triangle,* you explored patterns and relationships in that special array of numbers. You now know that the numbers in Pascal's triangle are actually combinatorial coefficients.

Your task now is to examine the patterns and relationships in Pascal's triangle in light of the connection between Pascal's triangle and combinatorial coefficients.

For each pattern or relationship you found in Pascal's triangle, do two things.

- Express the pattern or relationship in terms of combinatorial coefficients.

- Explain the pattern or relationship based on the meaning of combinatorial coefficients—for example, by using bowls of ice cream or another model for $_nC_r$.

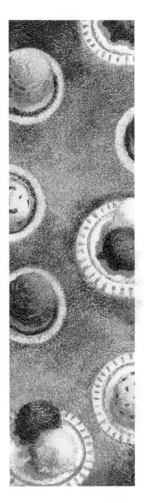

Binomials and Pascal—Part I

In *Binomial Powers,* you found powers of some binomials. Now you will look at powers of a special binomial and examine how the coefficients in the expansion are related to Pascal's triangle.

1. Expand and simplify each of these expressions, combining terms and writing each result as a sum without parentheses.

   a. $(a + b)^2$

   b. $(a + b)^3$

   c. $(a + b)^4$

   d. $(a + b)^5$

2. Examine the coefficients in your results. How are they related to Pascal's triangle?

Blaise Pascal (1623–1662)

Binomials and Pascal—Part II

In *Binomials and Pascal—Part I,* you examined powers of the binomial $a + b$, expanding expressions of the form $(a + b)^n$.

In each case, the coefficients form a row of Pascal's triangle. That is, they are numbers of the form $\binom{n}{r}$.

Now you will use the connection between the coefficients and Pascal's triangle to find the expansions for powers of some other binomials.

1. Find the expansion of $(a + b)^{10}$. Using your insights from the previous activity and your copy of Pascal's triangle, write the expansion as a sum of terms with powers of a and b and with appropriate coefficients from Pascal's triangle.

2. Find the expansion of $(a + 2)^5$.

3. Find the expansion of $(x - 1)^4$. Be careful about signs. It might help to think of $x - 1$ as $x + (-1)$.

A Pascal Portfolio

Write a summary of what you know about Pascal's triangle. Include these elements.

- How to create Pascal's triangle
- How to use Pascal's triangle to find combinatorial coefficients
- Properties of Pascal's triangle and explanations of these properties in terms of combinatorial coefficients
- Why the numbers in Pascal's triangle are called *binomial coefficients*

Another portrait of Blaise Pascal

The Baseball Finale

After many digressions, it's now time to solve the central problem of the unit. Remember—in this unit as in baseball—it's not over 'til it's over!

Jeff Kirilov records the probability of one of several possible outcomes for the teams competing in the pennant race.

Race for the Pennant! Revisited

Time is running out, and the season will soon be over. Here's your last chance to figure out the probability that the Good Guys will win the pennant.

Once again, here are the records of the two teams.

Team	Games won	Games lost	Games left
Good Guys	96	59	7
Bad Guys	93	62	7

Recall these key facts and assumptions.

- The Good Guys and Bad Guys do not play each other.
- In each game the Good Guys play, their probability of winning is .62.
- In each game the Bad Guys play, their probability of winning is .6.

Determine the probability that the Good Guys will win the pennant. Also determine the probability that the teams will be tied when they each finish the remaining seven games.

Graphing the Games

You've determined that there are eight possible overall outcomes for the Good Guys' final seven games. They can win all seven games, they can win six and lose one, and so on, down to losing all seven. You've also seen that these eight outcomes are not equally likely.

1. Make a bar graph showing the probabilities for the eight possible overall outcomes. Keep in mind that in each game they play, the Good Guys' probability of winning is .62.

The Bad Guys are almost as good a team as the Good Guys. For each remaining game, their probability of winning is .6. If you were to make a bar graph showing the probability of each overall outcome, it would not be much different from the graph for the Good Guys.

A fair coin, on the other hand, has a probability of .5 of coming up heads. Suppose you flipped a fair coin seven times and recorded the results. As with the baseball problem, there are eight possible overall outcomes (seven heads and no tails, six heads and one tail, and so on, down to no heads and seven tails).

2. Make a bar graph showing the probabilities for the eight possible overall outcomes for seven flips of a fair coin.

3. Discuss the similarities and differences between your two graphs.

Binomial Probabilities

In the central unit problem, the Good Guys play a series of seven games. For each game, the result is either a win or a loss, and the team's probability of winning is .62.

In a sequence of seven flips of a fair coin, the result of each flip is either heads or tails, and the probability of heads is .5 for each flip.

Although the probabilities are different in the two examples, the situations share two key features.

- There is some "event" with two possible outcomes.
- The event is repeated some number of times, but the probabilities of the two outcomes do not change. That is, the result of one repetition does not influence the results of other repetitions, so each occurrence of the event is *independent* of previous occurrences.

The probabilities associated with such a situation define the **binomial distribution.** Just as there are many variations of the normal distribution, with different means and standard deviations, there are also many variations of the binomial distribution. These variations depend on the probabilities for the two outcomes and the number of times the event is repeated.

1. The Good Guys are thinking about next year. Suppose their outcome for next season follows a binomial distribution. Specifically, assume that as in the unit problem, they have a probability of .62 of winning each time they play a game.

   If their season consists of 162 games, what is the probability that they will win exactly 100 games? Express your answer using a combinatorial coefficient. You do not need to get a numeric value for the probability.

continued ▶

2. Now consider the general case of the binomial distribution. As with the baseball and coin-flip examples, the event in question must have two outcomes. The two outcomes are generically referred to as *success* and *failure,* and each repetition of the event is called a *trial.* For instance, in the central unit problem, the event is a single game, success means winning the game, failure means losing the game, and the part of the Good Guys' season under consideration involves seven trials.

   Suppose the probability of success is p and the event is repeated n times.

   a. What is the probability of failure on each trial?

   b. How many failures will there be if there are r successes?

   c. What is the probability of getting exactly r successes out of the n trials?

Pennant Fever Portfolio

You will now put together your portfolio for *Pennant Fever*. This process has three steps.

* Write a cover letter that summarizes the unit.
* Choose papers to include from your work in the unit.
* Discuss your personal growth during the unit.

Cover Letter

Look back over *Pennant Fever* and describe the central problem of the unit and the key mathematical ideas. Your description should give an overview of how key ideas like combinations, permutations, and Pascal's triangle were developed and how they were used to solve the central problem. Also include ideas that were not directly part of the unit problem, such as the birthday problem and the binomial distribution.

In compiling your portfolio, you will select some activities you think were important in developing the unit's key ideas. Your cover letter should include an explanation of why you selected each item.

continued ▶

Selecting Papers

Your portfolio for *Pennant Fever* should contain these items.

- *Diagrams, Baseball, and Losing 'em All*
- *Which Is Which?*

  Include in your portfolio the activities you discussed as part of this activity.

- *A Pascal Portfolio*
- *"Race for the Pennant!" Revisited*
- *Binomial Probabilities*
- An activity illustrating the use or meaning of the binomial theorem
- A Problem of the Week

  Select one of the POWs you completed in this unit (*Happy Birthday!, Let's Make a Deal, Fair Spoons,* or *And a Fortune, Too!*).

- Other key activities

  Identify two concepts you think were important in this unit. For each concept, choose one or two activities that helped your understanding improve, and explain how the activity helped.

Personal Growth

Your cover letter for *Pennant Fever* should describe how the mathematical ideas were developed in the unit. In addition, write about your personal development during this unit. Also include any thoughts about your experiences that you wish to share with a reader of your portfolio.

SUPPLEMENTAL ACTIVITIES

Probability and counting techniques form the heart of this unit, and many of the supplemental activities continue those themes. Others follow up on ideas from the POWs. Here are some examples.

- *Programming a Deal* and *Simulation Evaluation* build on the activity *Simulate a Deal.*

- *Determining Dunkalot's Druthers* is a basketball probability problem quite similar to the central unit problem.

- *Sleeping In* and *My Dog's Smarter than Yours* are probability problems involving the combinatorial coefficients.

Putting Things Together

In the activity *Possible Outcomes,* you saw that the Good Guys can end up with any of eight possible records for their final seven games—from seven wins and no losses to no wins and seven losses. Similarly, there are eight different possibilities for the Bad Guys' final seven games. You also used this information to find the number of possible combinations of records for the two teams.

Here are some other problems involving finding the number of possibilities by making combinations from different lists.

1. The school cafeteria offers three main dishes (tacos, pasta, and chef's salad), four beverages (milk, iced tea, orange juice, and apple juice), and two desserts (peaches and pineapple). If you choose one main dish, one beverage, and one dessert, how many options do you have for creating your meal?

2. You're planning your weekend. You've decided to go to a movie Friday night, a concert Saturday night, and a sports event Sunday afternoon. There are five good movies showing, four excellent bands performing, and six local teams playing. How many different entertainment plans are available to you?

continued ▶

3. You will be away for 60 days and are planning what clothes to bring with you. For each day, you will need a shirt, a pair of pants, a pair of shoes, and a hat. You don't mind wearing an individual item more than once, but you don't want to wear the exact same outfit on two different days.

   You realize that if you bring one shirt, one pair of pants, one pair of shoes, and 60 hats, you could simply change hats each day to create exactly 60 different outfits, but that doesn't seem very interesting. Besides, all those hats would be pretty bulky!

   a. How many different shirts, pairs of pants, pairs of shoes, and hats should you bring? Find several possibilities that will give you exactly 60 different possible outfits.

   b. Find a combination that will require as few total items as possible.

4. What do Questions 1 to 3 have in common? Formulate some general principles for dealing with situations like this.

Ring the Bells!

After your experience with *Go for the Gold!,* you've decided that television game shows could be lots of fun. You apply and are accepted to be a contestant on *Ring the Bells!* You find out that you must pay a $200 fee to be on the show.

The show involves two buttons that are connected to colored bells and buzzers through a computer that uses a random number generator. Here's how the game works.

You begin by pushing button 1. There is a 40% chance that a green bell will ring, a 20% chance that a yellow bell will ring, and a 40% chance that a red buzzer will ring. If the green bell rings, you go on to button 2. If the red buzzer rings, the game is over and you lose and get no prize. If the yellow bell rings, you get a second try with button 1.

If you push button 1 a second time, the yellow changes from a bell to a buzzer, but the probabilities stay the same. If you get red or yellow (the buzzers), the game is over and you get a consolation prize of $100. If you get the green bell, you go on to button 2.

With button 2, there are only two possible outcomes: the green bell and the red buzzer. You have a 40% chance of getting the green bell and a 60% chance of getting the red buzzer. If you get the bell, you win $1,000. If you get the buzzer, the game is over and you lose and get no prize.

Do you accept the invitation to be on the show? Use both an area model (or sequence of area models) and a tree diagram to explain your decision. And don't forget about the $200 fee!

Programming a Deal

In the activity *Simulate a Deal,* you tested both the "switch" and "stay" strategies by carrying out a simulation. Like many simulations, this one can be accomplished by a calculator or computer program using a random number generator.

Your task now is to write such a program. Here are two options you might consider.

- **One-game-at-a-time program:** In this type of program, the user decides at the start of each game which of the two strategies to test. The program uses a random number generator to decide where the car is and then allows the user to choose the initial door. The game might end with a message like, "You decided to <'switch' or 'stay'> and you ended up with <'a car' or 'a worthless prize'>." With this type of program, the user has to keep track of the results.

- **Many-games-at-a-time program:** In this type of program, the user decides which strategy to test and also states how many games to play. The program then plays that many games one after another, using a random number generator to decide both where the car is and what the player's initial guess is. At the end of the game, the program gives a message like, "You used the <'switch' or 'stay'> strategy <some number> times. You got the car <some number> times and a worthless prize <some number> times."

To write your program, use one of these options or come up with a variation of your own.

Simulation Evaluation

When your class compiled its results from *Simulate a Deal,* you probably concluded that the "switch" strategy was better than the "stay" strategy. But whenever you use a simulation to estimate probabilities, it's a good idea to ask yourself how reliable your estimates are.

If you had no evidence about the strategies, you might take as your null hypothesis that the two strategies are equally good. Under this null hypothesis, you would expect the number of successes for the "switch" strategy to be the same as the number of successes for the "stay" strategy. (That's *not* the same as saying that each strategy has a 50% chance of success.)

Your class data probably did not show the two strategies having the same rate of success. Your task now is to evaluate whether the difference between your class results and the results expected under the null hypothesis just described might be due to sampling fluctuation.

Specifically, answer this question.

> *If the two strategies are actually equally good, what is the probability of getting results as far off from equal for the two strategies as your actual class results?*

Use the chi-square statistic to compare two populations: games played using the "switch" strategy and games played using the "stay" strategy. Treat the overall class results from simulations for each strategy as your sample from that population.

The Chances of Doubles

When you roll a pair of dice, getting a *double* means getting the same result on both dice.

1. Suppose you roll a pair of ordinary dice. Explain why the probability of rolling a double is $\frac{1}{6}$.

Now suppose you roll the pair of dice and then roll the pair again. You have a $\frac{1}{6}$ chance of getting a double the first time. You also have a $\frac{1}{6}$ chance of getting a double the second time. So it might seem reasonable that the probability of getting a double on at least one of the rolls would be $\frac{1}{6} + \frac{1}{6}$.

By that reasoning, if you rolled the pair of dice three times, your probability of getting a double on at least one of the rolls would be $\frac{1}{6} + \frac{1}{6} + \frac{1}{6}$. And if you rolled the pair six times, the probability would be $\frac{1}{6} + \frac{1}{6} + \frac{1}{6} + \frac{1}{6} + \frac{1}{6} + \frac{1}{6}$, which equals 1.

In other words, by this reasoning, you would be certain of getting a double on at least one of the six rolls—which is definitely not true.

2. a. Explain why the probability of getting a double on at least one of two rolls of the pair of dice is not simply $\frac{1}{6} + \frac{1}{6}$.

   b. Find the correct probability of getting a double on at least one of two rolls of the pair of dice.

3. What is the probability of rolling a double at least once if you roll the pair of dice three times? If you roll four times? If you roll n times?

Determining Dunkalot's Druthers

Tyler Dunkalot's team has tied with another team for the basketball league's championship. He and the other team's captain have to choose between two options for determining the champion.

- **Option 1:** A three-game series between the two teams, in which the first team to win two games is the champion
- **Option 2:** A five-game series between the two teams, in which the first team to win three games is the champion

Tyler estimates that in each game the teams play, his team has a probability of .55 of winning. His team has been getting better over the season, and the other team has stayed pretty much the same.

Which of the two methods for choosing the champion—two out of three or three out of five—would you advise Tyler to support?

Sleeping In

Cynthia's school has eight class periods, which follow this schedule.

1st period:	8:00–8:50
2nd period:	9:00–9:50
3rd period:	10:00–10:50
4th period:	11:00–11:50
5th period:	12:00–12:50
6th period:	1:00–1:50
7th period:	2:00–2:50
8th period:	3:00–3:50

Each student takes five courses and has three free periods. The free periods are assigned randomly, and students do not need to report to school until the period when their first course meets

Cynthia does not think she should be expected to be coherent at 8:00 a.m. Even 9:00 a.m. is a bit early for her to think clearly. She wonders what her chances are of being able to sleep late.

1. What is the probability that Cynthia will have the first period free?

2. What is the probability that Cynthia will have the first two periods free?

3. What is the probability that Cynthia will get her dream schedule and have the first three periods free?

Twelve Bags of Gold Revisited

If you did the *Twelve Bags of Gold* POW in Year 1, perhaps you can now improve on your previous work. Maybe you can give a clearer explanation or a simpler solution. Here's the original problem.

The king has 12 bags of gold. Each of his 12 bags holds exactly the same amount of gold as each of the others, and they all weigh the same. Except . . .

Rumor has it that one of his 12 trusted caretakers is not so trustworthy. Someone is making counterfeit gold. So the king sends his assistants to find the counterfeiter. They do find her, but she won't tell them who has the counterfeit gold that she made.

All the assistants learn from her is that one of the 12 bags contains counterfeit gold and that this bag's weight is different from the others. She refuses to reveal whether the different bag is heavier or lighter.

So the king needs to know two things.

- Which bag weighs a different amount from the rest?
- Is that bag heavier or lighter?

And, of course, he wants the answer found economically. He still has the old balance scale. He wants the solution in two weighings, but his court mathematician says it will take three weighings. No one else sees how it can be done in so few weighings. Can you figure it out?

Find a way to determine which bag is counterfeit and whether it weighs more or less than the others. Do so using the balance scale only three times.

My Dog's Smarter than Yours

Emiko claims her dog is very smart. When she opens the door in the morning, he runs out and brings in the newspaper.

You don't think that sounds very unusual? Well, Emiko lives in an apartment building. There are five newspapers outside every morning, and only one is a Japanese-language newspaper. That's the one that's delivered for Emiko's family.

Now, Emiko doesn't claim that her dog always brings in the right newspaper, but she says he does so more often than would happen if he were choosing randomly. Emiko's brother Hiro is skeptical. His hypothesis—the null hypothesis—is that the dog is simply picking papers at random.

Emiko and Hiro have devised a test. They will observe the dog for five straight days. Hiro says that if the dog brings in the right paper three or more times out of five, he'll reject his null hypothesis.

Suppose Hiro's null hypothesis is actually correct. What is the probability that he will end up rejecting it?

Defining Pascal

One way to define Pascal's triangle is by stating how each row is formed from the previous row. For example, the number 15 in the box here is the sum of the entries 5 and 10 just above it. In general, each entry in a new row can be found by adding the two closest entries in the previous row.

```
                1
              1   1
            1   2   1
          1   3   3   1
        1   4   6   4   1
      1   5  10  10   5   1
    1   6  [15]  20  15   6   1
```

Another approach is to define Pascal's triangle in terms of the combinatorial coefficients. To do this, label the top row of Pascal's triangle as "row 0," the next row as "row 1," and so on. Similarly, label the entry at the left of any row as "entry 0," the next entry as "entry 1," and so on. For example, the boxed number 15 is entry 2 of row 6.

Using this system, we can define Pascal's triangle by this statement.

Entry r of row n of Pascal's triangle is the combinatorial coefficient $\binom{n}{r}$.

For example, entry 2 of row 6 should be $\binom{6}{2}$. Sure enough, $\binom{6}{2} = 15$. The entries 5 and 10 that add to give the entry 15 are the combinatorial coefficients $\binom{5}{1}$ and $\binom{5}{2}$.

It's important that these two ways of defining Pascal's triangle give the same result. In this activity, you will explore the relationship between the two definitions.

continued

1. Applying both definitions to this particular case of the entries 15, 5, and 10 gives this equation

$$\binom{6}{2} = \binom{5}{1} + \binom{5}{2}$$

You can verify numerically that $15 = 5 + 10$, but your task here is to explain this equation in terms of the meaning of combinatorial coefficients.

For example, why should the number of possible two-scoop bowls of ice cream, chosen from among six flavors, be the same as the sum of the number of one-scoop bowls chosen from among five flavors and the number of two-scoop bowls chosen from among five flavors?

2. Write a generalization of the equation displayed in Question 1. That is, write a general equation expressing the pattern for extending Pascal's triangle in terms of combinatorial coefficients.

3. Explain why your equation in Question 2 must be true for all values of n and r. Base your explanation on the meaning of $\binom{n}{r}$ as the number of ways to select r objects from a set of n objects.

Maximum in the Middle

One of the reasons for the interest in Pascal's triangle is that combinatorial coefficients play an important role in many probability problems.

For example, the combinatorial coefficient $\binom{6}{2}$, which is the number shown as $\boxed{15}$ below, gives the number of ways to flip a coin six times and get exactly two heads.

$$
\begin{array}{ccccccccccccc}
 & & & & & & 1 & & & & & & \\
 & & & & & 1 & & 1 & & & & & \\
 & & & & 1 & & 2 & & 1 & & & & \\
 & & & 1 & & 3 & & 3 & & 1 & & & \\
 & & 1 & & 4 & & 6 & & 4 & & 1 & & \\
 & 1 & & 5 & & 10 & & 10 & & 5 & & 1 & \\
1 & & 6 & & \boxed{15} & & 20 & & 15 & & 6 & & 1
\end{array}
$$

If a coin is flipped six times, it makes sense that the most likely number of heads to get is three. This matches the fact that the greatest entry in the last row shown here for Pascal's triangle is 20. This entry corresponds to the combinatorial coefficient $\binom{6}{3}$. Remember that values for $\binom{n}{r}$ appear in what is actually the $(n + 1)$th row of Pascal's triangle, although we refer to this as "row n."

1. First consider the case in which n is even, so n is twice some other integer m. Prove that among all choices for r, the largest value of $\binom{2m}{r}$ occurs when r is equal to m. Base your proof on the formula for combinatorial coefficients.

2. State and prove a similar result for the case in which n is odd. You might begin by writing n as $2t + 1$ for some integer t.

The Whys of Binomial Expansion

You have expanded various expressions of the form $(a + b)^n$ and seen that the coefficients turn out to be combinatorial coefficients. In fact, this is true for every positive integer value of n. This principle is called the **binomial theorem.**

Your goal now is to find out why combinatorial coefficients appear in these expansions.

1. Use the distributive property to expand this expression.

$$(a_1 + b_1)(a_2 + b_2)(a_3 + b_3)(a_4 + b_4)$$

2. Each term in the expansion from Question 1 is a product of terms with some a's and some b's (or all a's or all b's). For instance, one of the terms is $a_1 b_2 b_3 a_4$, which has two factors that are a's and two factors that are b's.

   a. Altogether, how many terms in your expansion have two a's and two b's?

   b. What are the values of n and r for the combinatorial coefficient that best represents your answer from part a? Explain your answer.

3. Use your work from Questions 1 and 2 to write a general explanation of the fact that the coefficients of $(a + b)^n$ are combinatorial coefficients.

The Binomial Theorem and Row Sums

You have seen that the coefficients in the expansion of $(a + b)^n$ are the combinatorial coefficients that form row n of Pascal's triangle. This principle is called the *binomial theorem*.

In Pascal's triangle, the sum of the entries in row n is 2^n, as illustrated below. How can you prove this property using the binomial theorem? To begin, think about what can you substitute for a and b to make the expansion of $(a + b)^n$ equal to the sum of the entries from row n of Pascal's triangle.

$$
\begin{aligned}
1 &= 1 \\
1 + 1 &= 2 \\
1 + 2 + 1 &= 4 \\
1 + 3 + 3 + 1 &= 8 \\
1 + 4 + 6 + 4 + 1 &= 16
\end{aligned}
$$

High Dive

Circular Functions and the Physics of Falling Objects

High Dive—Circular Functions and the Physics of Falling Objects

Going to the Circus

The central problem of this unit involves a circus act. In the act, a diver falls from a turning Ferris wheel into a tub of water carried by a moving cart. To solve the problem—which involves various kinds of motion—you will need to learn quite a bit of new mathematics.

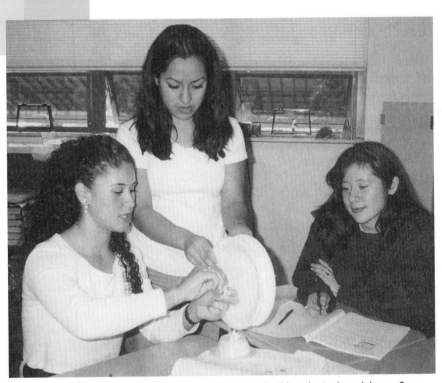

Maribel DeLoa, Vivian Barajas, and Caroline Moo build a physical model as a first step toward solving the unit problem.

The Circus Act

You may have seen or heard about a circus act in which someone dives off a high platform into a small tub of water. The Interactive Circus Troupe has come up with an exciting new variation on this act.

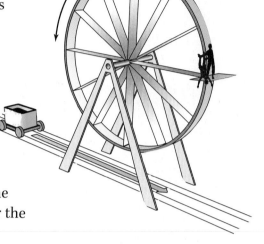

They have attached the diver's platform to one of the pivoting seats on a Ferris wheel so that the platform stays parallel to the ground. The platform sticks out, perpendicular to the plane of the Ferris wheel. The tub of water is on a moving cart that runs along a track, in the plane of the Ferris wheel, and passes under the end of the platform.

As the Ferris wheel turns, an assistant holds the diver by the ankles. The assistant must let go at exactly the right moment, so that the diver will land in the moving tub of water.

If you were the diver, would you want to trust your assistant's on-the-spot judgment? A slight error and you could go "Splat!" instead of "Splash!"

Your Task

The diver has insisted that the circus owners hire your group to advise the assistant. You need to figure out exactly when the assistant should let go. Your analysis will be tested on a dummy before it is used with an actual human being.

1. Make a physical model of the problem, using materials that your teacher provides.

2. Specify any other information you need to know about the circus act to determine when the assistant should let go.

continued ▶

Historical note: The first Ferris wheel was created for the 1893 Chicago World's Fair and was the brainchild of George Washington Gale Ferris. This creation was much larger than most Ferris wheels of today. It stood 265 feet high and was 250 feet in diameter. It carried 36 cars, each of which could hold 60 people. A single revolution took about 20 minutes. Admission was 50¢, ten times the cost of any other ride at the fair. The Ferris wheel was dismantled after the fair and made brief appearances at other major events before being sold for scrap metal in 1906.

The Tower of Hanoi

○ The Legend of the Golden Discs

Buddhism, one of the world's major religions, has roots in India and is practiced by over 300 million people throughout the world. An ancient legend describes an important task once given to a group of Buddhist monks.

According to the legend, a Buddhist temple contained 64 golden discs piled one on top of another. Each successive disc was slightly smaller than the one below it. This pile of discs sat upon a golden tray. Two empty golden trays lay next to this tray.

The monks' task was to move the pile of 64 discs from its original tray to one of the other trays. To do so, they had to follow certain rules. The monks could move only one disc at a time, taking it off the top of a pile and placing it either on an empty tray or on top of an existing pile on one of the trays. Moreover, a disc placed on top of an existing pile could not be larger than the disc below it.

The legend concludes with the promise that when the monks finish this task, the world will be filled with peace and harmony. As you will realize, the monks could not possibly have finished the task. (How unfortunate for the world!)

continued

○ *The Puzzle*

A famous mathematical puzzle, known as the Tower of Hanoi, is based on this legend. (Hanoi is the capital of Vietnam, which is in Southeast Asia. Many people in Vietnam are Buddhists.) The puzzle consists of three pegs and a set of discs of different sizes, as shown in the diagram.

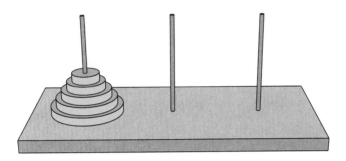

The discs have holes in their centers. To begin with, the discs are all placed over the peg at the left, with the largest disc on the bottom and with the discs decreasing in size as they go up. (This diagram shows only 5 discs instead of 64.)

The task in this puzzle is to transfer all 5 of the discs to the peg on the right. As in the legend, the discs must be moved according to certain rules.

- Only one disc can be moved at a time.
- The disc being moved must be the top disc on its peg.
- The disc being moved must be placed either on an empty peg or on top of a larger disc on a different peg.

○ *Getting Started*

Your POW is to answer this question.

If the monks move one disc every second, how long will it take them to complete their task?

Start your investigation of this question with just two or three discs. Work your way up, finding the *least number* of moves required to transfer the pile of discs from the peg on the left to the peg on the right.

continued ▶

As you work, consider these questions. The notation a_n represents the number of moves required to move n discs from the peg on the left to the peg on the right.

- If you know how many moves are needed to move 20 discs, how can you find the number of moves needed to move 21 discs? Can you generalize this process into a formula? That is, if you know a_n, how can you find a_{n+1}? Can you explain why this formula holds true?

- Look for a formula that gives a_n directly in terms of n. Test your formula with specific cases. If you knew that this formula worked for $n = 20$, could you prove that it worked for $n = 21$? Can you prove the formula in general?

When you have answered these questions as best you can, return to the question about the monks and their 64 discs.

○ *Write-up*

1. *Process*

2. *Results:* Give the results of your investigation, including these details.

   - The number of moves required for any specific cases you studied

   - The amount of time required for the monks to move the 64 discs

   - Any general formulas or procedures that you found, even if you aren't sure of them

3. *Solutions:* Explain your results, including how you know that the number of moves for each number of discs is the least possible. Also give any explanations you found for your generalizations.

4. *Self-assessment*

The Ferris Wheel

Al and Betty are at the amusement park to ride on a Ferris wheel. This wheel has a radius of 15 feet, and its center is 20 feet above ground level.

You can describe various positions in the cycle of a Ferris wheel in terms of the face of a clock, as indicated in the diagram. For example, the highest point in the wheel's cycle is the 12 o'clock position, and the point farthest to the right is the 3 o'clock position.

For simplicity, think of Al and Betty's location as they ride as simply a point on the circumference of the wheel's circular path. That is, ignore the size of the Ferris wheel seats, the heights of Al and Betty, and so on.

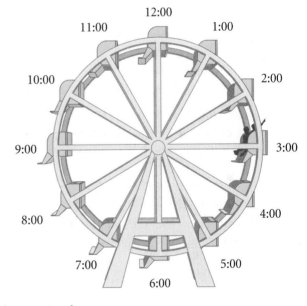

1. How far off the ground are Al and Betty when they are at each of these positions?

   a. The 3 o'clock position

   b. The 12 o'clock position

   c. The 9 o'clock position

   d. The 6 o'clock position

2. How far off the ground are Al and Betty when they are at the 2 o'clock position? (*Caution*: Their height at the 2 o'clock position is not a third of the way between their height at the 3 o'clock position and their height at the 12 o'clock position.)

3. Pick two other clock positions. Figure out how far off the ground Al and Betty are when they reach each of those positions.

As the Ferris Wheel Turns

To understand what happens when a diver is released from a moving Ferris wheel, you need precise information about the position of the diving platform as the Ferris wheel turns.

In this activity, you will look only at the *height* of the platform. Later, you will consider how far the platform is to the left or right of the center of the wheel.

You will need this information about the Ferris wheel.

- The radius of the Ferris wheel is 50 feet.

- The wheel turns at a constant speed, makes a complete turn every 40 seconds, and moves counterclockwise.

- The center of the wheel is 65 feet off the ground.

Use these facts throughout the unit, unless a problem specifically gives different information. *Reminder:* The circumference of a circle can be found from its radius using the formula $C = 2\pi r$.

1. At what speed is the platform moving (in feet per second) as it goes around on the Ferris wheel?

2. The rate at which an object turns is called *angular speed*, because it measures how fast an angle is changing. Angular speed does not depend on the radius. Through what angle (in degrees) does the Ferris wheel turn each second?

continued ▶

3. How many seconds does it take for the platform to go each of these distances?

   a. From the 3 o'clock to the 11 o'clock position

   b. From the 3 o'clock to the 7 o'clock position

   c. From the 3 o'clock to the 4 o'clock position

4. What is the platform's height off the ground at each of these times?

   a. 1 second after passing the 3 o'clock position

   b. 6 seconds after passing the 3 o'clock position

   c. 10 seconds after passing the 3 o'clock position

   d. 14 seconds after passing the 3 o'clock position

   e. 23 seconds after passing the 3 o'clock position

   f. 49 seconds after passing the 3 o'clock position

The Height and the Sine

You've seen that trigonometric functions can be helpful in describing where the platform is as it travels around on the Ferris wheel. But the basic right-triangle definitions of these functions work only for acute angles.

In the next several activities, you'll explore how to extend the definition of the sine function to arbitrary angles. You will also investigate how to use this extended definition to get a general formula for the platform's height.

Jason Weinstock presents the formula his group developed to express Al and Betty's height off the ground as the Ferris wheel turns.

At Certain Points in Time

In *As the Ferris Wheel Turns,* you found the height of the platform after it had turned for specific amounts of time. You probably saw that this is easiest when the platform is in the first quadrant.

Now you will generalize your work for the case of the first quadrant. The basic facts about the Ferris wheel are the same as in *As the Ferris Wheel Turns.* In particular, the period is 40 seconds, so the platform remains in the first quadrant for the first 10 seconds.

1. Suppose the Ferris wheel has been turning for t seconds, with $0 < t < 10$. Represent the platform's height off the ground as h, and find a formula for h in terms of t.

2. Verify your formula, which is for the first quadrant, using your results from Questions 4a ($t = 1$) and 4b ($t = 6$) of *As the Ferris Wheel Turns.*

A Clear View

As you may remember, the Ferris wheel at the amusement park where Al and Betty like to ride has a radius of 15 feet, and its center is 20 feet above ground level. This is not the same Ferris wheel as the one at the circus.

The park's Ferris wheel turns with a constant angular speed. It takes 24 seconds for a complete turn.

The fence around the amusement park is 13 feet high. Once Al and Betty get above the fence, there is a wonderful view.

1. During one revolution, what percentage of the time are Al and Betty above the height of the fence?

2. How would your answer to Question 1 change if the period were other than 24 seconds?

Extending the Sine

If the Ferris wheel at the circus turns counterclockwise at a constant angular speed of 9 degrees per second and the platform passes the 3 o'clock position at $t = 0$, then the platform will remain in the first quadrant through $t = 10$.

During this time interval, the platform's height above the ground is given by the formula

$$h = 65 + 50 \sin (9t)$$

However, the right-triangle definition of the sine function makes sense only for acute angles. To make this formula work for all values of t, we need to extend the definition of the sine function to include all angles.

The Coordinate Setting

The context of the Ferris wheel could be used to develop this extended definition. However, the standard approach uses a more abstract setting that makes it easier to apply the definition to other situations.

The angle θ is placed within a coordinate system, with its vertex at the origin. The angle is measured counterclockwise from the positive direction of the x-axis. The goal is to express $\sin \theta$ in terms of the x- and y-coordinates of a point on the ray defining the angle, such as point A in the first diagram. A is assumed to be different from the origin.

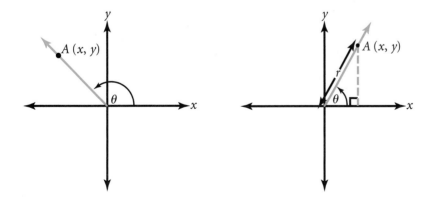

continued ▶

When θ is an acute angle, we get a diagram like the second one. It's helpful to introduce the letter r to represent the distance from A to the origin. This distance is also the length of the hypotenuse of the right triangle.

Based on the right-triangle definition of the sine function, we get

$$\sin \theta = \frac{y}{r}$$

Mathematicians use this equation to extend the definition of the sine function to arbitrary angles. That is, they define $\sin \theta$ as the ratio $\frac{y}{r}$ for *any* angle θ. (This automatically means that the new definition agrees with the old one for acute angles.)

The Ferris Wheel Analogy

You can think of A as a point on the circular path of the Ferris wheel, as shown in this diagram. In this context, r corresponds to the radius of the Ferris wheel, and y corresponds to the platform's height *relative to the center of the Ferris wheel.*

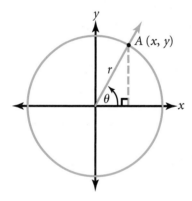

Testing the Definition

You've seen that the sine function can be extended to all angles using the *xy*-coordinate system. The big question is this.

> *If you use this coordinate definition of the sine function, does the platform-height formula work for all angles?*

In this activity, you will investigate that question.

1. If the platform has been turning for 25 seconds, it has moved through an angle of 225° and is in the third quadrant of its cycle.

    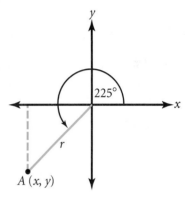

    a. Use a diagram like the one shown here to find the value of sin 225° based on the coordinate definition of the sine function. First choose a specific value for *r*. Then find the value of *y* using the right triangle.

    b. Substitute your answer from part a into the expression 65 + 50 sin 225°.

    c. Explain why your answer to part b is reasonable for the position of the platform after 25 seconds.

    d. Verify that your calculator gives the same value for sin 225° that you found in part a.

2. Go through a sequence of steps like those in Question 1 using the value $t = 32$, which places the platform in the fourth quadrant. You will first need to find the actual height of the platform for $t = 32$.

Graphing the Ferris Wheel

1. Plot individual points to create a graph showing the platform's height, *h*, as a function of the time elapsed, *t*. Explain how you get the value for *h* for each point you plot. Your graph should show the first 80 seconds of the Ferris wheel's movement. Use the basic information about the Ferris wheel from *As the Ferris Wheel Turns*.

2. Describe how this graph would change if you made each of the adjustments described in parts a to c of this question. Treat each part separately, changing only the item mentioned and keeping the rest of the information as in Question 1.

   a. How would the graph change if the radius of the Ferris wheel were smaller?

   b. How would the graph change if the Ferris wheel were turning faster—that is, if the period were shorter?

   c. How would the graph change if you measured height with respect to the center of the Ferris wheel instead of with respect to the ground? For example, if the platform were 40 feet above the ground, you would treat this as a height of −25 feet, because 40 feet above the ground is 25 feet below the center of the wheel.

Ferris Wheel Graph Variations

In Question 1 of *Graphing the Ferris Wheel*, you made a graph showing how the height of the platform depends on the time that has elapsed since the wheel began moving. That graph was based on the "standard" Ferris wheel, which has a radius of 50 feet, a period of 40 seconds, and a center that is 65 feet off the ground. The diagram shows two periods of that graph.

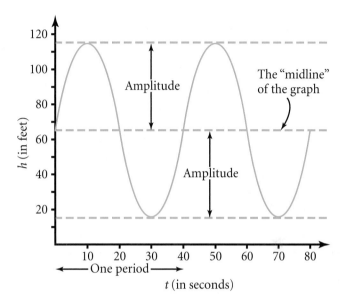

The dashed line at $h = 65$ shows the "midline" of the graph. The graph is as much above this line as it is below. The other dashed lines, at $h = 115$ and $h = 15$, show the maximum and minimum heights of the graph. The distance from the midline to the maximum or minimum is called the **amplitude** of the graph. The amplitude of this graph is 50.

In Question 2 of *Graphing the Ferris Wheel*, you described how the graph would change if you made certain adjustments to the Ferris wheel. In this activity, you will look at those changes in more detail.

Treat each question as a separate problem, changing only the item mentioned and keeping the rest of the information as in the standard Ferris wheel. Use the same scale for all your graphs, to make visual comparisons easier.

1. a. Pick a new value, less than 50 feet, for the radius, and draw the graph.

    b. Give an equation for your new graph, expressing h (the height of the platform, in feet) in terms of t (the time elapsed, in seconds).

    c. Pick a value for t, and verify that your equation from part b gives the value you used in your graph for that value of t.

continued ▶

2. a. Pick a new value, less than 40 seconds, for the period, and draw the graph.

   b. Give an equation for your new graph, expressing h in terms of t.

   c. Pick a value for t, and verify that your equation from part b gives the value you used in your graph for that value of t.

3. Suppose the Ferris wheel is set up inside a large hole so that its center is exactly level with the ground.

   a. Draw the graph based on this change.

   b. Give an equation for your new graph, expressing h in terms of t.

   c. Pick a specific value for t, and verify that your equation from part b gives the value you used in your graph for that value of t.

The "Plain" Sine Graph

The height of the Ferris wheel platform is given by a formula that involves the sine function. In previous activities, you've graphed this height function and examined how the graph changes as details of the Ferris wheel are changed.

Now you'll look at the graph of the "plain" sine function—outside of the context of the Ferris wheel.

1. Draw the graph of the function defined by the equation $z = \sin \theta$ for values of θ from $-360°$ to $720°$. (*Note:* To avoid confusion with x- and y-coordinates or the idea that t represents time and h represents height on the Ferris wheel, we are introducing new variables here.)

2. What is the amplitude of this function?

3. What is the period of this function? Why is the sine function periodic?

4. What are the θ-intercepts of the graph?

5. What values of θ make $\sin \theta$ a maximum? What values of θ make $\sin \theta$ a minimum?

6. Suppose the equation $h = \sin t$ describes the platform-height function for some Ferris wheel. What are the specifications of that Ferris wheel? That is, what are its radius, its period, and the height of its center? Indicate any ways in which this wheel differs from the standard Ferris wheel described in *As the Ferris Wheel Turns*.

Sand Castles

Oceana loves to build elaborate sand castles. Her problem is that her castles take a long time to build and often get swept away by the incoming tide.

Oceana is planning a trip to the beach next week. She decides to pay attention to the tides so that she can plan her castle building and have as much time as possible.

The beach slopes up gradually from the ocean toward the parking lot. Oceana considers the waterline to be "high" if the water comes farther up the beach, leaving less sandy area visible. She considers the waterline to be "low" if there is more sandy area visible. Oceana likes to position herself as close to the water as possible because damp sand is better for building.

According to Oceana's analysis, the water level on the beach for the day of her trip will fit this equation.

$$w(t) = 20 \sin (29t)$$

In this equation, $w(t)$ represents how far the waterline is above or below its average position. The distance is measured in feet, and t represents the number of hours elapsed since midnight.

continued ▶

In the case shown in the diagram, the waterline is above its average position, and $w(t)$ is positive.

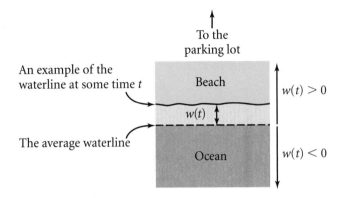

1. Graph the waterline function for a 24-hour period.

2. a. What is the highest position up the beach (compared to its average position) that the waterline will be during the day? (This is called *high tide*.)

   b. What is the lowest position that the waterline will be during the day? (This is called *low tide*.)

3. Suppose Oceana plans to build her castle right on the average waterline just as the water has moved below that line. How much time will she have to build before the water returns and destroys her work?

4. Suppose Oceana wants to build 10 feet below the average waterline. What is the maximum amount of time she can have for making her castle?

5. Suppose Oceana decides she needs only two hours to build and admire her castle. What is the lowest position on the beach where she can build?

Paving Patterns

Al and Betty are helping Al's family lay paving stones for
a path along the side of their house. The path will be exactly
2 feet wide. Each paving stone is rectangular, with dimensions
1 foot by 2 feet.

You might think this would be easy: simply lay one stone after
another across the path. But there is more than one way to place
the stones.

For example, a section of the path 3 feet long could use any of these
three arrangements. *Important:* These arrangements are all considered
different, even though the first two are very much alike.

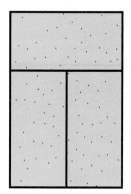 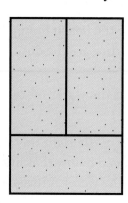 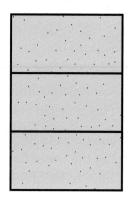

Al and Betty want to know how many different ways there are to lay
out the stones. The path is 20 feet long.

Al and Betty start to analyze the situation by using 1-inch-by-2-inch
plastic tiles set inside a 2-inch-by-20-inch rectangle, but they are soon
overwhelmed by all the possibilities.

Can you help? You might want to start with shorter paths and look
for patterns in the number of cases.

You do not need to show the patterns themselves, except to
explain your thinking. Instead, focus on *how many* patterns
there are for a path of a given length.

continued

○ *Write-up*

1. *Problem statement*

2. *Process*

3. *Results*

   - Give the numeric results for any specific cases you studied.
   - Give any general formulas you found, even if you aren't sure of them.
   - Give any explanations you found for your formulas.

4. *Self-assessment*

More Beach Adventures

1. After spending the day building sand castles, Oceana wants to take an evening walk with a friend along the shoreline.

   Oceana knows that one stretch along the shore is quite rocky. At that point, the rocks jut into the ocean. To walk around them, a person has to follow a path that is 14 feet below the average waterline.

   If Oceana and her friend don't want to get wet, they need to take their walk when the waterline is 14 feet or more below the average waterline. What is the time period during which they can take their walk?

   Remember that the position of the waterline over the course of the day is given by the equation $w(t) = 20 \sin (29t)$, where the distance is measured in feet and t represents the number of hours elapsed since midnight.

2. While she builds sand castles, Oceana likes to amuse herself by looking for numbers that have a sine of a given value. Here are four problems she thought about recently. In parts a and b, find exact values for θ. In parts c and d, give θ to the nearest degree. Your solutions should be between $-360°$ and $360°$.

   a. Find three values of θ, other than $15°$, such that $\sin \theta = \sin 15°$.

   b. Find three values of θ such that $\sin \theta = -\sin 60°$.

   c. Find three values of θ such that $\sin \theta = 0.5$.

   d. Find three values of θ such that $\sin \theta = -0.71$.

Falling, Falling, Falling

The diver on the Ferris wheel doesn't simply go round and round. At some point, the assistant lets go and the diver begins his fall.

How long will the diver be in the air? You'll have to learn some principles of physics to answer this question. The question is complicated by the fact that the diver does not fall at a constant speed.

Stephanie Lin records a formula for the height of an object falling from rest.

Distance with Changing Speed

1. Curt is traveling home from college to visit his family. He drives from 1 p.m. to 3 p.m. at an average speed of 50 miles per hour. Then he drives from 3 p.m. to 6 p.m. at an average speed of 60 miles per hour.

   a. Draw a graph showing Curt's speed as a function of time for the entire period from 1 p.m. to 6 p.m. Treat his speed as constant for each of the two time periods—from 1 p.m. to 3 p.m. and from 3 p.m. to 6 p.m.

   b. Describe how to use areas in your graph to represent the total distance Curt travels.

2. A triathlete is running at a steady speed of 20 feet per second. At exactly noon, she starts to increase her speed. Her speed increases at a constant rate so that 20 seconds later, she is going 30 feet per second.

   a. Graph the runner's speed as a function of time for this 20-second interval.

   b. Calculate the runner's average speed for this 20-second interval.

   c. Explain how to use area to find the total distance she runs during this 20-second interval.

Acceleration Variations and a Sine Summary

Part I: Acceleration Variations

In Question 2 of *Distance with Changing Speed,* you considered the case of a person running with constant acceleration. In other words, the runner's speed was increasing at a constant rate.

In that question, the runner's speed went from 20 feet per second to 30 feet per second over a 20-second time interval. The graph shows the runner's speed as a function of time.

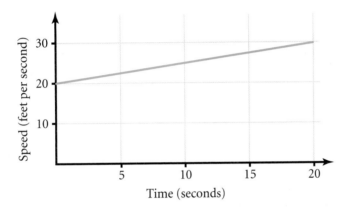

That question illustrates an important principle.

> If an object is traveling with constant acceleration, then its average speed over any time interval is the average of its beginning speed and its final speed during that time interval.

According to this principle, the runner's average speed for the 20-second interval was exactly 25 feet per second, which is the average of 20 feet per second (the beginning speed) and 30 feet per second (the final speed).

Your first task in this activity is to describe three variations on this situation. In each case, the runner's speed should increase, as before, from 20 feet per second to 30 feet per second over the same 20-second time interval. But in your examples, *the runner's acceleration should not be constant.*

continued

For each example, graph the runner's speed in terms of time.

- Give an example in which the runner's average speed is *more than* the average of her beginning speed and her final speed.

- Give an example in which the runner's average speed is *less than* the average of her beginning speed and her final speed.

- Give an example in which the runner's average speed is *equal to* the average of her beginning speed and her final speed. Remember that even with this example, her acceleration should not be constant.

Part II: A Sine Summary

The idea of extending the sine function to all angles—not merely acute angles—is an important concept. Your task now is to reflect on your work with the sine function. Include these things in your written work.

- A summary of what you have learned so far about this idea

- Any questions you still have about this extended sine function

- An explanation of how the extension of the sine function helps with the solution of the unit problem

Free Fall

Since the beginning of time, objects have fallen. But it wasn't until the sixteenth and seventeenth centuries that scientists understood the physics and mathematics of falling objects.

The Italian physicist Galileo Galilei (1564–1642) is one of those credited with figuring out the laws of gravitational fall based on experiments. The English physicist Isaac Newton (1642–1727) developed a broader theory of gravitation to explain Galileo's observations.

Free-Falling Objects

Using experiments and theoretical analysis, physicists have confirmed this principle.

> Falling objects have constant acceleration.

This principle assumes there is no air resistance or other complicating factors to interfere with an object's fall. That is, the principle describes the behavior of *free-falling* objects. In this unit, assume that unless you are told otherwise, falling objects are falling freely.

This broad principle of free-falling objects can be stated more precisely.

> The instantaneous speed of a freely falling object increases approximately 32 feet per second for each second of the object's fall.

Starting from Rest

The simplest case of a free-falling object is when an object starts from rest—that is, when its speed is zero at $t = 0$. In this case, the object's instantaneous speed after 1 second is 32 feet per second; after 2 seconds, its instantaneous speed is 64 feet per second; and so on.

continued

From Acceleration to Distance

Your task is to use the principles just stated to express the distance an object falls in terms of the amount of time it has been falling. Assume the object is dropped from rest and falls freely.

1. a. How fast is the object going at $t = 5$?

   b. How far does the object fall in the first 5 seconds?

2. Generalize your work from Question 1 to develop a formula for how far the object falls in the first t seconds.

3. Suppose the object starts falling from a height of h feet. What is its height after t seconds? Assume the object has not yet reached the ground.

4. Use your result from Question 3 to find an expression, in terms of h, for the amount of time it would take for the object to reach the ground.

Now apply your work to a simple version of the circus act.

5. Suppose the platform is fixed at 90 feet above the ground, the diver falls freely from rest, and the water level in the tub is 8 feet above the ground. How long will it take the diver to reach the water?

Not So Spectacular

The circus owner decides that to save money, he will fill in for the Ferris wheel diver from time to time.

This isn't actually a very good idea. The owner is not an experienced diver, so he can't safely fall great distances. In fact, he refuses to be dropped from more than 25 feet above the ground. He also insists there be a huge tub of water under him at all times.

Your task is to find all possible times when the owner will be 25 feet from the ground. You may want to describe the complete set of possibilities by writing an algebraic expression for *t*.

Here are the basic facts about the Ferris wheel.

- The radius is 50 feet.
- The center of the wheel is 65 feet off the ground.
- The wheel turns counterclockwise at a constant angular speed, with a period of 40 seconds.
- The platform is at the 3 o'clock position when the Ferris wheel starts moving.

A Practice Jump

After some not-so-high practice dives by the circus owner, the circus performers decide to do a practice run of the show with the diver himself. But they decide to set it up so that they will not have to worry about a moving cart.

Instead, the cart containing the tub of water is placed directly under the Ferris wheel's 11 o'clock position. As usual, the platform passes the 3 o'clock position at $t = 0$.

1. How many seconds will it take for the platform to reach the 11 o'clock position?

2. What is the diver's height off the ground when he is at the 11 o'clock position?

One purpose of this practice run is to find how long it will take for the diver to fall into the water. You should be able to predict this, based on the formula that an object falling freely from rest takes $\sqrt{\frac{h}{16}}$ seconds to fall h feet. Assume the diver is falling freely from rest.

3. How long will it take from the time the diver is released until he hits the water? Don't forget that the water level in the cart is 8 feet above the ground.

4. More generally, suppose the assistant lets go W seconds after the Ferris wheel starts turning. Here, W stands for "wheel time." Assuming the cart is in the right place, how long will the diver be in the air before he hits the water?

Moving Left and Right

Up to this point, you have mostly been considering the platform's position and the diver's motion in the vertical dimension. But as the Ferris wheel turns, the platform is also moving to the left or right, and the cart is moving steadily to the right (once it gets started).

The key to a successful dive is having the cart at the right place at the right time. It's now time for you to consider the horizontal dimension of the Ferris wheel problem.

Kevin Brandt and Jordyn Vincelet discuss the fact that the turning Ferris wheel also involves horizontal movement of the diver's platform.

Cart Travel Time

So far in the unit, you've focused mainly on the position and motion of the diver. Where's the cart of water in all this?

The cart starts moving when the Ferris wheel passes the 3 o'clock position. The goal is for the cart to be in the correct position when the diver reaches the level of the water in the cart. In this activity, you will consider only the cart's *travel time*.

Suppose the assistant lets go of the diver W seconds after the Ferris wheel passes the 3 o'clock position. Write an expression in terms of W for the length of time the cart will have traveled from the moment it starts until the moment the diver reaches the level of the water.

Where Does He Land?

Earlier in the unit, you found that the expression $65 + 50 \sin(9t)$ gives the diver's height off the ground while he is still on the platform. But what about the diver's *horizontal* position? This will be crucial in determining whether he lands in the tub of water on the moving cart.

To describe the diver's horizontal position, you will use a horizontal coordinate system, as shown here. In this coordinate system, an object's x-coordinate is based on its distance (in feet) to the right or left of the center of the Ferris wheel, with objects to the right of the center having positive x-coordinates.

For instance, the platform and diver have an x-coordinate of 50 when the platform passes the 3 o'clock position. The cart starts its motion with an x-coordinate of -240, because it is initially 240 feet to the left of the center of the Ferris wheel's base.

As usual, make these assumptions: The platform passes the 3 o'clock position at $t = 0$. The wheel turns counterclockwise at a constant rate, with a period of 40 seconds. The diver falls straight down once he is released.

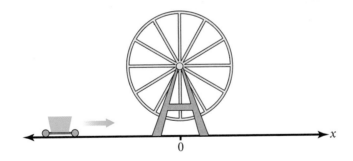

1. Where will the diver land if he is released at each of these times?

   a. $t = 3$

   b. $t = 7$

   c. $t = 12$

   d. $t = 26$

   e. $t = 37$

continued ⯈

2. Sketch a graph of the platform's *x*-coordinate as a function of *t*. Your graph should cover two complete turns of the Ferris wheel— from $t = 0$ to $t = 80$.

   Note: Although the platform's *x*-coordinate represents its horizontal position, in this context *x* is a function of *t*. That is, *t* is the independent variable and *x* is the dependent variable. That means you should show the value of *t* on the horizontal axis of your graph and the value of *x* on the vertical axis.

First Quadrant Platform

In Question 1 of *Where Does He Land?* you found the *x*-coordinate of the diver's landing position for five specific cases.

At the moment the diver is released, his *x*-coordinate is the same as the *x*-coordinate of the platform. In Question 2 of *Where Does He Land?* you sketched a graph of the platform's *x*-coordinate as a function of *t*.

Now focus on values of *t* between 0 and 10, so that the platform is still in the first quadrant. Develop an equation that gives the platform's *x*-coordinate in terms of *t*.

Carts and Periodic Problems

Part I: Where's the Cart?

In *Where Does He Land?* you looked at the horizontal coordinate of the diver when he falls. You also need to know where the cart is while the diver is falling—and especially where it is when the diver reaches the water.

The cart begins 240 feet to the left of the Ferris wheel's base, so its x-coordinate at $t = 0$ is -240. The cart moves to the right at 15 feet per second and begins moving at that speed at $t = 0$.

Based on this information, find the cart's x-coordinate at the moment the diver reaches the water level.

Part II: Periodic Problems

You have seen that the height of a platform on a Ferris wheel represents a periodic function. You have encountered periodic functions before. For instance, the swinging of a pendulum is periodic motion, and the bob's distance from the center line is a periodic function of time (assuming the pendulum isn't slowing down).

1. Describe three other situations that you believe are periodic. For each example, explain what is repeating and give the period for the repetition.

2. Sketch graphs of at least two of the periodic situations you described.

Generalizing the Platform

If the Ferris wheel platform starts at the 3 o'clock position, with the Ferris wheel turning counterclockwise at a constant angular speed of 9 degrees per second, then the platform will remain in the first quadrant through $t = 10$.

During this time interval, the platform's x-coordinate is given by this formula.

$$x = 50 \cos (9t)$$

This formula uses the facts that the Ferris wheel's radius is 50 feet and the angular speed is 9 degrees per second. But the right-triangle definition of the cosine function applies only to acute angles, so this formula isn't defined if t is greater than 10. In this activity, you will explore how to extend the definition of the cosine function.

Specific Cases

1. Consider the case $t = 12$.

    a. Find the platform's x-coordinate when $t = 12$. This was Question 1c of *Where Does He Land?* You may want to express your answer in terms of the cosine of some acute angle.

    b. What value should you assign to $\cos (9 \cdot 12)$ so that the formula $x = 50 \cos (9t)$ gives your answer from part a when you substitute 12 for t?

continued ▶

2. Consider the case $t = 26$.

   a. Find the platform's x-coordinate when $t = 26$. This was Question 1d of *Where Does He Land?* You may want to express your answer in terms of the cosine of some acute angle.

   b. What value should you assign to $\cos(9 \cdot 26)$ so that the formula $x = 50 \cos(9t)$ gives your answer from part a when you substitute 26 for t?

The General Case

3. How can you define $\cos \theta$ in a way that makes sense for all angles and that gives the results you needed in Questions 1b and 2b? You may want to look back at the activity *Extending the Sine*.

Planning for Formulas

You now have all the parts to the puzzle. You simply have to put them together! Suppose W represents the amount of time the Ferris wheel has been turning at the moment the diver is released. You have formulas that tell you each of these things in terms of W.

- The diver's height at the moment he is released
- The diver's x-coordinate at the moment he is released
- The length of time the diver falls until he reaches the water level
- The cart's x-coordinate when the diver reaches the water level

Write out each of these four formulas. Explain each formula clearly, including how the general definitions of sine and cosine and the principles of falling objects are used in them.

Also discuss how each of the following facts fits into your formulas.

- The Ferris wheel has a radius of 50 feet.
- The center of the Ferris wheel is 65 feet above the ground.
- The Ferris wheel turns counterclockwise at a constant rate, making a complete turn every 40 seconds.
- When the cart starts moving, it is 240 feet to the left of the Ferris wheel's base.
- The cart moves to the right along the track at a constant speed of 15 feet per second.
- The water level in the cart is 8 feet above the ground.
- When the cart starts moving, the platform is at the 3 o'clock position.

Finding the Release Time

You have developed a large collection of formulas that explain specific parts of the Ferris wheel problem. Now it's time to put them all together.

Shaleen Nand ponders how to pull together all the information she's developed and the various formulas she's collected.

Moving Cart, Turning Ferris Wheel

Your task is to figure out when the assistant should let go of the diver. Let $t = 0$ represent the moment when the platform passes the 3 o'clock position. Let W represent the number of seconds until the diver is released. You need to determine the right value for W.

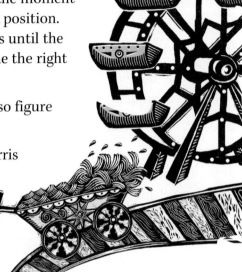

In addition to giving the value of W, also figure out these things.

- Where the platform will be in the Ferris wheel's cycle when the diver is dropped

- Where the cart will be when the diver hits the water

Putting the Cart Before the Ferris Wheel

What if you could change where the cart started? That might make things a little easier.

In this activity, assume that all the facts about the Ferris wheel and the cart are the same as usual except for the cart's initial position.

Suppose the diver is released exactly 25 seconds after the Ferris wheel begins turning from its 3 o'clock position.

1. What is the diver's *x*-coordinate as he falls?

2. Where should the cart start out so that the diver will fall into the tub of water? Assume the cart still starts to the left of the Ferris wheel and travels to the right at 15 feet per second.

What's Your Cosine?

You have seen that the cosine function is defined in a manner similar to that for the sine function. If θ is any angle, draw a ray from the origin, making a counterclockwise angle of that size with the positive x-axis. Pick a point (x, y) on the ray (other than the origin). Define r as the distance from (x, y) to the origin, so $r = \sqrt{x^2 + y^2}$.

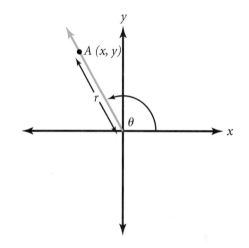

Then define the cosine function for all angles by this equation.

$$\cos \theta = \frac{x}{r}$$

As with the sine function, this definition gives the same values for acute angles as the right-triangle definition. In addition, the extended cosine function can give the same value for different angles.

1. Draw the graph of the function defined by the equation $z = \cos \theta$ for values of θ from $-360°$ to $720°$.

   a. What is the amplitude of this function?

   b. What is the period of this function? Why is the cosine function periodic?

   c. What are the θ-intercepts of the graph?

   d. What values of θ make $\cos \theta$ a maximum? What values of θ make $\cos \theta$ a minimum?

continued ▶

2. These questions are similar to the questions about the sine function in *More Beach Adventures*. As in that activity, your solutions should be between $-360°$ and $360°$. In parts a and b, find exact values for θ. In parts c and d, give θ to the nearest degree.

a. Find three values of θ, other than $81°$, such that $\cos \theta = \cos 81°$.

b. Find three values of θ such that $\cos \theta = -\cos 20°$.

c. Find three values of θ such that $\cos \theta = 0.3$.

d. Find three values of θ such that $\cos \theta = -0.48$.

Find the Ferris Wheel

1. Imagine that the equations in parts a and b each describe the *x*-coordinate of a rider on some Ferris wheel in terms of time, where the rider is at the 3 o'clock position when $t = 0$. In these equations, t is in seconds and x is in feet.

   Recall that *angular speed* is the rate at which the Ferris wheel turns. In this situation, it is given in degrees per second.

   Give the radius, period, and angular speed of the Ferris wheel that each equation represents.

   a. $x = 25 \cos (10t)$

   b. $x = 100 \cos (3t)$

2. a. Write an equation that would give the *x*-coordinate of a rider on a Ferris wheel that has a smaller radius than the wheel in Question 1a but a greater angular speed.

   b. Describe how the graph for the equation in Question 2a would differ from the graph for Question 1a.

A Trigonometric Conclusion

Congratulate yourself on a major achievement—finding out when the assistant should release the diver under the given conditions. Then consider this. Your work so far has involved a significant simplification of the problem. If the assistant uses the solution from *Moving Cart, Turning Ferris Wheel,* it could cost the diver his life. So there's still quite a bit of work to do on the Ferris wheel situation.

Before leaving the Ferris wheel problem, you will learn a bit more about trigonometry, including the use of polar coordinates and some important general principles called *identities.*

Vick Chandra uses the Ferris wheel problem to understand more about trigonometry.

Some Polar Practice

Polar coordinates and *rectangular coordinates* give us two ways to describe points in the plane. This activity focuses on the relationships between the two systems.

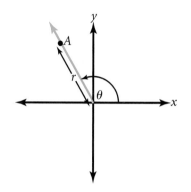

1. **a.** Find the rectangular coordinates for the point whose polar coordinates are (2, 30°).

   b. Find the rectangular coordinates for the point whose polar coordinates are (5, 140°).

2. **a.** Find a pair of polar coordinates for the point whose rectangular coordinates are (8, 2).

   b. Find a pair of polar coordinates for the point whose rectangular coordinates are (4, −9).

A Polar Summary

You know that the position of a point in the plane is usually described in terms of coordinates x and y, which are its **rectangular coordinates** (or Cartesian coordinates). A point's position in the plane can also be described in terms of **polar coordinates**, usually represented by the letters r and θ.

For example, in the first diagram, point P has rectangular coordinates (4, 7). The variable r represents the distance from P to the origin. The variable θ represents the angle made between the positive direction of the x-axis and the ray from the origin through P, measured counterclockwise.

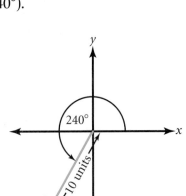

You can use the Pythagorean theorem to find that $r = \sqrt{4^2 + 7^2} = \sqrt{65} \approx 8.06$. To get θ, you can use one of the trigonometric functions.

For example, you can use the sine function, whose general definition is $\sin \theta = \frac{y}{r}$. For point P, this equation becomes $\sin \theta = \frac{7}{\sqrt{65}}$, or about 0.868, which gives $\theta \approx 60°$. In other words, point P can be represented approximately in polar coordinates as (8.06, 60°).

The process can be reversed, starting from a point's polar coordinates and finding the point's rectangular coordinates. For instance, in the second diagram, point Q has polar coordinates (10, 240°).

You can use the general definitions of the sine and cosine functions to find the rectangular coordinates of point Q.

For example, $\sin \theta = \frac{y}{r}$, so $y = r \sin \theta$. Therefore, the y-coordinate of Q is $10 \sin 240°$, or approximately -8.7.

Similarly, $\cos \theta = \frac{x}{r}$, which gives $x = r \cos \theta$. So, the x-coordinate of point Q is $10 \cos 240°$, which equals -5. The rectangular coordinates of Q are therefore approximately $(-5, -8.7)$.

continued ▸

Angles Greater Than 360°

The concept of polar coordinates is complicated by the fact that we don't restrict θ to angles between 0° and 360°. An angle of 360° or greater is simply interpreted as representing more than a complete rotation around the origin.

For instance, point P can be represented in polar coordinates as (8.06, 420°), because a counterclockwise rotation of 420° from the positive x-axis results in the same ray from the origin as a rotation of 60°. Similarly, point Q can be represented as (10, 600°), (10, 960°), (10, 1320°), and so on.

Negative Angles

We also allow the polar coordinate θ to be negative, by interpreting a negative angle as a *clockwise* rotation from the positive x-axis. For example, point Q can be described by the polar coordinates (10, −120°). The negative sign for the 120° angle indicates rotating 120° in the clockwise direction.

Negative Values for *r*

The final complication for polar coordinates is that we allow negative values for *r*. If *r* is negative, the point lies in the opposite direction from the point with the corresponding positive *r*-value.

For example, consider the diagram shown here. Suppose point *S*, in the first quadrant, has polar coordinates (2, 30°). Suppose point *T*, in the third quadrant, is in the opposite direction from the origin as point *S* and is also 2 units from the origin. Point *T* can be described by the polar coordinates (−2, 30°).

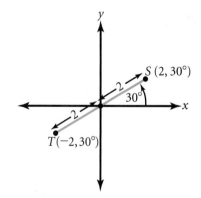

Note that point *T* can also be described by the polar coordinates (2, 210°).

continued ▶

Summary: Multiple Representations

The use of arbitrary angles for θ and of both positive and negative values for r means we can represent every point in the plane (except the origin) in polar coordinates in infinitely many ways. This creates some problems in working with polar coordinates, but it also leads to flexibility.

Because points have more than one representation, we sometimes speak of "a polar representation" of a point rather than "the polar coordinates" of the point. For convenience, you might refer to the representation with r positive and $0° \leq \theta < 360°$ as the *standard polar representation.*

Polar Coordinates on the Ferris Wheel

You may find it helpful to think of polar coordinates in terms of the Ferris wheel.

Picture a Ferris wheel with its center at the origin of the coordinate system. Then picture a rider on the circumference of the wheel, starting on the positive part of the x-axis and going counterclockwise.

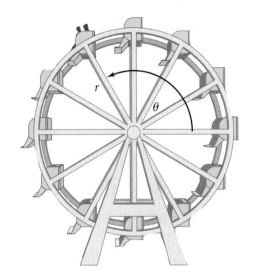

In this model, the rider's r-coordinate gives the radius of the Ferris wheel. The rider's θ-coordinate gives the angle through which the rider has turned (starting from the 3 o'clock position). For example, a person on a 30-foot wheel who has gone one-fourth of the way around the wheel has polar coordinates $(30, 90°)$.

1. Suppose a Ferris wheel has a radius of 40 feet and a period of 20 seconds. The rider passes the 3 o'clock position at $t = 0$. Find the rectangular coordinates and the standard polar coordinates for the rider when $t = 3$, using the center of the wheel as the origin.

2. a. Find a value of t different from 3 seconds, for which the rider would be at the same position as in Question 1.

   b. Use your answer to part a to find a different pair of polar coordinates for the position in Question 1.

3. Find general expressions for both the rectangular coordinates and the polar coordinates of a rider's position at time t. Use the Ferris wheel from Question 1, with radius 40 feet and period 20 seconds.

Pythagorean Trigonometry

As you have seen, the definitions of the sine and cosine functions are based on a coordinate diagram like this one.

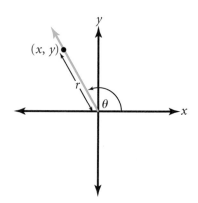

Specifically, to define $\sin \theta$ and $\cos \theta$, draw a ray from the origin that makes a counterclockwise angle θ with the positive x-axis. Then pick some point on that ray (other than the origin). Using r to represent the distance from the point to the origin, $r = \sqrt{x^2 + y^2}$.

If the point has rectangular coordinates (x, y), you define $\sin \theta$ as the ratio $\frac{y}{r}$ and define $\cos \theta$ as the ratio $\frac{x}{r}$.

Because the ratios $\frac{y}{r}$ and $\frac{x}{r}$ don't change no matter which point on the ray you choose, you can pick any point that is convenient. One common simplification is to pick the point that lies on the unit circle, which is the circle with radius 1 and center at the origin. Choosing this point simplifies matters because it means $r = 1$.

1. Suppose you choose the point (x, y) so that it is on the unit circle. How can you express x and y in terms of $\sin \theta$ and $\cos \theta$?

2. What is the equation of the unit circle? That is, what condition must x and y satisfy if (x, y) is 1 unit from the origin?

3. Use your answers to Questions 1 and 2 to write an equation relating $\sin \theta$ and $\cos \theta$ for points on the unit circle.

4. Choose four values of θ, one in each quadrant. Verify in each case that your equation in Question 3 holds true.

Coordinate Tangents

You've developed a way to define the sine and cosine functions for arbitrary angles. Now it's time to look at the tangent.

Remember that for a right triangle such as the one shown here, we define $\tan \theta$ by the formula

$$\tan \theta = \frac{\text{opposite}}{\text{adjacent}}$$

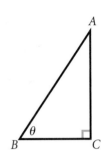

where *opposite* means the length of $\overline{AC}$ and *adjacent* means the length of $\overline{BC}$.

1. Suppose a point in the plane has rectangular coordinates (x, y) and polar coordinates (r, θ), as in the second diagram. How would you define $\tan \theta$ in terms of x and y? Explain and justify your decision.

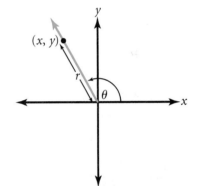

2. It's helpful to have equations connecting the various trigonometric functions. How can you express $\tan \theta$ in terms of $\sin \theta$ and $\cos \theta$, rather than in terms of the coordinates x and y? Think about how x and y might be expressed in terms of sine, cosine, and r.

3. Find each value, based on your definition in Question 1.
   a. $\tan 120°$
   b. $\tan 230°$
   c. $\tan (-50°)$
   d. $\tan 385°$

4. Sketch a graph of the equation $z = \tan t$, using t for the horizontal axis and z for the vertical axis. Include values for t from $-180°$ to $360°$ in your graph.

Positions on the Ferris Wheel

In *Pythagorean Trigonometry,* you developed the equation $(\cos \theta)^2 + (\sin \theta)^2 = 1$. You saw that this equation is true no matter what value you substitute for the angle θ.

Equations that are true no matter what values are substituted for the variables are called **identities.** In this activity and in *More Positions on the Ferris Wheel,* you will look at other identities involving the sine and cosine functions. The Ferris wheel model can help you develop and understand these identities.

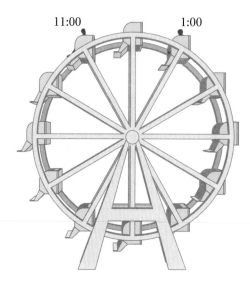

11:00   1:00

The diagram shows two riders on a Ferris wheel, at the 1 o'clock and the 11 o'clock positions. The rider at the 1 o'clock position has turned 60° from the 3 o'clock position. The rider at the 11 o'clock position has turned 120°.

Suppose the Ferris wheel's radius is 50 feet. A rider's height, compared to the center of the wheel, is then given by the expression $50 \sin \theta$. But these two riders are at the same height, so $50 \sin 60° = 50 \sin 120°$. Dividing by 50 gives the following relationship.

$$\sin 60° = \sin 120°$$

The equation $\sin 60° = \sin 120°$ can be generalized, using the diagram shown here, to get an identity involving the sine function.

In this diagram, points A and B represent the positions of two riders on a Ferris wheel. That means A and B are the same distance from the origin.

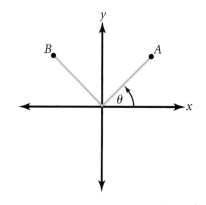

continued ▶

The angle θ represents the angle of turn for a rider at point A. Assume points A and B are at the same height on the Ferris wheel, so they have the same y-coordinate.

1. Find the angle through which the rider at point B has turned. Express your answer in terms of θ. First consider an example, such as $\theta = 20°$. Find the angle for point B and then generalize.

2. Use the fact that points A and B are at the same height to write a generalization of the equation $\sin 60° = \sin 120°$.

More Positions on the Ferris Wheel

In this activity, you will continue your exploration of trigonometric identities.

Part I: Clockwise and Counterclockwise

The two Ferris wheel riders shown here both started from the 3 o'clock position. The first rider turned 30° and is now at the 2 o'clock position. The second rider turned −30° and is now at the 4 o'clock position. Negative angles, you'll recall, are interpreted as clockwise motion.

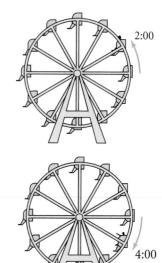

Assume the radius of the Ferris wheel is 50 feet. Recall that if a rider turns through an angle θ, then his x-coordinate is given by the expression $50 \cos \theta$. Therefore, the first rider's x-coordinate is $50 \cos 30°$ and the second rider's x-coordinate is $50 \cos (−30°)$.

1. a. Explain why these two riders have the same x-coordinate. That is, why are they the same distance to the right of the center of the Ferris wheel?

    b. What does your answer to part a tell you about $\cos 30°$ and $\cos (−30°)$?

Now consider the general situation. In the next diagram, points C and D represent two positions on a Ferris wheel. In the case of point C, the rider has turned through an angle θ. For point D, the rider has turned through an angle $−\theta$.

2. a. Explain why points C and D have the same x-coordinate.

    b. Use the diagram and your answer to part a to explain why $\cos \theta$ and $\cos (−\theta)$ must be equal.

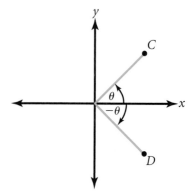

continued ◗

Part II: From Identity to the Ferris Wheel

In Part I, you started with a situation on the Ferris wheel and generalized it to get a trigonometric identity. Now you will start with the identity and create a Ferris wheel explanation.

Consider the equation $\sin(-\theta) = -\sin\theta$.

3. Substitute values for θ to confirm that the equation is true for those values. Try a variety of values, including angles that are negative and angles that are greater than $360°$.

4. Create a Ferris wheel situation to explain the equation in a manner similar to the one you used in Part I.

5. Create a coordinate system diagram like that in Part I to illustrate this situation.

A Trigonometric Reflection

In the activity *Moving Cart, Turning Ferris Wheel,* you figured out how many seconds after the Ferris wheel passes the 3 o'clock position that the assistant should let go of the diver to make sure the diver lands in the cart. Even though this is a simplified version of the problem, you couldn't have solved it without understanding mathematical concepts of trigonometry.

You first learned about trigonometry in the context of right triangles. Now you've found that the trigonometric functions can be defined for all angles. You have also learned some things about graphs, trigonometric identities, and polar coordinates.

Compile a summary of these ideas. Include diagrams as needed to help you explain any formulas. You don't need to include formulas that relate only to the unit problem, but do use the Ferris wheel to explain ideas about trigonometry.

High Dive Portfolio

It is time to put together your portfolio for *High Dive.*
Compiling your portfolio has three steps.

- Write a cover letter that summarizes the unit.
- Choose papers to include from your work in this unit.
- Discuss your personal mathematical growth in this unit.

Cover Letter

Look back over *High Dive* and describe
the central problem of the unit and the key
mathematical ideas. Your description should give an overview of how
the key ideas—such as extending the sine and cosine functions and
finding falling-time functions—were developed and how they were used
to solve the central problem.

In compiling your portfolio, you will select some activities that
you think were important in developing the key ideas of this unit.
Your cover letter should include an explanation of why you selected
each item.

Selecting Papers

Your portfolio for *High Dive* should contain

- *Moving Cart, Turning Ferris Wheel*
- A Problem of the Week

    Select one of the POWs you completed in this unit: *Tower of Hanoi* or
    Paving Patterns.

- *A Trigonometric Reflection*
- Other key activities

    Identify two concepts you think were important in this unit. For
    each concept, choose one or two activities that helped improve your
    understanding, and explain how the activities helped.

continued ▶

Personal Growth

Your cover letter for *High Dive* should describe how the mathematical ideas were developed in the unit. In addition, write about your own personal development during the unit. You may want to address this question.

How do you feel about your ability to solve a complex problem that has as many components as the "High Dive" problem?

Include any thoughts about your experiences that you wish to share with a reader of your portfolio

SUPPLEMENTAL ACTIVITIES

The supplemental activities in *High Dive* focus primarily on the trigonometric functions and their relationship with the Ferris wheel situation. Here are three examples.

- *A Shifted Ferris Wheel* examines how changing the starting time for the Ferris wheel would affect the function describing the platform's height.

- *A Change in Plans* presents an interesting twist on the original circus act problem in that you don't have to take into account the angular velocity of the dive.

- *Polar Equations* and *Circular Sine* continue the work with polar coordinates.

Mr. Ferris and His Wheel

The Ferris wheel is named after its inventor, George Washington Gale Ferris.

Many of us have probably ridden on or watched a Ferris wheel at some point in our lives. But it's unlikely we know very much about its fascinating history. Here are some questions about the Ferris wheel that you may want to research.

- Who was George Ferris?
- Where was he raised and educated?
- How did he come to invent the Ferris wheel?
- What was the first Ferris wheel made of?
- How did the invention of the Ferris wheel change George Ferris's life?
- Did Ferris have any other notable inventions?

Write a report about your findings. You may want to expand your investigation to the broader topic of amusement park rides or to some other aspect of carnivals and fairs.

A Shifted Ferris Wheel

In the main unit problem, the diver's platform is at the 3 o'clock position when the cart starts moving. Using this moment as $t = 0$, the platform's height after t seconds is given by the expression $65 + 50 \sin (9t)$.

Suppose instead that at $t = 0$, the platform was at the 6 o'clock position.

1. Find an expression that gives the platform's height as a function of t.

2. Sketch the graph of the height function. Compare it to the graph for the main unit problem.

3. Consider other positions for the Ferris wheel at $t = 0$. Describe in general how changing the position affects the function describing the platform's height.

Prisoner Revisited

Do you remember the prisoner from the Year 1 unit *The Pit and the Pendulum*? Well, he's back.

This time, he is lying on the table in the middle of a square prison cell that is 35 feet by 35 feet. A pendulum moves back and forth above him, as shown here. (There are no rats in this cell.) As before, a blade is attached to the end of the pendulum. The length of the pendulum does not change this time, but the table is gradually rising, moving the prisoner up toward the blade.

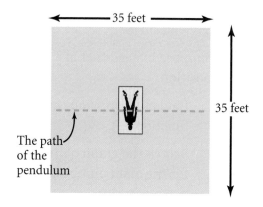

The path of the pendulum

The prisoner notices that the pendulum's motion follows a sine-like pattern as it swings back and forth. Specifically, the pendulum's horizontal distance $p(t)$ from the center of the cell (measured in feet) is given by the function

$$p(t) = 15 \sin (60t)$$

where t is the number of seconds the pendulum has been swinging.

The second diagram shows this horizontal distance, viewed from the front of the cell. (This diagram is not drawn to scale.)

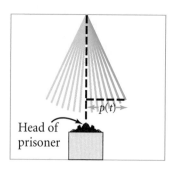

Head of prisoner

continued

Suddenly, a friend of the prisoner appears in the adjacent cell. The friend rushes to the bars that separate the two cells. The pendulum swings alternately toward him and away from him, as shown in this overhead view.

The prisoner's friend realizes that if the pendulum comes within 3 feet of the bars between the cells, he can reach through the bars and grab onto the pendulum, stopping its motion.

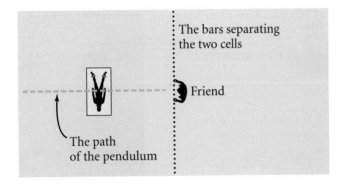

1. Will the pendulum come close enough to the bars between the cells so that the prisoner's friend can reach it? Explain your answer.

2. If so, for how long will the pendulum be in the friend's range each time it passes by?

Lightning at the Beach on Jupiter

As you may have noticed, the three variables *rate, time,* and *distance* are closely related.

In this activity, you are given information about two of these variables and asked to find the value for the third.

1. Light travels at about 186,000 miles per second. Jupiter is about 483,000,000 miles from the sun. (It's sometimes closer and sometimes farther away, but we'll use this average distance.)

    How long does it take for light to travel from the sun to Jupiter?

2. Amparo wants to spend the day at the beach, which is 100 miles away. She leaves at 8:00 in the morning and wants to be home by 7:00 that evening.

    For Amparo to have 6 hours at the beach, what should her average speed for the trip be?

3. You see a flash of lightning. About 6 seconds later, you hear the crash of thunder. Assume that the light reaches you instantly and that the sound travels at about 1100 feet per second. (The exact speed of sound depends on atmospheric conditions like temperature.)

    How far away was the lightning?

4. What general relationships exist among rate, distance, and time?

5. How do the concepts of rate, distance, and time relate to the main unit problem?

The Derivative of Position

In *Free Fall,* you developed an important general principle about free-falling objects.

> If an object at rest falls freely from a height of h feet, then its height after t seconds is approximately $h - 16t^2$ feet.

This principle builds on the fact from physics that a free-falling object accelerates at approximately 32 feet per second for each second it falls.

Your task in this activity is to confirm the formula $h - 16t^2$ using derivatives. You will need to show that if an object's height fits this formula, then its acceleration must be 32 feet per second for each second it falls.

1. Suppose a certain object is moving downward so that its height $f(t)$ after t seconds is given by the equation $f(t) = h - 16t^2$.

   a. At what rate is the object's height changing at $t = 1$? That is, what is the object's instantaneous velocity at $t = 1$?

   b. Explain why the number you found in part a is the same as the derivative of f at $t = 1$.

2. a. Find the derivative of f at $t = 2$, $t = 5$, and $t = 10$.

   b. Based on your answers to Questions 1 and 2a, give a general expression for $f'(t)$ in terms of t.

3. What does your result from Question 2b say about the object's acceleration?

A Change in Plans

Preparations for the circus act are coming along nicely. You need only a little more time to work out all the details for the jump from a moving Ferris wheel. But the investors are getting impatient! They want you to start generating more income right now. So you decide to go on the road with a modified act.

Here is the plan for the modified act.

> You ask a randomly selected audience member to choose an angle between 0 and 360 degrees. You then turn the Ferris wheel that many degrees and stop it. When the wheel stops, the cart starts moving along the track toward the wheel from 240 feet away at a speed of 15 feet per second.

> At the appropriate number of seconds after the cart starts moving, the diver drops and lands in the moving cart!

To make this modified act successful, you will need a function whose input is any number of degrees between 0 and 360 and whose output is the number of seconds after the cart starts moving that the diver should wait to drop.

Find that function.

Polar Equations

Over the years, you've worked with and graphed many equations involving x and y. The graph of such an equation consists of all points whose rectangular coordinates fit the equation. For example, the point with rectangular coordinates $(3, 4)$ is on the graph of $5x - 2y = 7$ because $5 \cdot 3 - 2 \cdot 4 = 7$.

You can also graph equations involving polar equations. As with equations using x and y, the graph of an equation involving r and θ consists of all points whose polar coordinates fit the equation.

For example, the point with polar coordinates $(3, 90°)$ is on the graph of the equation $r + \sin \theta = 4$ because $3 + \sin 90° = 4$.

For each of these equations, first find some number pairs for r and θ that fit the equation. Then use those number pairs as polar coordinates and plot the points they represent. Finally, use these points to sketch a graph of the equation. Find more solutions if you need them to get a good idea of what the graph looks like.

1. $r = \theta$

2. $r = \cos \theta$

3. $r = 2$

4. $\theta = 20°$

Circular Sine

If you were to plot some points for the polar coordinate equation $r = \sin \theta$ and connect them, you might find that the graph looks something like the one shown here. It appears to be a circle, but it's hard to tell for sure simply by plotting points and connecting them.

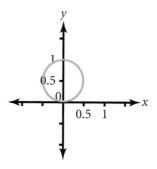

Your challenge in this activity is to show that the graph of the polar equation $r = \sin \theta$ is definitely a circle.

1. If this graph is a circle, what are the rectangular coordinates of its center and what is its radius?

2. What is the rectangular equation for the circle with the center and radius you found in Question 1? Suppose a point (x, y) is on this circle. Use the Pythagorean theorem to get an equation for the distance from this point to the center of the circle.

3. How can you use the relationships between rectangular and polar coordinates to confirm that the rectangular equation for Question 2 is equivalent to the polar equation $r = \sin \theta$?

A Polar Exploration

In this activity, you will investigate graphs and equations using polar coordinates and report on what you discover.

If you worked on the supplemental activity *Polar Equations,* you saw that the graphs of simple polar equations, such as $r = \theta$, can give very different graphs from simple equations with rectangular coordinates.

Here is one of the interesting graphs you can get from a fairly simple polar equation.

You might consult a trigonometry textbook or mathematics Web sites for ideas of interesting equations to explore. Your report should indicate any references you used and show clearly which ideas came from other sources and which are your own.

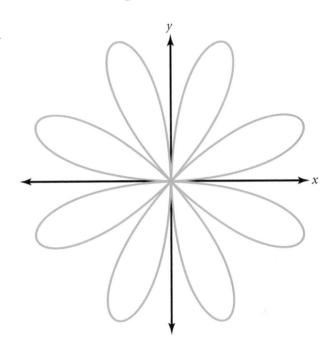

A Shift in Sine

You have observed that the graphs of the functions $z = \sin t$ and $z = \cos t$ are quite similar. One way to describe the relationship is that if you shift the graph of the sine function 90° to the left, you get the graph of the cosine function. Alternatively, shifting the graph of the cosine function 90° to the right produces the graph of the sine function.

1. Express this relationship between the graphs as a trigonometric identity, writing $\sin \theta$ as the cosine of a different angle.

2. Prove the identity you found in Question 1. Use the relationship $\sin \theta = \cos (90° - \theta)$, which you verified for all angles θ.

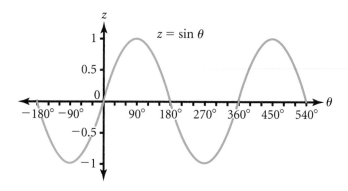

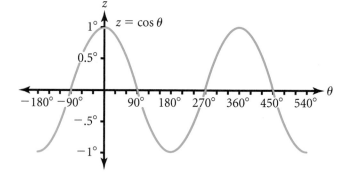

More Pythagorean Trigonometry

The Pythagorean theorem tells us that in a right triangle such as the one shown here, the lengths of the sides satisfy the equation $a^2 + b^2 = c^2$.

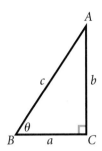

The sine and cosine functions are defined for right triangles by the equations $\sin\theta = \frac{b}{c}$ and $\cos\theta = \frac{a}{c}$.

In the activity *Pythagorean Trigonometry*, you developed an identity involving the sine and cosine functions that resembles the statement of the Pythagorean theorem.

1. State that identity and explain it for acute angles based on the equations $a^2 + b^2 = c^2$, $\sin\theta = \frac{b}{c}$, and $\cos\theta = \frac{a}{c}$.

2. Develop similar identities involving the other trigonometric functions—tangent, cotangent, secant, and cosecant—based on the definitions $\tan\theta = \frac{b}{a}$, $\cot\theta = \frac{a}{b}$, $\sec\theta = \frac{c}{a}$, and $\csc\theta = \frac{c}{b}$.

GLOSSARY

This is the glossary for all five units of IMP Year 3. This glossary may be useful when you encounter a term in **bold** text that is new or unfamiliar, or it can be used to confirm or clarify your understanding of a term.

Adjacent interior angle See **exterior angle.**

Amplitude Half the distance between the maximum and minimum of a periodic function.

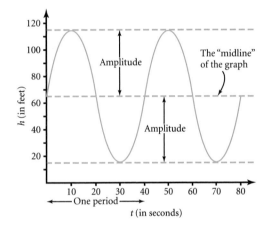

Analytic geometry The study of geometry using a coordinate system and principles of algebra; in contrast to **synthetic geometry.**

Angle bisector A line segment or ray that divides an angle into two smaller angles of equal measure.

Arithmetic sequence A sequence of numbers in which the difference between successive terms is constant.

Example: The sequence 5, 8, 11, 14, . . . is an arithmetic sequence in which each term is 3 more than the preceding term.

Associative   An operation $*$ is associative (or has the associative property) if the equation $(a * b) * c = a * (b * c)$ holds true for all values of a, b, and c.

Examples: The operation of addition is associative because for any numbers a, b, and c, $(a + b) + c = a + (b + c)$. The operation of division is not associative because, for example, $(12 \div 4) \div 2$ is not equal to $12 \div (4 \div 2)$.

Average rate of change   The ratio between the change in a quantity over an interval of time and the length of the time interval; in contrast to **instantaneous rate of change.**

Example: If the population of a town grows by 15,000 people over a period of 10 years, its average rate of change is 1500 people per year. The rate of change in any given year may be higher or lower than the average rate of change.

Binomial coefficient   A synonym for **combinatorial coefficient.**

Binomial distribution   A probability distribution describing the probability of each possible result of a fixed number of repeated independent trials of the same event with two possible outcomes, where the order of the outcomes is not significant. If a particular outcome has probability p for each trial, the binomial distribution says that the probability that this outcome occurs exactly r times in n trials is $_nC_r \cdot p^r \cdot (1 - p)^{n-r}$. (See **combinatorial coefficient** for the meaning of $_nC_r$.)

Example: Suppose the probability of a weighted coin coming up heads is 0.7. If the coin is flipped 50 times, the probability of exactly 30 heads is $_{50}C_{30} \cdot (0.7)^{30} \cdot (0.3)^{20}$. The binomial distribution would describe the probability for each of the 51 possible results (0 through 50 heads).

Binomial theorem   This theorem states that the expression $(x + y)^n$ is the sum of all terms of the form $_nC_r \cdot x^{n-r} \cdot y^r$, where r goes from 0 through n. (See **combinatorial coefficient** for the meaning of $_nC_r$.)

Central angle   An angle whose vertex is the center of a circle with its sides determined by radii of the circle.

Circle   The set of all points in a plane at a specific distance (the *radius*) from a specific point (the *center*). The *standard form* for the equation of a circle is $(x - a)^2 + (y - b)^2 = r^2$, where (a, b) are the coordinates of the center and r is the radius.

Circumference   The perimeter of a circle, or the distance around a circle. Circumference can also refer to a circle's boundary.

Circumscribed and inscribed figures   If a circle passes through all of the vertices of a polygon, then the circle is circumscribed about the polygon, and the polygon is inscribed in the circle.

> *Example:* In this diagram, the circle is circumscribed about $\triangle ABC$ and the triangle is inscribed in the circle. This circle is the *circumcircle* of the triangle, and its center is the *circumcenter* of the triangle.

If a circle is tangent to all of the sides of a polygon, then the circle is inscribed in the polygon, and the polygon is circumscribed about the circle.

> *Example:* In this diagram, the circle is inscribed in $\triangle DEF$ and the triangle is circumscribed about the circle. This circle is called the *incircle* of the triangle and its center is called the *incenter* of the triangle. (*Note:* Not all polygons have a circumcircle or incircle.)

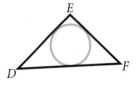

Coefficient   Usually, a number used to multiply an algebraic expression. In some cases, a variable is used as a coefficient.

> *Example:* In the expression $3x + 4\sin x$, the numbers 3 and 4 are coefficients. In the expression ae^{kx}, the variables a and k are coefficients.

Coefficient matrix   The **matrix** representing the **coefficients** of the variables in a system of linear equations.

> *Example:* For the system
>
> $$3r + 2s = 9$$
>
> $$-5r + 4s = 16$$
>
> the coefficient matrix is
>
> $$\begin{bmatrix} 3 & 2 \\ -5 & 4 \end{bmatrix}$$

Collinear Contained by the same line.

Column vector A **matrix** that contains exactly one column.

Combination Each way of selecting a set of size r from a specific set of size n. See also **combinatorial coefficient.**

Combinatorial coefficient The number of ways of selecting a set of size r (without regard to the order of selection) from a specific set of size n. This number is written as $\binom{n}{r}$ or $_nC_r$. Each way of selecting the set of size r is called a **combination.**

Combinatorial coefficients are the coefficients in a **binomial distribution.**

Combinatorial coefficients are also called **binomial coefficients** because of their relationship to the expansion of powers of binomials (see **binomial theorem**).

> *Example:* You can select two numbers from the set $\{1, 2, 3, 4, 5\}$ in these ways: $\{1, 2\}, \{1, 3\}, \{1, 4\}, \{1, 5\}, \{2, 3\}, \{2, 4\}, \{2, 5\}, \{3, 4\}, \{3, 5\},$ and $\{4, 5\}$. Because there are exactly ten distinct ways, $_5C_2 = 10$.

See also **permutation.**

Commutative An operation $*$ is commutative (or has the commutative property) if the equation $a * b = b * a$ holds true for all values of a and b.

> *Examples:* The operation of addition is commutative because for any numbers a and b, $a + b = b + a$. The operation of subtraction is not commutative because, for example, $5 - 9$ is not equal to $9 - 5$.

Completing the square The process of adding a constant term to a quadratic expression to make it a perfect-square trinomial.

> *Example:* To complete the square for the expression $x^2 + 10x$, add 25, because $x^2 + 10x + 25$ is the square $(x + 5)^2$.

Conclusion See **"If-then" statement.**

Constant term In any polynomial, a term that does not contain the variable. If no such term appears in the expression, then the constant term is 0.

> *Example:* In the polynomial $x^3 - 2x^2 + 7$, the number 7 is the constant term. In the polynomial $2x^4 + 5x$, the constant term is 0.

Constant term matrix   For a system of linear equations expressed by the single matrix equation [A] [X] = [B], the column matrix [B] that contains the constants to the right of the equal signs in the linear equations. See also **constant term.**

Example: For the pair of equations

$$2x + 3y = 5$$
$$-5x + y = 13$$

represented by the matrix equation

$$\begin{bmatrix} 2 & 3 \\ -5 & 1 \end{bmatrix} \begin{bmatrix} x \\ y \end{bmatrix} = \begin{bmatrix} 5 \\ 13 \end{bmatrix}$$

the matrix $\begin{bmatrix} 5 \\ 13 \end{bmatrix}$ is the constant term matrix.

Constraint   A limitation or restriction. In a **linear programming** problem, any of the conditions limiting the variables.

Converse   The statement obtained by interchanging the hypothesis and conclusion of an "if-then" statement.

Example: The converse of "If a polygon has three sides, then it is a triangle" is the statement "If a figure is a triangle, then it is a polygon with three sides."

See also **"if and only if"** and **"if-then" statement.**

Coordinate plane   In the **three-dimensional coordinate system,** any of the three planes that includes two of the perpendicular, scaled coordinate axes. In the two-dimensional coordinate system, the set of all points.

Example: The *xz*-plane is the plane containing the *x*- and *z*-axes, and consists of all points whose *y*-coordinate is 0.

Cosine   The ratio of the length of the leg adjacent to one non-right angle of a right triangle to the length of the hypotenuse.

Cylinder   Commonly, a solid figure with two parallel circular bases and having sides perpendicular to those bases, such as a tin can is shaped. More exactly, this describes a right circular cylinder.

Dependent system   See **system of equations.**

Derivative   Given a function f at the point $(a, f(a))$, the instantaneous rate of change of f at $x = a$. The derivative at $(a, f(a))$ [written $f'(a)$] is also the slope of the line tangent to the graph of f at that point. The derivative of a function does not necessarily exist at every point.

For a given function f, the derivatives at each point together define a new function, also called the *derivative* (or *derived function*) and represented by the symbol f'.

Dimensions of a matrix   The number of rows and columns in a matrix.

> *Example:* This matrix has dimensions 2×3 because it has two rows and three columns.
>
> $$\begin{bmatrix} 1 & -3 & 0 \\ 5 & 6 & -4 \end{bmatrix}$$

Directrix   A fixed line that, together with a point not on the line called the **focus,** determines a parabola, ellipse, or hyperbola. The directrix and focus are used differently to define each of those figures. See also **ellipse, hyperbola,** and **parabola.**

Distance formula   A formula (based on the **Pythagorean theorem**) for determining the distance between two points using the coordinates of the points. In a two-dimensional coordinate system, the distance formula states that the distance between the points (x_1, y_1) and (x_2, y_2) is $\sqrt{(x_2 - x_1)^2 + (y_2 - y_1)^2}$.

Elimination method   A method of solving a **system of equations** that involves adding or subtracting the equations to create a new system with one fewer variable. The goal of the method is to eventually create an equation with only one variable. Also called *Gaussian elimination.*

Ellipse   A two-dimensional geometric shape formed as the intersection of a circular cone with an oblique plane.

Also, the set of all points the sum of whose distance from two fixed points (foci, plural of **focus**) is a given positive constant.

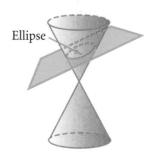

Ellipse

Entry   One of the numbers in a **matrix.**

Equidistant   At the same distance.

Exponential   Informally, any function, equation, or expression in which the variable is in the exponent. Used to refer to a function defined by an equation of the form $y = k \cdot b^{cx}$, where k, b, and c are specific numbers, $b > 0$, and k and c are both nonzero.

Exterior angle   An angle formed outside a polygon by extending one of the sides of the polygon.

> *Example:* The diagram shows exterior $\angle BAF$ for polygon $ABCDE$. $\angle BAE$ is the *adjacent interior angle.* The angles of the polygon at B, C, D, and E are *nonadjacent interior angles.*

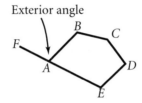

Feasible region   The region consisting of all points whose coordinates satisfy a given set of **constraints.** A point in this set is called a *feasible point.*

First octant   In three-dimensional coordinate space, the set of points for which all three coordinates are positive. See **octant.**

Focus (of an **ellipse, hyperbola,** or **parabola**)   A point on the coordinate plane used with the **directrix** to define an ellipse, hyperbola, or parabola. (Plural: foci)

Geometric sequence   A sequence of numbers in which the ratio between successive terms is constant.

> *Example:* The sequence 3, 6, 12, 24, . . . is a geometric sequence in which each term is 2 times the preceding term, or the ratio between successive terms is

$$\frac{6}{3} = \frac{12}{6} = \frac{24}{12} = 2$$

Hyperbola   A two-dimensional geometric shape formed as the intersection of two circular cones with a plane that is parallel to the axis of the cones.

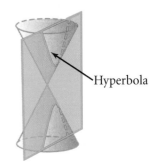

Hyperbola

Also, the set of all points for which the difference between the distance to each of the two fixed points (foci, plural of **focus**) is a given positive constant.

Hypothesis   See **"If-then" statement.**

Identity   A statement of equality that holds true no matter which numbers are substituted for the variables, as long as the expressions on both sides of the equation make sense.

> *Examples:* The equation $(a + b)^2 = a^2 + 2ab + b^2$ is an identity because it holds true for all real numbers a and b. The equation $\sin(-\theta) = -\sin\theta$ is an identity because it holds true for all values of θ.

Identity element   For a given operation, an identity element (or *identity*) is an element that, when combined with any element using that operation, yields the second element as the result.

> *Examples:* The number 0 is the identity for addition (or *additive identity*) because $x + 0$ and $0 + x$ are both equal to x for any number x. Similarly, the number 1 is the identity for multiplication (or *multiplicative identity*).

"If and only if"   A phrase used to indicate that both a given **"if-then" statement** and its converse are true.

> *Example:* The statement "If a triangle is equilateral, then it is equiangular" and its converse, "If a triangle is equiangular, then it is equilateral," are both true. These two statements can then be combined to create this "if and only if" statement: *A triangle is equilateral if and only if it is equiangular.*

"If-then" statement   A specific form of mathematical statement saying that if one condition—the *hypothesis*—is true, then another condition—the *conclusion*—must also be true.

> *Example:* This is a true "if-then" statement: *If two angles of a triangle have equal measure, then the sides opposite these angles have equal length.* The statement "two angles of a triangle have equal measure" is the hypothesis; the statement "the sides opposite these angles have equal length" is the conclusion.

Inconsistent system   See **system of equations.**

Independent system   See **system of equations.**

Inscribed (polygon or circle)   See **circumscribed and inscribed figures.**

Instantaneous rate of change   The rate at which a quantity is changing at a given instant; in contrast to **average rate of change.** An important example is the instantaneous speed of an object. The instantaneous speed can be thought of as the average speed over an infinitely small time period and can be found by evaluating the **derivative** of the function at the desired instant.

Inverse   An element that, when combined through an operation (such as addition or multiplication) with a given element, yields the **identity element** as the result.

> *Examples:* The number -7 is the inverse element for 7 for the operation of addition (or the *additive inverse* of 7) because both $7 + (-7)$ and $(-7) + 7$ are equal to 0, which is the identity element for addition. Similarly, the number $\frac{1}{5}$ is the inverse for 5 for the operation of multiplication (or the **multiplicative inverse** of 5).

Inverse trigonometric function   Any of the functions used to find an angle when the value of a trigonometric function of the angle is known.

> *Example:* The sine of $30°$ is 0.5. Conversely, the inverse sine of 0.5 (written $\sin^{-1} 0.5$ or arcsin 0.5) is $30°$.

Lattice point   A point in a coordinate system with integer coordinates.

Limit   A process used to investigate the behavior of a function at a given point by examining the value of the function at points that are successively closer to the given value.

> *Example:* For the function defined by the equation $f(x) = \frac{\sin x}{x}$, the limit as x approaches 0 can be found intuitively by examining the value of the function at $x = 0.1$, then 0.01, then 0.001, and so on. The notation used for this limit is

$$\lim_{x \to 0} \frac{\sin x}{x}$$

In defining this expression formally, one must consider negative values near 0, such as $-0.1, -0.01, -0.001$, and so on, as well as positive values. *Note:* A function does not necessarily have a limit at every value of x.

Limits are especially useful in finding the **derivative** of a function, which is studied in detail in calculus.

Linear algebra   The branch of mathematics dealing with linear expressions and systems of linear equations.

Linear programming   A problem-solving method that involves maximizing or minimizing a linear expression subject to a set of **constraints** that are linear equations or inequalities.

Matrix   A rectangular array of numbers or expressions. The study of operations with matrices is called *matrix algebra.*

Median   In a triangle, the line segment connecting a vertex to the midpoint of the opposite side.

Midline   The line segment connecting the midpoints of two sides of a triangle.

Midpoint formula   A formula for determining the midpoint of a line segment using the coordinates of the endpoints of the segment. In a two-dimensional coordinate system, the midpoint formula states that the midpoint of the segment with endpoints (x_1, y_1) and (x_2, y_2) is

$$\left(\frac{x_1 + x_2}{2}, \frac{y_1 + y_2}{2} \right)$$

Multiplicative inverse   For a given element, an element that, when multiplied by the given element, yields the multiplicative **identity element** as the result.

   Example: The number $\frac{1}{5}$ is the multiplicative inverse of 5 because $\frac{1}{5} \cdot 5 = 1$, and 1 is the multiplicative identity element.

For a square matrix, a matrix that, when multiplied on the left or right by the given matrix, yields the multiplicative identity matrix.

   Example: The multiplicative inverse of the matrix $\begin{bmatrix} 5 & 6 \\ 7 & 8 \end{bmatrix}$ (often called simply the inverse of the matrix) is $\begin{bmatrix} -4 & 3 \\ 3.5 & -2.5 \end{bmatrix}$ because $\begin{bmatrix} -4 & 3 \\ 3.5 & -2.5 \end{bmatrix}\begin{bmatrix} 5 & 6 \\ 7 & 8 \end{bmatrix}$ equals the identity matrix $\begin{bmatrix} 1 & 0 \\ 0 & 1 \end{bmatrix}$. The inverse of a matrix [A] is denoted $[A]^{-1}$.

Natural logarithm   A logarithm using the base e (where e is the special number that is approximately 2.718).

   Example: The natural logarithm of 25, written ln 25, is approximately 3.22 because $e^{3.22}$ is approximately 25.

Nonadjacent interior angle   See **exterior angle.**

Octant   One of the eight regions into which three-dimensional space is divided by the **coordinate planes,** as shown in the diagram. Points with one or more coordinates equal to 0 do not belong to any of the octants.

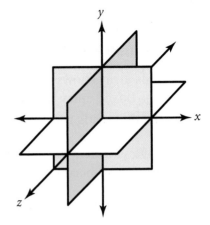

Example: The set of points (x, y, z) for which $x > 0$, $y < 0$, and $z < 0$ is one of the eight octants—the right-hand, lower, rear region in the diagram. The **first octant** is the set of points for which all three coordinates are positive. The other octants are not numbered.

Parabola   The type of curve that occurs as the graph of a quadratic function. The maximum or minimum point of the graph is called the *vertex* (or turning point) of the parabola.

Examples: The graphs of the equations $y = x^2$ and $y = -x^2 + 2x + 2$, shown here, are both parabolas. The first is described as "opening upward," and its vertex is at its minimum point, $(0, 0)$. The second is described as "opening downward," and its vertex is at its maximum point, $(1, 3)$.

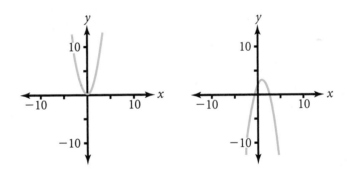

Also, the set of all points such that the distance from each point to the **focus** is equal to the distance from the same point to the **directrix.**

Pascal's triangle A specific triangular array of numbers in which each entry is the sum of the entries to its right and left in the preceding row. Entries at the ends of rows are 1. The entries in Pascal's triangle are all **combinatorial coefficients.**

$$
\begin{array}{ccccccccccc}
 & & & & & 1 & & & & & \\
 & & & & 1 & & 1 & & & & \\
 & & & 1 & & 2 & & 1 & & & \\
 & & 1 & & 3 & & 3 & & 1 & & \\
 & 1 & & 4 & & 6 & & 4 & & 1 & \\
1 & & 5 & & \boxed{10} & & 10 & & 5 & & 1
\end{array}
$$

This array shows the first six rows of Pascal's triangle. The boxed entry $\boxed{10}$ is the sum of the entries 4 and 6 in the preceding row.

Permutation Generally, an arrangement of objects in a particular order. The number of permutations for r distinct objects selected in a specific order from a specific set of size n is written as $_nP_r$.

Example: You can select two distinct numbers in a particular order from the set $\{1, 2, 3\}$ in these ways: $\{1, 2\}, \{2, 1\}, \{1, 3\}, \{3, 1\}, \{2, 3\}$, and $\{3, 2\}$. Because there are exactly six ways to select two distinct numbers, $_3P_2 = 6$.

See also **combinatorial coefficient.**

Perpendicular bisector A line that is perpendicular to a given line segment at that segment's midpoint.

Pigeonhole principle The principle that if m objects are placed in n disjoint sets, with $m > n$, then at least one of the sets must contain at least two of the objects. Often stated as, "If you place m pigeons in n pigeonholes, with $m > n$, then you have to put at least two pigeons in the same pigeonhole."

Polar coordinates A pair of coordinates (r, θ) identifying a point in the plane by its distance (r) from the origin and the angle (θ) between the positive x-axis and the ray from the origin through the point, measured counterclockwise.

Example: Point B in the diagram, whose rectangular coordinates are $(-1, 1)$, has polar coordinates $(\sqrt{2}, 135°)$ because the distance from $(0, 0)$ to B is $\sqrt{2}$ and the angle from the positive x-axis to the ray through B is $135°$.

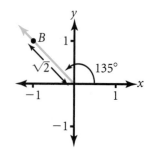

[*Note:* Point B has other polar coordinate representations, such as $(-\sqrt{2}, 315°)$ and $(\sqrt{2}, 495°)$.]

Profit function In a **linear programming** problem, the function that describes how the value to be maximized or minimized (often the profit) is calculated using the constraint variables.

Proportionality constant A number that represents a fixed ratio between two quantities. Also known as *constant of proportionality*.

> *Example:* The area of any triangle is proportional to the product of the base and the height of the triangle. In the formula $A = \frac{1}{2}bh$, $\frac{1}{2}$ is the proportionality constant.

Proportionality property An informal term for the property stating that for functions of the form $y = k \cdot b^{cx}$, the **derivative** of the function is proportional to the function itself.

Pythagorean theorem This theorem states that in a right triangle with legs of lengths a and b and hypotenuse of length c, the lengths satisfy the equation $a^2 + b^2 = c^2$.

Pythagorean triple Any set of three positive whole numbers a, b, and c that satisfy the equation $a^2 + b^2 = c^2$.

> *Examples:* The set 3, 4, and 5 and the set 7, 24, and 25 are Pythagorean triples.

Rectangular coordinates A pair of coordinates that identifies the position of a point in the **coordinate plane** in relation to each of two mutually perpendicular coordinate axes. These axes are usually called the x-axis (horizontal) and y-axis (vertical). The horizontal coordinate is given first.

Row vector A **matrix** that contains exactly one row.

Secant line A line passing through two points on a graph, especially two points on a curve; in contrast to a **tangent line.**

Sine The ratio of the length of the leg opposite one nonright angle of a right triangle to the length of the hypotenuse.

Skew lines In three-dimensional space, lines that do not intersect but are not parallel.

Slope Informally, the steepness of a line. The slope of a nonvertical line in the xy-coordinate system is defined formally as the ratio $\frac{y_2 - y_1}{x_2 - x_1}$, where (x_1, y_1) and (x_2, y_2) are any two distinct points on the line. Slope is not defined for vertical lines.

Square matrix A **matrix** in which the number of rows is equal to the number of columns.

Step function   A function whose output values remain constant over each of various intervals of input values before "jumping" to a different value. The graph of a step function often looks like a series of steps.

Substitution method   A method for solving a **system of equations** in which one equation is solved for one variable and the resulting expression is substituted into another equation.

Synthetic geometry   The study of geometry using theorems and observations to create theorems or solve problems, without using measurements; in contrast to **analytic geometry.**

System of equations   A set of two or more equations being considered together for the purpose of finding a solution common to all of the equations, if it exists. If the equations have no common solution, the system is **inconsistent.** If one of the equations can be removed from the system without changing the set of common solutions, that equation is dependent on the others, and the system as a whole is also **dependent.** If no equation is dependent on the rest, the system is **independent.**

In the case of a system of linear equations with the same number of equations as variables, the system is *inconsistent* if there is no solution, *dependent* if there are infinitely many solutions, and *independent* if there is a unique solution.

Tangent (of an angle)   The ratio of the length of the leg opposite one nonright angle of a right triangle to the length of the leg adjacent to the same angle.

Tangent line   Informally, a line that "just touches" a curve, passing through only a single point; in contrast to a **secant line.**

Example: In this diagram, line *m* is tangent to the circle at point *P*.

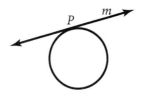

Three-dimensional coordinate system   A system in which a point is identified by a triple [such as $(3, 7, -2)$] that gives its position relative to each of three mutually perpendicular coordinate axes, usually labeled as the x-, y-, and z-axes. There are different systems for identifying the three axes. The system used in this book orients the x-axis horizontally (with positive values to the right of the origin), the y-axis vertically (with positive values upward from the origin), and the z-axis into and out of the viewing plane (with positive values toward the viewer from the origin).

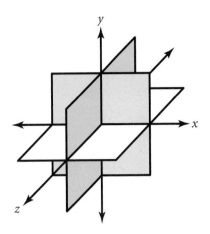

3-space   The set of all points in the **three-dimensional coordinate system.**

Triangular numbers   The numbers obtained by finding the sum of the first n positive integers, for different values of n; that is, the numbers $1, 1 + 2, 1 + 2 + 3, 1 + 2 + 3 + 4$, and so on. These are called *triangular numbers* because they give the number of elements in triangular arrays like those shown here.

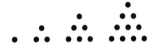

Trigonometry   The study of the relationship between any angle of a right triangle and the ratios of the sides of the triangle. See *A Geometric Summary* in *Orchard Hideout.*

Unit circle   A circle whose radius is 1 unit.

Vertical angles   A pair of "opposite" angles formed by a pair of intersecting lines.

   Example: Angles 1 and 2 are vertical angles.

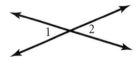

INDEX OF MATHEMATICAL IDEAS

The phrase "concept development" indicates that the associated term is previewed or developed on the page, but may not be named.

cylinders
    defined, 497
    surface area of: concept development, 57
    volume of: concept development, 57

D

decibel scale, defined, 276
deductive reasoning, concept development, 12, 16, 27, 29, 40, 67, 71–79, 82–86, 158, 250, 305, 309, 374, 407, 409, 412–413, 470–471, 488, 490–491
degree of a function, defined, 317
dependent systems of equations,
    defined, 498
    concept development, 151, 156, 188–189, 195, 205, 218
depreciation, concept development, 283
derivative
    and concavity: concept development, 288
    defined, 259, 498
    of an exponential function, 271, 278–280, 320–321
    as a function: concept development, 271, 275, 278–280, 288, 317, 320
    graph of, 288
    as instantaneous rate of change: concept development, 253–255, 258–261, 273, 306, 485
    notation for: concept development, 278–280
    proportionality property of: concept development, 271, 273, 278–280, 285, 320–321
    sign of, 275, 288, 314
    as slope of tangent to the curve: concept development, 257, 259–262, 288, 309
    zeroes of: concept development, 288, 314
    concept development, 265
determinants, defined, 218

diagonals of a rectangle bisect each other, 86
directrix
    defined, 89, 498
    of an ellipse or hyperbola, 93
    of a parabola, 89–93
discrete graphs. *See* graphs, discrete
displacement. *See* distance traveled; falling objects, physics of
distance
    from a point to a line, defined, 30
    from a point to a line: concept development, 28–29, 46, 55, 60
    See also distance formula; distance traveled
distance formula
    defined, 498
    and the Pythagorean theorem, 23
    concept development, 19, 22, 25, 27, 32, 46, 50–51, 70, 79
distance traveled
    area model for: concept development, 442
    finding with constant acceleration: concept development, 442
    See also falling objects, physics of; rate of change
distributive property, application of, 41, 379, 388–389, 412
division. *See* divisibility; greatest common divisor; remainders
divisibility, application of, 328, 332
divisors. *See* divisibility; greatest common divisor; remainders
domain
    defined, 314
    concept development, 440
doubling time (with compounding), 286

E

e
    as the base of an exponential expression, 291
    concept development, 271, 281, 285–287, 290, 319–320

eccentricity, 93

elimination method for solving systems of equations
  defined, 147, 498
  concept development, 144–146, 148–151
  See also systems of equations

ellipse
  as conic section, 89
  defined, 498
  equation of, 97–100
  geometric definitions, 93–95
  sketching, 95

equations
  as constraints. *See* constraints, as equations
  of line through two points, 125–127, 136, 164, 204
  See also equivalent equations

equidistance
  defined, 499
  concept development, 12–17, 28, 30, 70–72, 78, 83, 86

equivalent equations, concept development, 51–53

estimation, application of, 18, 34–39, 326

expected value, application of, 81, 334, 338, 401

exponential equations
  concept development, 269
  converting to logarithmic equations, 272, 314
  defined, 499
  finding: concept development, 272, 283, 286–287, 290, 318
  fitting, 284, 291–295
  See also exponential functions; logarithms

exponential functions
  change of base, 282, 285
  domain and range: concept development, 314

derivative of: concept development, 271, 278–280, 285, 290, 320–321
  general form of, 321
  graphing, 227, 293–294
  and population growth: concept development, 227, 244, 266, 268, 273, 278–281, 284, 291–292, 294–295
  concept development, 227–228, 267, 272
  See also derivative, proportionality property of; exponential equations

exponents
  logarithms. *See* logarithms
  See also exponents, laws of

exponents, laws of
  additive law, 269, 314
  raising exponential expressions to powers, 269, 314
  repeated exponentiation, 269, 314
  application of, 282

expressions. *See* algebraic expressions

exterior angle
  defined, 75, 499
  and nonadjacent interior angles, 75

extrapolation, concept development, 224, 228, 244, 284, 295

F

factorial, concept development, 355, 357, 364

failure of events in probability, defined, 394

falling objects, physics of
  acceleration due to gravity, 445, 485
  distance fallen as a function of time, 445
  freely-falling: defined, 445
  height as function of time, 251, 485
  instantaneous speed: concept development, 253–254, 261, 445, 485
  time to fall a given distance, 251, 254, 445, 448, 450, 457, 486

concept development, 418, 441, 459, 460, 477

feasible regions
corners of, 119, 141, 161
corners of: concept development, 115
defined, 499
with three variables, 141
concept development, 110
See also linear programming

Fibonacci sequence, concept development, 438

fitting lines and curves
with a calculator, 293, 295
exponential equations, 284, 291–295
linear equations: lines, 125–127, 136, 164, 213, 248, 256, 297, 305, 309
linear equations: planes, 204, 213
quadratic equations, 172, 190

fluctuation, sampling: application of, 403

focus
defined, 499
of an ellipse, 93–99
of a hyperbola, 93–97
of a parabola, 89–92

functions
degree of: defined, 317
domain and range of: defined, 314
exponential. *See* exponential functions
linear. *See* linear functions
logarithmic. *See* logarithms
notation: application of, 125, 251, 253–255, 257–262, 273, 278–280, 285, 288, 306, 309, 316, 320
quadratic. *See* quadratic functions
range of. *See* functions, domain and range of
sine. *See* periodic functions

G

Galilei, Galileo, 445
Galileo. *See* Galilei, Galileo
Gaussian elimination. *See* elimination method for solving systems of equations

geometric sequences, defined, 312, 499
geometric series, concept development, 312
graphing calculators. *See* calculators
graphs and graphing
circular functions. *See* circular functions, graphing
conic sections, 89–100
derivatives. *See* derivatives, graph of
discrete and continuous: concept development, 227, 259
exponential. *See* exponential functions, graphing
inequalities, 200. *See also* linear programming
intersection. *See* intersection (as common solution of equations)
linear equations. *See* linear equations, graphing
linear inequalities. *See* linear inequalities, graphing
plotting points, 27, 70, 131, 190, 227, 242, 288, 295, 302, 487
polar equations. *See* polar equations, graphing
quadratics. *See* quadratic graphs
rate vs. time. *See* rate of change, graphing vs. time
scale's effect on steepness, 235
step functions: defined, 506
step functions: concept development, 230
in three dimensions, 130–131, 134, 141, 156, 195, 204, 217
x- and *y*-intercepts. *See* intercepts

gravity
acceleration due to, 445, 485
See also falling objects, physics of

greatest common divisor, concept development, 42

greatest integer function, concept development, 263

growth. *See* absolute growth; percentage growth; rate of change

H

half plane
    concept development, 200
    See also linear inequalities, graphing
hexagon, area and perimeter of regular, 37
history of mathematics
    Galilei, Galileo, 445
    Newton, Isaac, 445
    Pascal, Blaise, 383
hyperbola
    as conic section, 89
    defined, 500
    equation of, 97
    geometric definitions, 93–95
    sketching, 95
hypotenuse
    defined, 6
    length of. *See* Pythagorean theorem
    median to, 86
    midpoint of, 79
hypotheses
    defined, 500
    concept development, 16, 67, 78
    See also conjecture; null hypothesis

I

identities, trigonometric
    cosine of a negative angle, 474
    cotangent and cosecant, 491
    defined, 472, 500
    Pythagorean: concept development, 470, 472, 491
    sine and cosine of complementary angles: concept development, 424, 490
    sine of a negative angle, 474
    sine of supplementary angles, 472
    tangent as function of sine and cosine, 471
    tangent and secant, 491
    concept development, 476

identity element for multiplication
    defined, 500
    See also identity matrices
identity matrices, concept development, 185, 187
incenter
    defined, 84
    concept development, 30
incircle, concept development, 30
inclination, angle of, 302
inconsistent systems of equations, concept development, 124, 156, 161, 188–189, 195, 205, 218, 304
independent events, defined, 394
independent systems of equations, concept development, 122
inductive reasoning, concept development, 19, 23, 25, 27, 34–39, 41–42, 108, 253–254, 271, 286, 305, 356, 383–384, 409, 420, 427, 438, 445, 448, 485
inequalities
    graphing, 119, 200
    linear. *See* linear inequalities
    systems of, 200
    concept development, 19, 107, 110, 132
    See also linear programming
inflation, 267, 286
    concept development, 287, 290
    See also percentage growth
inscribed
    angles, 73–74
    circle, 83–84
    defined, 32, 501
    concept development, 30, 34–39
instantaneous rate of change. *See* rate of change, instantaneous
intercepts
    concept development, 131, 230, 435, 461
    See also linear equations, graphing: slope-intercept form
interest, compound
    defined, 272

See also functions; linear equations; linear equations, graphing; linear inequalities

linear inequalities
finding, 107, 200
See also inequalities; linear programming

linear inequalities, graphing
feasible region, 141
See also linear programming

linear programming
defined, 502
feasible regions. *See* feasible regions
in more than two variables, 111, 119, 141, 157, 211
in more than two variables: concept development, 120–121, 132, 142, 153, 161–162, 192–194
summary of issues in, 112
concept development, 104–107, 110, 115–118, 152, 202–203, 376

lines. *See* intersection; fitting, lines; linear equations; linear equations, graphing; line segments

locus, concept development, 12–16, 19, 28, 30, 50, 92–100

logarithmic equations, concept development, 276, 314

logarithms
common: concept development, 290
decibel scale, 276
defined, 314
exponential equations, solutions to, 269, 272, 314
laws of, 314
natural: defined, 291, 502
natural: concept development, 290, 295
application of, 263, 268

logic and reasoning
counterexamples, 186
"If . . . , then . . ." statements: concept development, 16, 19, 67, 78, 500

"If and only if" statements: concept development, 19, 30, 50, 87, 500
concept development, 158
See also converses; deductive reasoning; inductive reasoning; proof

M

mathematical modeling, concept development, 4, 12, 46, 50, 60, 107–110, 115, 125, 135, 148, 162, 190, 206, 230, 291, 294–295, 308, 436, 459

mathematicians. *See* history of mathematics

mathematics, history of. *See* history of mathematics

matrices
addition of, 169, 216
and the associative property, 186, 216
with a calculator, 179
coefficient, defined, 184
and the commutative property, 186, 216
column vectors, 168
constant term, defined, 184
defined, 168, 502
determinant of, 218
dimensions of, 168, 498
identity: concept development, 185
inverse of, 187–189
invertibility: concept development, 188, 217
multiplication of: concept development, 174–187, 214
notation of, 168
row vectors, 168
in solving systems of equations: concept development, 182–189, 194, 196, 218
square, 168, 506

maxima and minima of functions, 435–436, 461

maximizing a linear function over a region. *See* linear programming measure, units of. *See* units of measure

median of triangle

    defined, 84–86, 502

    to hypotenuse, 86

midline

    defined, 76, 502

    and base of triangle, 76

midpoint

    of hypotenuse, 79, 86

    line through, 28, 78

midpoint formula

    defined, 502

    concept development, 25, 27, 32, 70–71, 79

mile, equivalent in feet, 61

minimizing a linear function over a region.

    See linear programming

modeling

    See mathematical modeling

multiplication

    of matrices. *See* matrices, multiplication of

    multiplicative inverse. *See* matrices, inverse of

    See also distributive property

multiplicative inverse

    defined, 502

    See also matrices, inverse of

multiplication principle for counting combinations. *See* combinations, multiplication principle for counting

N

natural logarithms. *See* logarithms, natural

Newton, Isaac, 445

nonadjacent interior angles, 75

notation. *See* derivatives, notation for; functions, notation; scientific notation

null hypothesis, application of, 378, 381, 403, 408

number sense

    concept development, 42, 69, 82, 158, 263

    See also estimation

number theory, 82

numbers

    irrational. *See* irrational numbers

    rounding. *See* rounding numbers

    triangular: concept development, 384

    See also scientific notation

O

oblique prisms, 6

octagons, area and perimeter of, 38

octant

    defined, 499, 503

    numbering, 128

P

parabolas

    defined, 172, 503

    determining the focus and directrix, 89–92

    directrix of, defined, 89

    fitting, 172, 190

    focus of, defined, 89

    geometric definition, 89–93

    See also quadratic graphs

parallel

    lines. *See* inconsistent systems of equations

    lines, slope of. *See* slope, of parallel lines

    lines crossed by a transversal, 6

    lines crossed by a transversal: application of, 250

    planes: concept development, 130, 134

parallelogram

    defined, 76

    and midpoints of quadrilateral, 27, 76

Pascal, Blaise, 383

Pascal's triangle

    and binomial expansions, 388–390, 413

    and combinatorial coefficients, 384–387, 390, 409–411, 413

    defined, 383, 409, 504

    numbering of rows and entries, 385, 409

    concept development, 382, 390, 396

application of: equation of a circle, 19
application of: length of a line segment, 11, 16, 46, 431
application of: trigonometric identities. *See* Pythagorean identity
concept development, 41
See also Pythagorean triple

Pythagorean triple
defined, 41, 82, 505
primitive: defined, 82

Q

quadratic equations
finding with focus and directrix, 89
fitting, 172, 190
graphs of. *See* quadratic graphs
standard form of, 172
See also quadratic functions

quadratic functions
graphs of. *See* quadratic graphs
application of, 251, 253–255, 258–259, 306, 445, 485
concept development, 172, 273

quadratic graphs
directrix of, 89–92
focus of, 89–92
as parabola, 89–92
vertex of: concept development, 89–92
application of, 190
concept development, 288

R

radius, concept development, 4, 12

range
defined, 314
concept development, 440

rate of change
absolute growth: concept development, 228, 294
angular speed's relationship to speed: concept development, 424
average, 227–230, 233–236, 239, 243–244, 251, 253–258, 306, 442–443, 484

average: defined, 256, 494
average: finding with constant acceleration, 443–445
constant, 236–239, 294, 454, 457–460, 484, 486
doubling time, 286
graphing vs. time, 442–443
instantaneous: concept development, 233, 253–261, 265, 306, 445, 485
instantaneous: defined, 501
percentage growth, 228, 267–269, 272–273, 283–287, 290–291, 294–295, 318
relationship to distance and time, 484
relative growth. *See* rate of change, percentage growth
concept development, 44, 59–60
See also acceleration; derivative; distance traveled; slope

ratio
trigonometric. *See* trigonometry
application of, 81, 276, 312
See also probability

rectangles, diagonals of, 86

recursion, concept development, 267, 420, 438

reference angles, concept development, 431, 461

regular polygons, area and perimeter of, 37–39

remainders, applications of, 328, 332

replacement, sampling without. *See* sampling without replacement

rhombus, defined, 27

right angle, inscribed in semicircle, 73

right prisms, defined, 6

right triangles
defined, 6
midpoint of hypotenuse, 79
special (30°-60° and 45°-45°), 66, 80
special (30°-60° and 45°-45°): concept development, 302, 431
See also Pythagorean theorem; triangles; trigonometry

roots (of numbers)

> application of, 284
>
> *See also* exponents

rounding numbers, dangers of: concept development, 267

row vector

> defined, 505
>
> concept development, 168

Rule of 72, concept development, 286

S

sampling fluctuation, application of, 403

sampling without replacement, concept development, 361

scale, how change affects area, perimeter, and volume: concept development, 48, 57, 61, 88, 258, 308

scale factor. *See* proportional reasoning

scientific notation, application of, 226–227

secant line

> defined, 262, 505
>
> slope as average rate: concept development, 251, 257, 265

semicircle, inscribed angle of, 73

sequences

> arithmetic: defined, 310
>
> arithmetic: concept development, 246
>
> geometric: defined, 312

series

> arithmetic: concept development, 246, 310
>
> geometric: concept development, 312

similarity

> defined, 6
>
> of triangles, 6
>
> of triangles: application, 41, 46, 55, 60, 76, 250, 305

simulations

> random number generators, 402
>
> concept development, 341–343, 403

sine

> as a circular function: concept development, 424–427, 431–436, 440, 443, 447–448, 457–460, 465–466, 476–477, 481–482, 486
>
> and the cosine of the complementary angle: concept development, 424
>
> defined as circular function, 429, 470
>
> defined for right triangle, 6, 491, 505
>
> exact values, 66, 80
>
> graphing the function, 432–436, 440, 481, 490
>
> inverse. *See* inverse trigonometric functions
>
> of a negative angle, 474
>
> shifting horizontally: concept development, 481
>
> of supplementary angles, 472
>
> *See also* identities, trigonometric

skew lines

> defined, 505
>
> concept development, 134

slope

> defined, 240, 505
>
> of horizontal lines, 248, 262
>
> negative: concept development, 243, 248, 251, 253–254, 259–262
>
> of parallel lines: concept development, 230, 242, 304
>
> and rate of change: concept development, 230, 240–242, 256–257, 259–262, 265
>
> scale and steepness, 235
>
> of vertical lines, 248
>
> concept development, 227–233, 236–239, 244, 250, 301–302, 305
>
> *See also* derivative; linear equations, graphing; rate of change

slope-intercept form of linear equation. *See* linear equations, graphing

tangent to a curve
    defined, 262, 507
    finding the equation of, 309
    slope of: concept development, 257,
        259–262, 265, 275, 309
    See also derivative
technology. *See* calculators
three-dimensional coordinate system. *See*
    coordinate system, three-dimensional
transcendental numbers, 319
transformations. *See* translations
translations, of an ellipse, 100
transversal, 6
trapezoids, area of: application of, 442
tree diagrams for probability, application
    of, 333, 334–335, 337–339, 344–345,
    348, 401
triangles
    altitudes of: defined, 84
    angle sum property, 6
    congruence of, 6
    isosceles. *See* isosceles triangles
    medians of. *See* median of triangle
    midline, 76
    midpoint of hypotenuse, 79
    right. *See* Pythagorean theorem; right
        triangles; trigonometry
    right triangle trigonometry. *See*
        trigonometry
    similarity of, 6
    See also angle sum property;
        Pythagorean theorem; right
        triangles
triangular numbers
    defined, 507
    concept development, 384
trials in probability, defined, 394
trigonometry
    circular functions. *See* circular
        functions
    defined, 507
    identities. *See* identities, trigonometric
    inverse functions. *See* inverse
        trigonometric function

    as ratios, 6
    right-triangle: application of, 30, 37–39,
        46, 55, 60, 66, 80, 423–424, 431
    and special right triangles, 66, 80, 302
    unit-circle. *See* circular functions, unit
        circle

U

unit circle
    defined, 470, 507
    concept development, 431
units of measure
    for length, 6
    for surface area, 6
    for volume, 6
    application of, 44, 47, 57
    concept development: 34–39, 120, 169
    concept development: conversions of,
        48, 59–61, 88, 203, 226

V

velocity. *See* rate of change
vertex (of a parabola), concept
    development, 89–92
vertical angles, defined, 29, 507
volume
    and area, relation of, 57
    of cylinders, 57
    defined, 6
    of prisms, 6
    and scale factors, 57, 88, 308
    of spheres: defined, 308
    of spheres: concept development, 88

X

x-intercepts. *See* intercepts

Y

y-intercepts. *See* intercepts; linear
    equations, graphing: slope-intercept
    form

INDEX OF ACTIVITY TITLES

PHOTOGRAPHIC CREDITS

Front Cover Photos

(From top left, clockwise) Jonathan Wong, Johnny Tran, Lindsey Macloud, Caroline Williams, Giovanni Guzman, Armani Wilson, Alida Jekabson, Eden Ogbai, Dylan Matthews, Thao Nguyen, Jenna Balch

Front Cover and Unit Opener Photography

Berkeley High School and Lincoln High School: Stephen Loewinsohn
Stock photos: iStockphoto

Orchard Hideout

3 Lincoln High School, Stephen Loewinsohn; **4** Wilburn D. Murphy/ SuperStock; **6** iStockPhoto; **7** Trans-World Photos/SuperStock; **9** James Strachan/Robert Harding; **14** Hillary Turner; **17** PhotoDisc; **20** Lincoln High School, Stephen Loewinsohn; **26** Lincoln High School, Stephen Loewinsohn; **31** PhotoDisc; **33** Lincoln High School, Stephen Loewinsohn; **34** SuperStock/SuperStock; **36** iStockPhoto; **38** iStockPhoto; **45** Lincoln High School, Stephen Loewinsohn; **46** Mia & Klaus Matthes/SuperStock; **48** Ulf Huett Nilsson/Getty Images; **54** Lincoln High School, Stephen Loewinsohn; **57** Shutterstock; **60** iStockPhoto; **61** PhotoDisc; PhotoDisc; **63** Lincoln High School, Stephen Loewinsohn; **66** SuperStock; **80** Graeme Outerbridge/SuperStock; **85** iStockPhoto; **88** iStockPhoto

Meadows or Malls?

103 Lincoln High School, Stephen Loewinsohn; **104** iStockPhoto; **107** Rayman/Photolibrary; **111** Lincoln High School, Stephen Loewinsohn; **113** Lincoln High School, Stephen Loewinsohn; **119** nick baylis/Alamy; **123** Lincoln High School, Stephen Loewinsohn; **124** Photodisc; **132** Hillary Turner; **133** Hillary Turner (both); **138** Lincoln High School, Stephen Loewinsohn; **140** Lincoln High School, Stephen Loewinsohn; **141** Shutterstock; **142** iStockPhoto; **143** Shasta High School, Dave Robathan; **144** iStockPhoto; Shutterstock; Hillary Turner; **145** Hillary Turner; **146** iStockPhoto; Hillary Turner; **152** Lincoln High School, Stephen Loewinsohn; **162** David Forbert/Superstock; **163** Thinkstock/ Getty Images; **166** iStockPhoto; **167** Lincoln High School, Stephen Loewinsohn; **168** Lincoln High School, Stephen Loewinsohn; **170** Hillary Turner (all); **173** Shutterstock; **176** Hillary Turner; **178** iStockPhoto; **180** Lincoln High School, Stephen Loewinsohn; **181** Lincoln High School, Stephen Loewinsohn; **182** Redlink Production/Corbis; **189** Lincoln High

School, Stephen Loewinsohn; **191** Santa Maria High School, Chris Paulus; **193** iStockPhoto & Rayman/Photolibrary; **195** Hillary Turner; **196** Hillary Turner; **197** Lincoln High School, Stephen Loewinsohn; **205** Shutterstock; **206** Photodisc; **209** Shutterstock; **210** Lincoln High School, Stephen Loewinsohn; **212** Lincoln High School, Stephen Loewinsohn; **213** Shutterstock

Small World, Isn't It?

223 Los Altos High School, Judy Strauss, Lynne Alper; **224** Photodisc; **225** age fotostock/SuperStock; **229** Kapa'a High School, Elaine Denny; **233** Shutterstock; **238** Santa Cruz High School, Kevin Drinkard, Lynne Alper; **239** iStockPhoto; **249** Shutterstock; **252** Lincoln High School, Stephen Loewinsohn; **254** iStockPhoto; **256** Shutterstock; **259** Shutterstock; **261** Lincoln High School, Stephen Loewinsohn; **266** Brookline High School, Terry Nowak; **267** Hillary Turner (both); **268** Dr. David J. Patterson/Photo Researchers, Inc.; **272** iStockPhoto; **279** Palazzo Farnese, Rome, Italy/Bridgeman Art Library, London/Superstock; **280** Kordcom/Photolibrary; **281** Santa Cruz High School, Kevin Drinkard, Lynne Alper; **282** United Archives GmbH/Alamy; **283** Randy Faris/Corbis; **284** The Huntington Library, Art Collections, and Botanical Gardens, San Marino, California/Superstock; **286** KCP; **292** Lincoln High School, Stephen Loewinsohn; **296** Photodisc; **297** Lincoln High School, Stephen Loewinsohn; **303** ImageSource/Photolibrary; **314** Lincoln High School, Stephen Loewinsohn; **317** Spencer Platt/Getty Images; **318** Shutterstock; **321** Shutterstock

Pennant Fever

325 Lincoln High School, Stephen Loewinsohn; **327** iStockPhoto; **329** Klaus-Peter Wolf/Photolibrary; **332** Shutterstock; **333** Lincoln High School, Stephen Loewinsohn; **335** Shutterstock; **337** Tetra Images/Getty Images; **340** Silver Lake Regional High School, Kevin Sawyer, Lynne Alper; **344** Lori Adamski Peek/Getty Images; **346** iStockPhoto; **349** Lincoln High School, Lori Green; **360** SuperStock/SuperStock; **361** Hillary Turner; **364** iStockPhoto; **365** Shutterstock; **367** Bruce Ayres/Getty Images; **369** Lincoln High School, Stephen Loewinsohn; **377** Rayman/Photolibrary; **380** Creatas/Photolibrary; **381** iStockPhoto; **382** Kapa'a High School, Elaine Denny; **384** Photodisc; **388** PHOTOEDIT/PhotoEdit; **390** Wikipedia Public Domain; **391** Lincoln High School, Lori Green; **394** David Spindel/Superstock; **397** Lincoln High School, Stephen Loewinsohn; **399** Hillary Turner; **401** iStockPhoto; **408** iStockPhoto

High Dive

417 Oxnard High School, Jerry Neidenbach; **419** FEV Create Inc/Getty Images; **426** Capuchino High School, Chicha Lynch, Hillary Turner, Richard Wheeler; **432** Shutterstock; **435** Shutterstock; **441** Lincoln High School, Stephen Loewinsohn; **445** Chigmaroff/Davison/SuperStock; **448** Harry How/Getty images; **449** Lincoln High School, Stephen Loewinsohn; **452** Photodisc/Getty Images; **454** Paul & Lindamarie Ambrose/Getty Images; **455** Shutterstock; **456** Shutterstock; **458** Capuchino High School, Peter Jonnard, Hillary Turner, Richard Wheeler; **462** iStockPhoto; **463** John Warden/Superstock; **464** Capuchino High School, Chicha Lynch, Hillary Turner, Richard Wheeler; **465** Hillary Turner; **480** Bettmann/Corbis; **481** Shutterstock; **484** Shutterstock; **485** Steve Vidler/SuperStock